Flower Arranging in colour

Flower Arranging in colour

Betty Massingham

HAMLYN
LONDON · NEW YORK · SYDNEY · TORONTO

Published by
THE HAMLYN PUBLISHING GROUP LIMITED
LONDON · NEW YORK · SYDNEY · TORONTO
Hamlyn House, Feltham, Middlesex, England

SBN 600 01303 0

Second impression 1970
Printed in Hong Kong by Toppan

Contents

to Lady Georgina Coleridge

Introduction

It is said that arranging flowers can give peace of mind and can also lead to the attainment of patience and strength in adversity. If only the first of these claims is correct how worth while it is to spend precious time in selecting flowers and putting them into a vase for the pleasure and delight of those who will enjoy them. The simple fact of dealing with living material, whose beauty is worthy of respect, and of working with one's hands at something which is peaceful in itself and creative in its function — these seem to be reasons enough for the widespread interest and appeal of flower arrangement. One further recommendation is that it is not an expensive pursuit — indeed, it is often the smaller and less extravagant vases, sometimes composed of wild flowers or of only a little material, which are the most satisfying and the easiest to live with.

If I may strike a personal note I should like to take this opportunity of mentioning the pleasure I have had, over the years, through arranging flowers. My husband encouraged me to 'do the flowers' and from this has grown an interest in vases — porcelain, glass, copper, etc. and an almost unquenchable enthusiasm for antique shops and 'junk' stalls where treasures for holding flowers may sometimes be found. I have also discovered a deeper interest in paintings, especially those of flowers or of 'conversation pieces' where a vase of flowers may be a component of an interior scene. Old flower prints, secondhand gardening and poetry books and early herbals have all become objects of interest and often contain information about the plants and flowers one has got to know when arranging them.

It is now an added pleasure, too, to visit other people's gardens, to notice cottage gardens in the country lanes and villages, or town gardens — some of them seen from a train window.

The Chinese have a typically Chinese saying: 'If you want to be happy for a week, take a wife. If you want to be happy for a month, kill a pig. If you want to be happy all your life, make a garden.' Making a garden is not an essential of doing flowers, but it is a great step towards it, and even a window box or a tub or a small paved yard can make their contribution, and can provide the kind of plant which it is not practicable for the florist to stock. But the florist, on the other hand, can produce such a wealth of material, such a variety of colour and contrast that it is almost always possible to have at least one small flower arrangement in the house.

It is pleasant to recall, I think, that while large, formal arrangements for 'special' occasions have their own importance, it is the small domestic bunch of flowers which becomes part of the decorative scheme in one's own home that is of real value. Wild flowers in a jug on the kitchen table can make as great an impact as lilies in a silver vase for a wedding. It is, after all, the affection and respect that are felt for them that counts in the end.

Betty Massingham.

The art of flower arrangement

Flower arrangement is an art which was created and studied in Eastern countries for hundreds of years but it is a comparatively recent development in the Western world. This is an art which is a purely personal one, depending as much on the preferences of the arranger as on any set rules or ideas which have been laid down as guide lines.

Some flower arrangers do follow these rules or guide lines closely, perhaps even to the extent of thinking along the lines of a 'Hogarth curve' for a bunch of daffodils or a 'crescent curve' for half a dozen roses. But this seems to me to be a departure from the true essence of flower arranging, which, I think, should express not only the love of the materials being arranged but also the personality and taste of the arranger.

The less affectation there is the better the chance of the flowers being arranged in a natural way,

Right, The importance of
a few flowers in a simple container
is one of the facts which have emerged
in the art of flower arrangement
during recent years. Here two or three
Rhododendron praecox are
arranged with the rose pink flowers
of bergenia and sprays of ivy.

Left, A recent development
in contemporary flower arrangement
is the use of a piece of natural board
or bark in place of a container.
Here branches of cistus
are arranged with false fig leaves
in a dish of water
kept in place on the wood by plasticine
and concealed by moss.
Such an arrangement
gives a clear outline and,
against a plain background
will fit into most furnishing schemes.

Far left, Contemporary and traditional:
this group, arranged by Stella Coe
shows an Ikebana style interpretation
of 'silence' depicted by
aspidistra leaves and one arum lily,
in a Rosenthal container.

and so shown off to their best advantage.

The pleasure and satisfaction that can be obtained from arranging a bowl of flowers would be difficult to express or describe generally, since these must vary with the individual concerned and be involved with his love of flowers and green, growing plants, as well as his reaction to 'beauty', which this art is.

The idea that man should not be too far removed from his native earth is not a new one, and in these days of industrial and commercial interest, when the machine seems to take an undue precedence in our lives, arranging flowers in a vase seems to have even more significance than ever before.
This interest develops and widens one's horizons, especially if one is the fortunate owner of a garden, however small. Then one becomes interested in the flowers and plants, their names and their native habit, their flowering times, foliage, buds and stems. Nursery gardens, and florists' shops, gardening catalogues, books written about flowers and their histories, about the plant pioneers who ventured afar and discovered so many exotic plants, paintings of flowers—all become of great interest and value. A walk round a friend's garden, a random glance at a garden from a train or bus window, or a visit to some of the large estate gardens opened to the public—these too are enriched. To someone who may not previously have thought much about flowers beyond noticing them on sale in a shop window or on a market stall, flower arranging and the various associated interests create a new world. (The wish to reproduce two or three special flowers may lead to a desire to paint in order to do so. This can provide satisfaction of a high order and can sometimes even produce financial reward).

This is not an 'art' to be reserved only for a party or a 'special occasion'. A few flowers on the kitchen table can be as important in their own way as a full scale dinner party decoration. A *good* flower arrangement, fortunately, does not depend on the amount of money spent on it, nor on the amount of material used (in fact twenty flowers are not necessarily twice as beautiful as ten). Two or three geranium flowers taken from a plant in a cottage window can, in the right surroundings, be as effective when arranged with suitable foliage (either their own or with contrasting leaves) as many larger and more opulent arrangements. We have all seen the charm of buttercups in a blue jug or the brightness of scarlet hips in a copper can, or one Ophelia rose in a specimen vase.

What is essential in flower arrangement is good design, using the right shape and colour of container, and considering the surroundings and relating the arrangement to it. Every colour we select in a room, every piece of porcelain, each wallpaper or curtain or cushion – all have their own value, the binding on the cushion or the trimming on the lampshade or the band of gold on a Worcester saucer – all should be chosen to emphasise or harmonise with the general furnishing scheme. In the same way the flower arrangement must be considered; each flower and leaf carefully chosen for size, shape and colour, all in relation to the surroundings. To me a vase of flowers is probably more indicative of the character of the home maker than any other one thing.

Perhaps 'characteristic' is the key word when what is produced is the best of its kind and also characteristic of its origin and surroundings.

For instance, to be characteristic in an Oriental arrangement the flowers may stand in a barely furnished room. In the Orient they may be in an alcove, with perhaps a scroll picture as the only other decoration.

I feel strongly that it is largely through learning about other arts that we can hope to present Western ideas on a bowl of flowers as an art.

'Virgil does not speak of the beauty of ducks.. the softness of their voices and their round, black eyes so intelligent, but I should not have known how beautiful they are.. if I had not read Virgil. It is strange that he should have no word about water-lilies, yet he taught me to see their great leathery leaves'. (*Heloise and Abelard* – trans. George Moore.)

Left, This is an example of the art of contemporary flower arrangement. It was awarded the 1st prize in the 1965 autumn show of the Royal National Rose Society of Great Britain.

Right, An example of the art of a contemporary foliage arrangement. This is a simple group of rose leaves and hips, arranged, as far as possible as though they were growing.

Autumn arrangements

In this arrangement the container is white marked with greenish blue spots, dictating the green and white colour scheme of the group. The material includes long thin branches of the hedge plant *Lonicera nitida*, green and white leek heads and white anaphalis.

About this time of the year, there may be less colour in the garden. One feels that as autumn closes in with shorter evenings and early frosts in comparison with the wealth of summer, the flower border will soon have little to offer. And then, perhaps, there comes a St. Luke's summer, bringing more sunny days which 'set budding more, and still more later flowers for the bees'. Fortunately (although Keats did not mention it) there are later flowers not only for the bees, but also for the imaginative flower arranger.

What beauty such days can give to the garden, with colours turning and the air either crisp with frost or warm and drowsy with the late summer sun. And there is almost a double flowering season–the true autumn flowers, such as dahlias, chrysanthemums, Michaelmas daisies, monbretia, and so on, and at the same time still more buds from the summer flowers, fooled, perhaps, by the sunshine, like the bees: roses, delphiniums, mignonette, masterwort (*Astrantia*), Japanese anemones, foxgloves, myrtle and Californian lilac (*Ceanothus*).

As is well known, some of these only come on again if the dead flower spikes have been cut off at their early flowering. This applies especially to foxgloves, delphiniums and masterwort (*Astrantia*).

I am writing generally of gardens in Britain, but as far south as the Channel Islands I have seen a still greater variety of summer flowers and half hardy shrubs out at this time of the year. Indian mallow (*Abutilon*), coleus in flower, feverfew, godetia, cornflowers, love-lies-bleeding (*Amaranthus*), cross vine (*Bignonia*), thorn apple (*Datura stramomium*), pepper bush (*Piper*) and cup and saucer plant (*Cobaea scandens*), were some of the plants still producing material for flower arrangement at this comparatively late time of the year.

I also saw Californian poppies (*Eschscholtzia*) Kaffir lilies, blue salvia and some sprays of laurustinus. This was in a sheltered garden in St. Martin's, Guernsey, but it is highly probable that the same might be found in Somerset or Cornwall.

At this time of year there is a wealth of foliage suitable for arrangements in the house. Besides the wonderful colouring of azalea and peony leaves, not to mention many of the flowering shrubs, especially berberis, there are also the magnificent leaves of the globe artichoke. Hydrangea and begonia are two other reliable assets of the garden. Plantain lily (*Hosta*) is still available, as are, of course, garden ragwort (*Senecio laxifolius*), sea lavender (*Santolina*) and rosemary.

Yet another autumn delight is to have a small arrangement of massed colour which might be described as 'clashing' except that it is intentional. Two or three polyantha roses perhaps of Moulin Rouge and Aurora, with a variety of geraniums (pelargoniums) in pink, crimson and scarlet, arranged quite short on a pin holder, make a good contrast on a green dish or plate for a dining table, with the geranium leaves cut almost without any stalk to conceal the holder. This 'clashing' red colour scheme (with the addition of zinnias and dahlias) is equally effective for a larger arrangement in a white porcelain vase.

Now too, we should, perhaps, concentrate on leaves and berries. The berberis family provides the greatest variety of berries in tones of pale green, orange, pink and yellow. The colours are almost breath-taking in the effects they produce. There is, however, one obvious drawback to using berberis for flower arrangement: the copious prickles which decorate the branches. They are surely the most deadly and the sharpest of all prickles!

The only answer seems to be to wear thick gloves and have sharp secateurs for cutting. Most of the thorns must be removed before arranging and the branches at the base of the stem either crushed or split. The colours of the berries make this extra trouble well worthwhile, but it is advisable to bear in mind that it all takes time. Because of the prickles it is sometimes difficult to use berberis with other foliage or flowers and for that reason it may be more successful alone.

Cotoneaster provides bright scarlet berries without the difficulty of prickles and with the added attraction of dark green leaves; also available at this time are skimmia, which produces good clusters of scarlet berries later, and the orange tinted rowan berries.

When arranging branches of berries it is helpful to have a container with a narrow enough neck to support them without the additional props of wire netting or pin holders. This is especially true of berberis, which is usually curving and slightly top heavy. Often the chief contrast comes from the colour of the berries against the colour or texture of the vase.

Foliage is, of course, invaluable at this time of the year and a background of evergreen is often the means of showing up a small number of flowers. Portugal laurel with a few pink chrysanthemums, or camellia foliage with two or three flowers to the front (these can be changed to make a new group as the leaves will last for some weeks) are two of the many possible suggestions.

Horse chestnut, dramatic in size, shape and colouring, is especially beautiful when the leaves are turning to yellow but still have some of the fresh green in them. (There is one point to remember: the leaves must be cut some time before they are ready to drop.) The Spanish chestnut, especially valuable with its almost sculptural ser

In complete contrast is the silver birch – slender branches with numbers of small dancing leaves usually all one colour not unlike raw sienna. They give a charming lightness of touch where the horse chestnut and Spanish chestnut provide solidity and sturdiness and a definite outline.

Then there is beech, which is popular on account of its reliability when treated with glycerine. It is useful and produces a wonderful variety of colour if cut well before it is ready to fall. Similar to beech in many ways, but more angular in growth and turning from clear yellow and burnt sienna to a magnificent flame, is Persian iron wood (*Parrotia persica*). (This also reacts well to the glycerine treatment, turning a deep chocolate brown and lasts from one year to another.) Quite a different leaf and colouring comes with the gingko tree. This has a most distinguished foliage – clear yellow and almost key shaped. The branches may be rather tough and knobbly and therefore sometimes difficult to arrange, but it is worth taking the extra trouble which may be necessary to manipulate them.

Copper beech and prunus come into a class of their own and are as valuable in the autumn as they are earlier on in the year. The same applies to golden privet, radiant like sunshine if used with discrimination and going on well into the winter. The cucumber tree (*Magnolia acuminata*) is another reliable tree for cutting in the autumn, although it does not indulge in vivid autumn colouring but remains cool and elegant in its usual soft olive green backed with chocolate – this is dramatic foliage on the same scale of grandeur as the horse chestnut.

Rhododendron foliage deserves a special mention. It is always available whatever the season, with large dark pointed leaves (arranged almost in a rosette) in the winter but with fresh green shoots in the spring which give a two tone effect against the older darker foliage. The rhododendron is one of the most valuable shrubs for any time of the year.

There is almost no limit to the size of a group which can be constructed on a basis of rhododendron foliage, since both the long tall branches or the graceful curving ones are equally available on full grown shrubs. Cut from the country, where they have been washed by frequent rain and are not encrusted with dust and grime from a town, the colour of these leaves is a good, rich, green, which combines well with most flowers and makes a splendid contrast with other foliage.

R. ponticum the purple flowered shrub seen growing wild in many areas of Britain, especially near the Dorset coast south of Puddletown and all over the Lake District, is a plant which has great value and yet has been much despised; the familiar sight of the quantities of purple flowers are now rather taken for granted. This may be due to the introduction of many new and rather rare varieties of rhododendrons in the last few years.

R. ponticum was brought to England as long ago as 1763, and is a shrub much valued by Miss Gertrude Jekyll in her book *Wood and Garden*. Writing of her own rhododendrons she comments on the variety and shapes of leaf the various species produce: 'Now that the rhododendrons planted nine years ago have grown to a state and size of young maturity it is interesting to observe how much they vary in foliage, and how clearly the leaves show the relative degree of relationship to their original parents, the wild mountain plants of Asia Minor and the United States. These, being two of the hardiest kinds, were the ones first chosen by hybridisers, and to these kinds we owe nearly all of the large numbers of beautiful garden rhododendrons now in cultivation. The ones related to the wild *R. ponticum* have long, narrow, shining leaves, while the varieties that incline more to the American *R. catawbiense* (from the Catawba Mountains in the south eastern United States where it grows on mountain summits as well as on mountain slopes) have leaves twice as broad, and almost rounded at the shoulder where they join the stalk; moreover, the leaf has a different texture, less polished, and showing a grain like Morocco leather.'

From rhododendrons one is led to think of flowering shrubs such as azalea and forsythia, both of which take on a richness of autumn colouring probably unequalled by any other shrub, with the possible exception of the smoke tree (*Cotinus coggygria*). Azalea is inclined to turn to deep purple tones of wine or flame, whilst forsythia sometimes varies from a rather clear yellow, streaked with maroon, to the more conventional darker reds and purples of autumn.

The smoke tree is dramatic indeed—with its feathery plumes and lobe shaped leaves in colours which almost defy description—seen in any quantity this shrub seems to be on fire.

Other leaves which turn well in the autumn are those of the tree peony (in addition to the beauty of the colouring there is also the most distinctive shape of the leaves) and *Rosa hugonis*. Both of these will sometimes take on colourings of deep plum during this season.

In addition there is other foliage which does not excel in autumn colouring, but which goes on well into November and provides reliable material for arrangement as well as interesting contrasts in shape and colour. First on the list is the blue-grey of the globe artichoke, a leaf of almost architectural beauty. Second comes the bright clear green of the hydrangea, solid and definite in outline, and then in complete contrast the dark, rather feathery green of summer jasmine, or the trailing stems of the evergreen honeysuckle (with lighter, slightly mottled green leaves) or the curving stems of periwinkle—either dark and shining, or variegated. Mention of variegated periwinkle reminds one of the dogwoods and also of the variegated spindle tree.

These variegated shrubs and plants are invaluable, acting as an important contrast in colouring to the reds, purples, russets, browns and copper colourings of many of the deciduous shrubs and trees. Usually in a mixed group of autumn colourings only a touch of something variegated is necessary to bring the whole arrangement to life. This may, of course, depend on the texture and shading of the material used, and if there is already a lighter tone of foliage, such as pale yellow privet, the variegated material may not be necessary at all.

Bergenia goes on bravely through the autumn and winter and there are still many of the grey foliaged plants available: garden ragwort, everlasting flower (*Helichrysum*), bells of Ireland (a definite fresh green), old man's beard (*Clematis*), alliums (greenish white or mauve grey) and poppy seedheads (still blue green if they have been allowed to remain on the plants) and quantities of berries.

Then comes St. John's Wort, (small or slender stems) cotoneaster, bright red on fan-like branches berberis of all kinds, viburnum, darker red and very long lasting.

Early autumn is the time of year for cutting branches of beech etc. if one wishes to press or treat them with glycerine and water. This method of preserving is a well known one. The usual proportions are three quarters of glycerine to a quarter of water, although I have known equal quantities to be sufficient in some cases. The branches should be cut whilst still green, and the bases of their stems crushed or split open, then they should stand in the glycerine mixture for about a fortnight to three weeks. (It is advisable to let them stand in a tall, narrow container, so that

Right, An arrangement in a copper urn of autumn leaves and berries including lilac foliage, berberis berries, Persian iron wood, bracken and variegated dogwood. Lighter touches are provided by wild clematis, love-in-a-mist seedheads and a branch of the yellow ginkgo tree. The bright red rounded leaves come from the smoke tree and bells of Ireland seedheads; spiraea and *Rosa hugonis* foliage provide a note of clear green.

the liquid comes as far up the stems as possible).

At this stage some people arrange them in a jug or other suitable container and leave them throughout the winter as a decoration. However, when they seem to have absorbed as much liquid as they need they can be taken out and used with other material.

It is possible, of course, to experiment with various types of branches, sometimes successfully, sometimes not. I have found that the blue-grey of eucalyptus turns a lovely deep wine shade in glycerine, whereas dried off in the sun it sometimes turns a pale coffee colour. Either of these can be useful in a mixed group to provide contrasts of shape and colour. I have also experimented with branches of wild roses at the stage when the hips were bright and red but before the leaves had turned. These leaves, too, went a dark wine colour. Their small size and slightly serrated shape gave yet another note of interest amongst other leaves.

They lasted well in this condition and put away after one winter could be brought out again for the next.

The pressing of leaves can provide one with an even greater variety of material than perhaps the glycerine method. All types of foliage can be tried with such a simple method. The leaves should, of course, be in a good condition when they are laid flat between sheets of newspapers under a carpet, large rug, or any heavy, even weight, such as a pile of books or magazines. Spanish chestnut, ivy, Virginian creeper, garden ragwort, beech, bracken, silver birch are some of the materials which should be successful. For long lasting results, and to prevent any possibility of leaves curling up at the sides owing to too short a time under pressure, I would recommend that foliage should remain flat for at least a month.

Baskets

If there were no other containers available for arranging flowers, we could perhaps manage, in most circumstances, with baskets. These vary not only in shapes and sizes, but also in texture and to such an extent that there is usually something suitable, somewhere.

There are baskets made from Suffolk or Kentish reeds – with a soft grey-blue-green colouring – or from Norfolk willows, dark brown interlaced with pale buff; baskets in highly varnished materials, less sympathetic in outline but perhaps suggesting a more formal appearance; closely woven baskets, and ones with openwork designs, some in a large mesh and others in minutely worked patterns which almost give the feeling of fine needlework. From China there are delicate circular baskets as light as the proverbial feather – and finally in complete contrast are the sturdy brightly coloured baskets from Andorra.

From the point of view of flower arrangement a very important aspect of a basket is its handle. In some types of shapes a spreading arrangement is indicated, and when this is the case, the handle can become a focal point, being most useful for twining branches – especially in the case of plants with graceful stems, such as summer jasmine, hop, periwinkle and clematis. In any case, the handles should be allowed to show clearly, otherwise the shape of the basket will not be complete.

Containers holding the water must, of course, fit into the basket as neatly as possible. These may consist of Pyrex cooking dishes, biscuit tins or lids, baking tins (sandwich, cake, or loaf baking tins are especially suitable), and jam jars. The tins will be less noticeable if they are painted a soft colour. This also applies to the large mesh wire netting that will act as an anchorage for the flowers.

One of the soundest considerations for using a basket is that it can serve a dual purpose. Bread baskets, flat baskets, wine carriers, baskets to hold house plants, sewing baskets, log baskets, shopping baskets, etc. – these can all be used for different types of arrangements.

It could be suggested that a basket is not suitable for the sophisticated type of flower arrangement needed to fit in with sophisticated furnishings. My answer to this would be that I have used a basket for a dried arrangement in such surroundings

Left, A shallow basket showing off the interesting pattern of veronica foliage. The arrangement of the leaves on the stem gives a step ladder appearance, and when this is seen against a plain background the effect can be dramatic.

Right, A cluster of flowers arranged in this attractive small basket could be carried by a bridesmaid or, taken to hospital, already, arranged, as a gift for a patient. The basket is also suitable to use for fruit or bread.

Top, A trug is one of the most versatile of all basket shapes. Here it is lined with an oblong cake tin and used to hold a collection of foliage including bergenia leaves, rosemary, garden ragwort and branches of broom.

and that it did fit it. The design was good and the texture unfussy and simple but it was a sophisticated type of basket, and the dried material chosen was unusual and had a certain dignity.

I think that it is true to say that the colour and texture of many baskets is especially suitable for dried flowers. The colours of dried flowers are soft – there is nothing strident or unsympathetic about them – coming either in the tones and shades that are associated with a Corot or a Brueghel – or in the deep velvet colours of van Dyck or in aubergine, tawny buffs, grey-blues, olive, off white and pale pinks. All these combine well with the material used in baskets.

Finally, because there is no need for water, the stems of dried flowers can be arranged directly into the basket, and in some cases an even more natural effect can be obtained by actually fixing them through the weave.

The most useful of all baskets is probably the 'trug' basket. Everyone knows the usefulness of these baskets for gardening, and this is amplified by the fact that trugs come in a variety of sizes. A large one is invaluable for weeding or collecting cut flowers for the house, and the smaller ones for holding string, scissors, wall nails, secateurs, and all the paraphernalia required for tidying up the garden.

A trug basket also makes an attractive container for holding house plants, e.g. geraniums, tradescantia etc., and for those living in the country with open log fires it is an ideal receptacle for kindling wood.

Many types of baskets are suitable for holding flowers to give as gifts to patients in hospital. Some are manufactured in a close white wickerwork, equipped with a green tin lining and these come in a variety of shapes and sizes, some with handles and others without. One type of basket is even made with a lid.

With some of the smaller posy baskets it is sometimes better to have damp moss or sand for the flowers than to trust to a little jar of water. These so easily get spilt and the arrangement will have a very short life. If all the stems are safely anchored in a larger area of moss or sand they have more chance of absorbing moisture and of keeping fresh. But if you decide on water it is as well to fill up on arrival at the hospital so as to ensure that one does not have a dripping basket.

A much larger basket of quite a different type is the most useful for a pedestal arrangement to decorate a marquee or dance hall. These are baskets constructed specifically to hold flowers or plants, and are usually fitted with tin linings. They are sometimes painted in gold or silver and often have tall curved handles which give ample scope for trailing effects. This is the kind of basket used for presentations to visiting diplomats, V.I.P.s, Royalty, and other distinguished members of the community. If one of these is attempted by an amateur it may be as well to give a word of warning. These baskets are deceptive in size. The actual space to hold the flowers does not seem very large, but they do, in fact, take a quantity of flowers, and can work out to be rather expensive decorations. Also, considering the number of flowers they contain, these baskets do not hold a large amount of water, and so the tin container must be kept well filled to the brim.

A last suggestion, for another type of basket – the punnets. These, too, may either be filled with damp moss or else fitted with a small glass container. They are most suitable, I think, for primroses, gentians, etc., and may provide one of the first steps in flower arrangement for a child. If the punnet is filled with wet moss it will have to stand on a plate or saucer so that there will be no leaks on polished furniture.

Left, Branches of larch provide a dark background and a clear outline for seven white chrysanthemums arranged in a nut brown basket.

Right, A collection of baskets which provide containers for many different types of arrangements, including one for a wall group, an upright group and a bridesmaid's basket.

Top, The flowers in this 'blue' group illustrate the need for a variety of shades of one colour. The African lily is the only true blue flower in the group. The gladioli are deep purple and pale mauve. The onion heads are wine coloured and the clove carnations are pinky mauve.

Right, Bluebells have their own particular shade of blue and are arranged here with a few white ones and with lupin leaves. The contrast of the white with the blue seems to bring out the depth of colour as well as to lighten the whole arrangement.

Left, Delphiniums come in an extensive variety of shades of blue. Much of the charm of these flowers is in the buds and opening flowers. The bright green hydrangea leaves in the arrangement contrast with the clear blue of the delphiniums.

Blue arrangements

One of the usual difficulties about a blue arrangement is to bring it to life. Blue as a colour is impossible, I think, to define. It varies from dark purple-blue, ultramarine, or deep cobalt, to soft dove-grey, and palest sky blue. In between these extremes of colour are all the variations to be found when one looks closely into a cornflower or a scilla, a gentian or a forget-me-not, a bluebell or a delphinium.

How is it that these flowers never look lifeless in themselves? I think the answer is simply that there is always some form of contrast – either a coal-black pistil, creamy-white stamens, pinky mauve outer petals or the shading of a blue petal from quite a deep colour to almost white. An example of this is the scabious with soft grey-blue petals – though perhaps the field scabious is slightly

more blue than mauve – set off by numbers of stamens, some of them pearl coloured and some of them off-white.

The contrast of green leaves is something which one is inclined to take for granted, but which has the effect of throwing up the blue tones and giving them a different emphasis. This point reminds me of the occasion when I saw the painting by Jan Van Eyck of the Arnolfini Portrait, for the first time after it had been cleaned. It was then that the blue and green of the woman's dress made a definite impact, and since that time I have often arranged these two colours together. Delphiniums with hosta foliage or bluebells with wild arum leaves, chimney bellflowers *(Campanula pyramidalis)* with lupin foliage, field scabious with foxglove leaves – any of these suggestions illustrate the point which emerges, that blue often requires another colour in order to bring out the richness of its tones.

Miss Jekyll, one of the greatest lady gardeners, was trained first as an artist. She had an exceptional feeling for the right use of colour, and clearly stated her views on this subject in relation to planting a blue border or blue garden. What she writes has only to be translated into flower arrangement terms and applies in the same way: 'It is a curious thing that people will sometimes spoil some garden project for the sake of a word. For instance, a blue garden, for beauty's sake, may be hungering for a group of white lilies, or for something of palest lemon-yellow, but it is not allowed to have it because it is called the blue garden, and there must be no flowers in it but blue flowers. I can see no sense in this; it seems to me like fetters foolishly imposed. Surely the business of the blue garden is to be beautiful as well as to be blue. My own idea is that it should be beautiful first, and then just as blue as may be consistent with its best possible beauty'. Then Miss Jekyll adds a painting note learnt from her student days: 'Moreover, any experienced colourist knows that the blues will be more telling – more purely blue – by the juxtaposition of rightly placed complementary colour.' (Ibid)

When is a blue arrangement likely to be required? There are certain decoration schemes and certain occasions which demand a blue group. Cornflowers and delphiniums can be effective against a primrose wall and can also look particularly cool against a lime green background. Mention of cornflowers reminds me of the decorations for a

Short stemmed delphiniums cut from the side of the main stalk and arranged in a ginger jar. By using the small stalk flowers the central stem is left in the garden.

wedding some years ago. The colour scheme was to be blue and white. I had suggested a touch of scarlet to bring some life into what seemed to me a rather cold colour scheme, but this idea was refuted. The bride's father was the late John Drinkwater and his favourite flowers had always been cornflowers. For this reason no other flowers were to be used in the church or at the reception afterwards. Imagine my delight, when, just as I was leaving to go to the church for the service, the caterers arrived carrying large trays of the most delicious looking strawberries. This was exactly the colour I had had in mind to introduce into the flower decorations. And so the touch of warmth was there, after all, although not quite as I had thought of it.

Weddings and cocktail parties, dances and receptions often impose rather rigid restrictions in the field of colour, and have to be dealt with tactfully. One is told that the bridesmaids are wearing dresses of blue organdie and require the flower decorations to be blue to match them. Or that a dance hall is to be decorated in 'Cambridge' blue or a reception for a film star must be done in blue because the leading lady is wearing an 'ice-blue' dress. A twenty-first party may require blue arrangements as the young woman in question has always thought of blue as her favourite colour. These are all possible reasons for a blue flower group. The same reasons obviously apply to many other colours, but blue may be more difficult than most of them as one is not able to fall back on roses, chrysanthemums, or even carnations to any extent, whereas with most other colours these flowers are a safe standby.

Depending on the time of year, there are various possibilities which may be helpful. Delphiniums spring to mind, coming as they do in various heights and in every conceivable tone and shade of blue. If arranged when they are still in bud they will last well. Cornflowers, bluebells, scabious, love-in-a-mist (Nigella) hydrangeas, bellflowers, clematis, Californian lilac (Ceanothus) globe thistle, hyacinths, iris, larkspur, veronica, monkshood and beard tongues (Penstemons) are others which will introduce a lively variety of blues. With certain of these it would be interesting to introduce either two or three Madonna lilies, the pale yellow pot marigold (Calendula), clove carnations, or the striking contrast of a bright Zéphirine Drouhin rose.

A blue arrangement can also be helped by the colour of the container. White vases give a lightness to blue flowers (which they may badly need) or one may try a complete contrast, such as arranging deep blue delphiniums in an orange coloured container or softer toned blue scabious in a lemon-yellow vase. Pale blue flowers such as flax or love-in-a-mist can show up well in a lime-green container and the deeper purple-blue of monkshood or larkspur looks attractive and is considerably lightened by copper or brass.

Then there is the question of background and also the considerable problem of artificial light. Both these can make blue arrangements lifeless and undistinguished.

Remember that a blue group will always show up best against backgrounds of yellow or pale lime green or white, and can even look attractive against a clear red – although this tends to give a purple tone to the overall effect. But it is a waste of time putting blue flowers against a darkish ground, with no brightness in the colour itself. An exception is dark wood, which if it shines and gleams can be most successful.

Artificial light is well known to be difficult for blue; and if blue flowers are being arranged specifically for an evening event of some kind it is wise to introduce plenty of white, yellow or bright red.

Various tones of blue – the soft lilac blue of scabious, the more definite blue of hydrangea and the grey Wedgwood blue of globe thistle; the brighter blue of anchusa is lightened with a touch of white hedge parsley – the white is repeated in the gold and white jug.

27

Carnations – *dianthus* and pinks, were fashionable long before many of the other plants and shrubs now growing in our borders were even thought of, much less discovered. They are long lasting, and perhaps the most reliable of all cut flowers, with the exception of arum lilies. Besides being charming in shape, they are available either at the florists' or in the garden throughout the whole of the year, and have foliage that is distinguished both in its soft blue-grey colouring and in its unusual shape.

Pinks have been written about and grown and loved since the days of Chaucer, when they were known as picotees, gilly-flowers or cloves. It was a clove which was plunged into the wine goblet to give it a spicy flavour and a rare fragrance, just as rosemary was added to a tankard of ale.

As early as 1629 John Parkinson in his *Paradisi in Sole Paradisus Terrestris* named as many as nineteen sorts of carnations and thirty pinks (gilly-flowers) which permits one to assume that both flowers must have been cultivated at least during the reigns of Elizabeth I and James I. (In fact Chaucer mentions the 'clove gilofrer and nutmeg'.)

At the beginning of the nineteenth century there was a golden revival in the art of the florist and accordingly a large increase in the various types of carnations. These were divided into three: flakes, bizarres, and picotees, and in the early 1800's Queen Adelaide had a good collection of picotees in her Windsor Great Park garden.

Pinks also were much loved and grown in the Persian Empire in the sixteenth century and in Turkey in the seventeenth century. It is reported that a plant of pink called 'St. Phocas's Nosegay' was sent back to England from Smyrna in 1726.

Sweet Williams seem only to have been cultivated as a florist's flower at one period, namely the beginning of the Victorian era. The place was in Buckingham where at least a hundred varieties were raised, but the whole stock was sold in 1854 and much of it has since, to all intents and purposes, been lost.

Dianthus is the generic name for all uncultivated carnations, and the wild dianthus, still found growing in parts of Asia, is the forerunner of the many different varieties now available in our gardens. (The parent of the florist's carnation is thought to be *Dianthus caryophyllus,* described by medieval writers as the clove gilly-flower.)

We all have our special favourites and most keen gardeners have their own well tried methods of growing them, but I would like to suggest that more

Carnations

Far left, Carnations are available throughout most of the year in a wide variety of colours, which adds to their usefulness in flower arrangement. A handful of clove carnations arranged with two or three yellow ones can immediately add a note of interest to a furnishing scheme where one or both of these colours are featured.

Top, Arranged as naturally as possible, a bunch of pinks will bring into the house, the scent and feeling of a garden. In this arrangement the stems are cut different lengths— some are much shorter than others, so that the flowers can be seen separately.

Left, The carnations, in this arrangement, add brightness to the buff and cream coloured dried grasses. They last well and can be replaced independently of the grasses.

and more pinks and border carnations should be planted with a view to cutting for decoration. There seems to be no end to the variety and colour, some plain, some two shaded, some frilled, some with a bordered petal, some with more petals than others, and all almost without exception with an intense scent.

Since when growing wild they flourish in sunny positions on open hillsides where there is good soil drainage, these must obviously be the conditions they prefer in the garden. One may not be able to duplicate an 'open hillside' but one can at least build up a flower bed to a height of one foot to eighteen inches above the ordinary level–that is if the soil happens to be of heavy clay and not, therefore, well drained.

Dianthus (which includes pinks and border carnations as well as greenhouse carnations) like an alkaline soil, sandy if possible–although it must be admitted that sometimes these plants have been known to do quite well on soils with a certain amount of clay in them. For extra food they prefer rotted farmyard manure. However, they are not hungry plants and one of the best methods of having healthy plants and promoting their sturdy growth is to keep the top soil well hoed, staking the plants if it seems to be necessary. Watering is not usually needed.

Border carnations and pinks that winter outside in the garden should, in most climates, always be allowed to have air circulating freely round their stems and foliage. They do not like protection in the shape of layers of bracken or pieces of matting such as are often provided for most other silver foliaged plants in order to keep out the frost. They prefer currents of air all round their stems and so require, first and foremost, an open position away from wind breaks, overhanging trees, etc. and dislike especially the drifts of damp leaves which might fall in the autumn from nearby trees and settle around them like wet mattresses.

There are pinks and border carnations to suit everyone, as illustrated by the following remark, overheard at one of the British National Carnation Society's Shows in the Royal Horticultural Society's Old Hall:

'There is a carnation or pink for everybody, no matter how odd his taste'.

A winter arrangement using the bright colours of seven carnations against hazel catkins and the distinctive foliage of the Lenten hellebore.

Here are some of the plants given awards at the Wisley Trials a few years ago:

Pink Model: plant with very vigorous stout stems, 24-inches long. Flowers 2 – 2¾ inches in diameter, freely produced, centre crowded, scent slight clove; petals broad, entire, a colour near porcelain rose.

Cottage Primrose: plant vigorous with stout stems, 20-24 inches long. Flowers 2-5 inches in diameter, very freely produced, centre full, scent slight clove; petals broad, entire primrose yellow.

Downs Clove: plant vigorous with stout stems 24-30 inches long. Flowers 2¾ inches in diameter, freely produced, centre crowded, scent very strong clove; petals broad, entire, a rich velvety red near cardinal red.

Sussex Fortune: plant very vigorous with fairly stout stems 24 inches long. Flowers 2½-2¾ inches in diameter, freely produced, centre full, scent strong clove; petals broad, slightly serrated, a velvety shade of geranium lake.

Cottage Jester: plant vigorous with stout stems, 18-20 inches long. Flowers 2¼-2½ inches in diameter, very freely produced, centre full, scent strong clove; petals broad, primrose yellow.

Mendip Huntsman: plant vigorous with fairly stout stems, 30-34 inches long. Flowers 2-2½ inches in diameter, fairly freely produced, centre full, scent strong clove; petals broad, entire Orient red.

Apollo (a variety for the rock garden): plant vigorous, compact bushy erect habit; flower stems 6-8 inches long, slender, rigid, very erect; flowers 1¼ inches in diameter, double, centre tufted, scent slight clove; petals broad, cut, deeply serrated. Magenta rose when first open, changing to a shade of magenta when fully open, faint maroon marking at base of petal; calyx strong.

Helen (a variety for the open border): plant vigorous, compact, erect habit; flower stems 14-16 inches long, slender, very rigid; flowers 2¼-2½ inches in diameter, double, centre full, scent strong clove; petals broad, finely serrated, margins slightly incurving, a shade near porcelain rose.

Thor (a variety for the rock garden): plant vigorous, compact bushy erect habit, flower stems 6-7 inches long, slender, rigid; flowers 1¼ inches in diameter, double, centre full, scent-strong clove; petals broad, serrated, a deep glowing red.

Pink, ruby red, red and white and white sweet williams (*Dianthus barbatus*) arranged in a shallow pedestal Leeds dish. Sweet williams are one of the most suitable of the dianthus family for flower arrangement.

Christmas decorations

Holly was used by the Romans and Greeks for their festivals. Ivy is the symbol of everlasting life in Christian art, and mistletoe was considered sacred by the Druids of ancient Gaul and held in high esteem in Norse mythology. The early Christians called holly 'the righteous branch' and it was used for decorations by the Teutons in the belief that it would keep away evil spirits. There are some parts of the country today where it is still considered unlucky to bring holly into the house before Christmas Eve and other parts where it must be burnt on Twelfth Night. Even when the Puritans abolished most Christmas festivities, these evergreens survived for adorning churches and homes. Is it any wonder that there is magic in our Christmas decorations, especially when we mainly use these evergreens which have been bearers of tradition throughout the centuries?

Christmas seems to me, also, an occasion when children can enter into the decorating as at no other time. If they are too small to do anything else, they can at least drape the tree with tinsel and silver strands. Apart from the dining table– and even that would come within the scope of older children–there is very little that they cannot make themselves, or with the help of an adult.

And so, thinking in terms of evergreens and children, here are some ideas for decorating the house. None of these is particularly original or new but just as recipes for making a cake vary from

person to person, either because of ingredients or of different measurements, I may have included here something new or different from what you have known before.

Let us begin with the front door. There is a street in London where, just before Christmas, one can look down and see a holly wreath hanging on almost every door. Most of the doors happen to be painted different colours, and the effect of the decorations, many of them tied with red ribbon, is very attractive. Some people may feel that this is rather too much of a pattern to follow, and in the country the need is not quite the same. There is so much green of one kind or another near the front door and quite possibly a holly tree heavy with scarlet berries amongst it. However, in the city the whole effect is quite different, and some kind of green is very welcome.

The wreath which many people like for their doors can be made completely of evergreens, or of silvered branches and coloured balls, or a mixture of all three. I have compromised with a mixture including holly, berberis, mistletoe, silver ruscus, silver tape, stiff gold crinkly ribbon and a bow of red satin ribbon. There is really no end to what you can put into the holly wreath for the door, altering its character from one year to another. The base may consist of a wire frame, padded with moss and tied down with string. (This would have to be bought from your florist, unless you happen to have a wholesale gardening shop near by.) The wire frame may also be interlaced with holly, laurel, etc., to form a background for whatever else you wish to add, dispensing with the mossing, which comes near to the professional touch. It is most satisfactory to have a packet of wires, (again obtainable from a gardening shop), by which the different additions to your wreath can be fixed in position or alternatively they may be secured by fuse wire or by green string.

Coming inside the hall there are various possibilities. Some children like to cut out streamers, making patterns in the red and green coloured paper. KISSING RINGS can be made in many forms. The ring itself may be made from three wooden embroidery frames which are bound before being put together with red and green satin ribbon. They are then fixed in sphere like formation by pieces of

Left, A simple table decoration is arranged here in silver, red and white. The small tree is silver
and stands on a red ribbon. The bright red gladioli in the porcelain baskets are arranged with the silver-grey leaves of *Senecio cineraria;*
more silver and white is provided by the candlesticks, salt cellars, candles, plates and mistletoe.

Right, A Christmas wreath can be made from holly or from many different leaves.
In this case the wreath is made from mistletoe, berberis, holly, silvered ruscus and beech branches,
corrugated gold ribbon and a red satin bow.

wire or string where they touch each other; and after the basic work done, it is easy to think out variations in decoration. Sometimes the hoops have lengths of tinsel twisted in and out, and sprigs of mistletoe caught in the wires at intervals. The kissing ring may be suspended on a hook from the ceiling by a cluster of gold and red ribbon, and two gold and silver bells hung from the base.

Another variation on this ring is to paint the wooden hoops white and decorate them with red ribbon, substituting a bunch of red apples for the bells. The apples may be either wrapped in a single layer of cellophane or painted with natural-coloured nail varnish, to preserve their skins without wrinkles. Sprigs of holly look pretty with the white paint, especially if there are any red berries. A CANDLE WIRE STAND is yet another decoration for the hall. This is so simple to make that, except for fixing the candle in position, the whole thing can be made by a child of seven. The wire netting (large mesh) is cut into a strip about eighteen inches in width and a yard long. This should be laid out quite flat and painted white. (It is helpful to lay this on strong sheets of newspaper, so that it can be given a second coat of paint if necessary when the first one has dried.) Then it should be rolled into a kind of pillar, with some of the wire tucked in to form a base. The candle, which must be an outsize one, by its weight will help to keep the edifice in position on an old plate but the candle must also be fixed with wire to the sides of the pillar. After that there is little difficulty in decorating the wire with different coloured balls and a line of silver tinsel round the top. Sprays of Portugal laurel inserted into the wire mesh at the base will help to make it look more attractive, and conceal some of the necessary network.

This design may be repeated once or twice in

Branches of holly are used here as a background for chrysanthemums. The holly leaves must be in good condition and the branches trimmed before being arranged.

Right, To make the most of a few flowers, it is helpful to arrange them in a narrow necked container such as the copper jug in the photograph. The group is given extra size and height with silver branches, teasels, holly, grey backed grevillea and two or three stems of rhododendron foliage. All this material forms a background for the bright red carnations.

a big hall if more light is required. The candles burn slowly and will often last for more than one Christmas.

A good idea for a small Christmas tree is to put it in a front window on a table, decorate it chiefly with tinsel and white and sparkly things, and have a good sized candle in a solid holder at each side. If the candles are kept away from the edges of the branches there will be no danger of fire (if there is no draught from the window) and the tree will show up most attractively to passers by.

The crib (from a child's point of view) is perhaps the favourite of all our decorations. It could be arranged on a small window sill in the hall or some other suitable position, and then lit by a tall white candle in a solid candlestick kept well away from the straw. A flat baking tin is filled with sand and the figures are arranged in this. (The figures can now be bought separately and much more cheaply than was possible at one time, but with a little imagination they could be drawn, pasted on to cardboard, and then cut in silhouette.) The background is provided by sprays of evergreens, and there should be a lighted candle at each end of the shelf. To be still more ambitious, a back-cloth, on which is painted a deep night sky and a shining evening star, can be pinned against the wall behind.

Suggestions for dried or fresh flowers and foliage include:

1   For a large vase, dried flowers and evergreens together can produce a feeling of Christmas. Dark teasels, bulrushes, silver honesty, white larkspur, skeleton magnolia leaves all look well with red berried holly and camellia foliage.

2   For a small table arrangement—either Christmas roses or a few red carnations in a white porcelain dish, or a bunch of sweet-smelling narcissi with a bunch of violets. Sprays of red or white geraniums are valuable at this time of the year, and are not too difficult to produce if one has well cared for plants. A useful table decoration can be made in a punnet filled with damp moss. Sprays of fir, two or three sprigs of holly and mistletoe, a small tight bow of cellophane paper, two or three coloured candles, and one or two baubles will all make quite a pretty arrangement. The small candles can be omitted, and all the material grouped round one large red candle, held in position with a bow of red satin ribbon. The moss must be kept damp if the holly and mistletoe are to last any time, and in that case the punnet should stand on a dish.

3   A large arrangement of evergreens and foliage will last well – camellia green, pittosporum,

rosemary, eucalyptus leaves, holly, silk bark oak (*Grevillea*) and mistletoe.

4   An idea for a splash of colour to break away from the traditional red is to have branches of eucalyptus with the tufted salmon pink flowers, two or three sprays of stove spurge (*Euphorbia fulgens*) some orange lanterns (*Physalis alkekengi*) and a bunch of marigolds.

Other ideas for table decorations–not exactly flower arrangements, but including branches, sprays of evergreen, and candles are:

1   Green magnolia leaves pasted flat on a cardboard circle, decorated with clusters of red holly berries, and, at intervals round the circle, thick and short white and red candles glued in position. This makes a pretty centrepiece.

2   A tall column of wire netting, painted gold or silver, hung with coloured glass balls and decorated round the base with small branches of pine. Into the centre of the column is fixed a tall, wide, red candle. (The bottom of the wire should be folded in to make a base for the candle to stand on.)

3   Spreading bare branches picked from the country may be painted white, sprinkled with silver glitter, hung with red and white Christmas balls, and fixed firmly into painted flowerpots–gold, silver, or white.

4   A nest of tall candles arranged on a concealed wire mesh base, which is covered by sprays of evergreen decorated with artificial snow. Colour may be introduced either in the candles, or by a flat bow of satin ribbon at one side of the base.

5   Ivy is one of the most decorative and co-operative of Christmas evergreens. Arranged round the base of gleaming silver or glass candlesticks, or winding its way across a damask white tablecloth to show off the beauty of its pointed leaves, it can produce a natural and unfussy decoration.

6   Coloured Christmas balls and marbles piled high in a rare piece of old glass, as a centre-piece, surrounded by different coloured candles standing on flat silver stars.

7   Colour schemes with tablecloth, table napkins, candles, glasses, porcelain, etc. in red, white, pink, or green, etc. built round the centre piece of a contrasting colour.

8   Honesty, silvered ruscus, gold painted twigs, and a cluster of gold painted honesty arranged together with a wide double red satin bow securing

firmly two or three gold and silver baubles at the centre, and right through the middle of the group a very large double bow of cellophane paper. If possible this arrangement should be placed in a position with a light behind it, and the effect of the light shining through the gold and silver will be almost fairy-like. If this material can also stand against a mirror, the result will be better still.

9   A small basket, standing on a cake stand and filled with silvered twigs, branches of holly, mistletoe, red candles, and silver bells. Round the base of the stand place five of the small trees- like tiny fir trees, dark green and frosted-one can buy at Christmas time, standing in bright red tubs.

Other ideas for Christmas include small glasses or pieces of porcelain with two or three red or white flowers in them-scarlet geraniums in a white swan, or roses, or white chrysanthemums against dark, glossy leaves.

Sometimes one is lucky enough to have Christmas roses (*Helleborus niger*) out, if the preceding weeks have been reasonably mild or if, in colder climates, one has made sure of them by giving them the protection of a cloche. These look enchanting arranged either with their own leaves or/and with the dark, slightly more slender, leaves of the *H. foetidus*. I have arranged them sometimes in a white container and kept the whole colour scheme to green and white, with white candles, green table mats and white table napkins, with tinsel round silver candle sticks to give extra sparkle.

White geraniums also look attractive with a few leaves, either their own or cut from a zonal pelargonium with variegated periwinkle, especially when arranged in a small piece of white porcelain such as a basket or a figure with a container for water attached.

Another idea for the traditional red of Christmas is to have two bunches of anemones, taking out the purple and mauve ones, and making one small arrangement from the bright red-again, if possible, in a white container. (The purple anemones can be arranged in something suitable for a side table where the red and white colour scheme may not penetrate.)

If a large group is needed which would prove extravagant to fill with fresh materials, it is possible to use dried white larkspur and delphiniums, with pressed foliage of garden ragwort (with the white side of the leaf uppermost), silver honesty, pearly everlasting *(anaphalis)* all arranged with skeleton branches painted white-if possible of beech or

Right, A background of berried holly with pine and clusters of fir cones would be suitable for a Christmas arrangement. A few pure white Christmas roses could also be used. This arrangement stands on a piece of wood to give it a pedestal effect.

A basket of walnuts, a few red candles, some heavily berried sprays of holly and clusters of mistletoe make this cheerful Christmas decoration which will need no replenishment throughout the season.

hazel—and towards the centre a cluster of holly with red berries. This would show up to advantage if it was well lit from behind, especially if a few skeleton magnolia leaves were also included.

The addition of holly to almost any group immediately seems to give a feeling of Christmas, whatever other material is used, even if the colours of the other flowers are not in the traditional red or white. Branches of holly, for instance, kept as far as possible in their original shape and arranged with a gay mixture of chrysanthemums in yellow, white and bronze, certainly give this feeling, and will prove to be economical as well as attractive. A few rhododendron leaves might also be used towards the centre of such a group if they are available, or else a cluster of mistletoe. These would all be held in place by large mesh wire netting as holly is rather too heavy to be successful on a pin holder. If the water supply is watched carefully both the holly and the chrysanthemums will last for some time, especially if the stems of the chrysanthemums have been well smashed first.

This last suggestion might be too clumsy for a dining table and would, perhaps, be more suitable for a side table or for a table in the hall or on a landing. The flowers are sturdy and would stand up well to draughts which they might possibly encounter from the front door.

If gold or silver paint are brought into use, as is sometimes not only necessary but attractive if done with restraint, one would make the plea that it is not depended on to the exclusion of natural evergreens. It might also be well to remember that 'a little goes a long way'. However, there are occasions when an all-gold decoration, for instance, may not only be suitable but also economical and a few dried materials sprayed with gold paint can give quite a pleasing effect.

Fixed in Plasticine and on a pin-holder towards one end of a flat piece of bark the following small sprays and branches made an effective decoration: a sprig of dock, a small spray of honesty, a few poppy-heads, two or three sprigs of ruscus, a large head of achillea cut short and arranged towards the centre, and two curving stems of eucalyptus foliage which gave the outline shape to the whole group. (Eucalyptus is especially successful when sprayed owing to the interesting arrangement of the leaves and to their flat shape which catches and reflects the light.) Such decoration is useful for a hall or anywhere which might be draughty and difficult for fresh flowers, or it could be made as an all-round group for a table centre. But its main point is the economy of material – many other small stems of dried materials could be used – as long as they are selected with regard to their possibilities of contrast either in shape or texture.

Left, Red berried variegated holly and branches of rhododendron foliage provide the background for creamy white spray chrysanthemums.
The flowers stalks are cut different lengths, those towards the front and centre of the group are quite short.

Right, A small collection of evergreens, berries and dried woodheads form a cheerful arrangement for Christmas.
The dark shining camellia leaves provide contrast for the variegated ivy and golden privet.
The dried globe artichoke heads towards the centre of the group look almost as if they are carved out of wood.

Chrysanthemums

One of the most dependable and long lasting of all flowers for arrangement is the chrysanthemum. For this reason it has been appreciated by the Japanese for some hundreds of years. Although lately greatly increased in varieties, types, etc., many of its chief characteristics remain the same. More than anything else, it is the overall length of the flowering period which has been altered and extended almost beyond belief.

First cultivated in England, as far as is known during the eighteenth century, the chrysanthemum flowered on October 15th and not before—a hundred years later it is recorded as still doing the same. Then French horticulturists worked on the possibilities of earlier flowering types, realising the commercial potentialities of success. But it was not until thirty years ago that in England results were achieved.

Now, by keeping some chrysanthemums under glass for most of the year outdoor crops are available from July onwards into October and there is an almost constant source of supply, supplemented by shipments from abroad.

And so, there is seldom a shortage of chrysanthemums for flower decoration. Is this a good thing? Do we tend to depend too much on their almost permanent availability, knowing how reliable they are, to the detriment of other flowers? (This also applies to gladioli.)

The Japanese, who rule that flowers must only be used in their proper season, would not approve of such a procedure. What is their objection? Why should one only arrange flowers which are appropriate to a certain time of the year, such as branches of blossom in the spring and sprays of chrysanthemums in the autumn? The Japanese answer to this is that only by using what is in season does one learn about other flowers and plants. This thesis seems quite reasonable, for, if one only arranged chrysanthemums, gladioli, carnations and florists' roses, the chances are that they would be the only flowers one was familiar with or liked to use.

In this way, one of the main points of Japanese flower arrangement would be lost—that of getting to know not only the name but also the habits of various flowers and plants that are useful and suitable. The more extensive this knowledge the greater one's respect for the growing plant.

Here is a short list of recommended varieties suitable for the garden, decoration and cutting:
WHITE: Evelyn Bush, Whiteball, Jacqueline.
YELLOW: J.R. Johnson, Yellow Snowdance and Betty Wiggins.
BRONZE: Bill Speat, Westfield Bronze and Hector Morris.
PINK: Catherine Porter, Florist and John Woolman.
RED: Red Flare and Super Star.
PURPLE: Regalia and Wyvern.
BRONZE-APRICOT: Morley Jones.
CHAMPAGNE-PINK: Shantung.

Others which do not need debudding and can be grown for garden display and cutting are:
WHITE: Lilly Wisbech and Garden White.
YELLOW: Joke and Golden Orfe.
BRONZE: Wally Ruff and Nerina.

Returning to the point of a longer flowering period for chrysanthemums brings us to their

In this group two or three stems of spray chrysanthemums are arranged on a pin holder which stands in a small bowl of water on a flat dish. One of the sprays is kept to almost its full height, but the others are cut into shorter sprays and fill in the base of the arrangement and conceal the pin holder.

usefulness in certain types of flower arrangement. They survive equally well, unlike some other flowers, either arranged on a pin holder or in a mesh of wire netting or in 'Florapak' or 'Oasis'. They seem to have no preference. They will stand up (probably more successfully than any other flower) to the conditions imposed by central heating, and they come in different lengths of stem, some of the taller spray chrysanthemums being especially valuable for large arrangements.

But this is not all: there is a fantastically large range of colours, varying from white, creamy white, lemon yellow, sunshine yellow and deep gold, through all the various tones of orange, copper and bronze to pink, rose and deep wine. White chrysanthemums for weddings and funerals, or for occasions when white flowers are required, are invaluable. They are also important for use at Christmas and will fit into any holly and white flower schemes, e.g. group consisting of Christmas roses, white anemones, white carnations, and white orchids (in this case the small spray chrysanthemum would be most suitable, cut short), or else arranged alone. Chrysanthemums are also

suitable for taking to a patient in hospital, for they will contend with draughts and abrupt changes of temperature with more good nature than almost any other plant.

Two or three flowers, arranged with their foliage (which is original in shape and usually a good, dark green in colour) will comprise a group, if the stems are cut different lengths so that each flower can be clearly seen. The single chrysanthemums are especially attractive in this type of group, as are the early flowering chrysanthemums named 'radar', with thin narrow petals which give a shaggy appearance to the flower.

So far I have been referring to the chrysanthemum as something which comes into its proper season in the autumn. But there are, of course, many other members of this family which are available in their proper season, namely summer. Some of these are amongst the most valuable material for large arrangements which require bunches of flowers, economical in price, reliable in staying power, and attractive in shape.

Of these perhaps the best-known to flower arrangers is the Shasta daisy or Esther Read (*C. maximum*). A first cousin to Esther Read is Wirral Perfection, recommended especially as being good in the border as well as for cutting. Sometimes large groups for weddings or receptions need a great deal of what is known in the trade as 'padding'. This means material which is unobtrusive enough not to clash with or detract from the more important flowers, but which will provide the much needed body and substance. Such a flower is the Esther Read chrysanthemum, described as 'anemone centred'. Coming chiefly in white they are valuable either with other white flowers for a wedding or as a contrast with different colours. They last, one could almost claim, for weeks.

Then there is the wild ox-eye daisy, *(C. leucanthemum)*, which is, again, long lasting and one of the most charming in this chrysanthemum family. With their wide open white petals and golden centres, these daisies are simple and beautiful. They give a light touch to more solidly con-

This arrangement illustrates the use of an uneven number of flowers. Seven large copper coloured chrysanthemums are arranged with branches of the silver backed evergreen elaeagnus in an early porcelain jug. Elaeagnus is an invaluable shrub for cutting.

A collection of various types of chrysanthemums arranged in a wine cooler with branches of camellia, rosemary, garden ragwort, veronica, garden rue, phlomis, silver backed elaeagnus and silver leaved *Senecio cineraria*.

structed flowers and have a grace which some cultivated flowers from the border might well envy.

Rather like a bigger edition of the ox-eye daisy is *C. frutescens* the large white marguerite common to many gardens and sometimes found growing by the roadside. This is another invaluable flower for arrangement, because of its size, clear white petals, golden centres, long stems, and dark green foliage. Being simple in shape *C. frutescens* is singularly effective in a large arrangement or looks charming when arranged in a group on its own.

Yet another of this group of chrysanthemums is the plant known as feverfew, with clusters of small daisy like flowers at the ends of branching stems. There is a variety with yellow leaves known as golden feather, but this is not as attractive as the similar feverfew which has fresh green leaves, making a cooler background for the gold and white daisies. These sprays of flowers are attractive either for small arrangements or to give a light, branched effect with more solid material such as pansies, godetias, phlox and the Esther Reads already discussed.

The mention of small flowered feverfews reminds one of the chrysanthemum (as we think of it) belonging to the pompon variety. This is one of the outdoor kind. Some of the smallest of this group are useful in early autumn in much the same way as the feverfew is in the summer to lighten a large group or to use in a small arrangement. These flowers may also be cut into short sprays.

Church flowers

Each week, all over the world, people are arranging flowers in their churches. They do so because they want their church to look beautiful and cared for, just as the people who clean the brasses, polish the pews or scrub the tiled floors all want to make their church look as tidy and shining as possible. Cleaning brass and polishing woodwork are fairly straightforward. We all do it at home, and there is little difficulty.

But doing the flowers is often another matter. Theoretically, since we also arrange the flowers at home just as we do the housework it would seem to be a simple matter to do two vases of flowers for the altar or a large pedestal vase by the pulpit. But it is not quite as simple as that.

Let us go into the points to be considered carefully one by one. Containers for flowers on the altar are important for the same reasons that they are important in home decoration. They should show off the flowers well, be easy to arrange, hold plenty of water and fit in with their surroundings. But how often does this happen? Frequently, vases provided by the church are beautiful in texture

and design as vases, but when it comes to putting flowers into them their shapes are almost impossible from the point of view of arranging a dozen daffodils or a bunch of chrysanthemums. Narrow necks, which seem to prevail, are ideal for two or three branches with long stems, but not easy or suitable for a bunch of stocks or marigolds.

However, from the arranger's point of view, much more interest is now being shown in church vases and if suggestions are made tactfully it may well be possible to have ones which are made not only from fine brass or silver, often with exquisite craftsmanship, but which also have a good shape suitable for flower arrangements. Another requisite is that vases hold a good supply of water. They may not be topped up every day even though the verger has the best intentions, he may not have the time or opportunity, and so the more water they can hold the better.

Now comes the most important point that of the vase fitting in well with its surroundings. The usual arrangement on an altar is to have the cross in the middle and a candlestick at either end. In

between stand the vases. If possible they should combine well both in the metal they are made of and in their shapes, (particularly at the base), with the candlesticks and the cross.

Often vases are given in memory of someone, and so may be beautiful in themselves.

Flowers suitable for an altar arrangement should fulfil certain qualifications. First and foremost they should be sturdy and long lasting. In most cases, they must continue to look fresh for about a week. This is quite a tall order and can be fulfilled only by certain ones.

Here is a short list of long lasting flowers which I have personally found useful when doing church decoration, but there is no guarantee that they will always last the required week: African lily *(Agapanthus),* allium, carnation, chrysanthemum, yarrow *(Achillea),* gladiolus, larkspur, ixia, foxtail lily *(Eremurus),* Peruvian lily *(Alstroemeria),* Corsican hellebore, marguerite, globe thistle, Michaelmas daisy, zinnia, narcissus and daffodil (only if just cut before being arranged), London pride, godetia, sea holly *(Eryngium),* globe flower *(Trollius),* arum *regale* and *longiflorum* lilies.

Foliage for an altar arrangement, one must remember, should be clearly seen right down the church. As long as foliage is given a good supply of water, it will usually last through the week without difficulty. Here is a list of leaves and branches which might prove helpful: rosemary, pussy willow, eucalyptus, berberis, periwinkle, camellia, veronica, bergenia, whitebeam, Portugal laurel, magnolia, garden ragwort, *Garrya elliptica,* hydrangea, golden privet, tradescantia.

The background of the altar is obviously a most important factor in deciding what flowers and foliage to select, and, in the case of a reredos, whether to have any flowers at all. If the reredos does not permit having flowers actually on the altar a big vase on the altar step or on a pedestal can sometimes be used. Pedestal vases are discussed

in the section on weddings. The only possible place for them when there is an ornate altar is at the side, otherwise the carvings or other decorations would be concealed and the whole character of the altar spoilt. On very elaborate altars it is really unnecessary to have any flowers although small vases may be placed there for the benefit of the clergy or brides. Small vases do not show up even at a short distance away, and if they were made more important they would obscure the reredos.

As regards the relation of flowers to their surroundings, the flowers should not stand out on their own but should bring into close relationship the cross with the candlesticks, the altar with its background and the cross again with a window, picture or curtain which may be above or behind it.

A children's chapel, or a small table for which the children are responsible is included in many churches. Small children like to arrange a small vase and often like to provide the vase themselves, which may well turn out to be an old honey jar or a meat paste pot. Using a bunch of anemones in such a vase, the child may learn one of the first principles of flower arrangement–i.e. to cut the stems at different lengths.

Now let us turn to harvest festivals and christenings. It always seems to me slightly impertinent to make suggestions for harvest festival decorations. Many churches already adorn their pulpits, choir stalls, window ledges and lecterns with the fruits of harvest so beautifully that further ideas seem unnecessary. There is such a generosity of material available at this time–vegetables, flowers, fruit, corn, wine, etc. – and it is generally displayed attractively in all its bounty. Flower arrangement may play a part in this festival, but it cannot be regarded as the most important one.

However, there are a few points which apply equally to the arrangement of fruit and vegetables as they do to flowers. One is that they should be in a position which enables them to be seen by most of the congregation, and the other is the consideration of colour.

Positions in which the produce is arranged must, therefore, be selected with an eye to their sitting, and at a harvest festival great use can be made of ledges and sloping window sills, which are difficult to decorate at any other time of the year. Pillars can be brought into use by twining seed heads of wild clematis spirally, which are kept in position by thin bands of wire. Corn and wheat look effective tied in clusters in this way too.

Colour in a harvest festival gives a feeling of abundance just as much as the quantity of material used. There are scarlet hips, deep brown reed mace, nasturtiums, zinnias, Michaelmas daisies, the purple-pink of Comtesse de Bouchard clematis, dahlias, chrysanthemums, the good, clear yellow of golden privet, scarlet oaks, wine-red azalea leaves, scarlet and red and purple Virginian creeper, dark green, clear cut fig leaves, trailing ivy and periwinkle, and long curving stems of summer jasmine. Sometimes there are still some pure white Japanese anemones in bloom and always the bunchy hydrangeas. Imagine this riot of colour with shining red apples, great yellow and green marrows, scarlet carrots, the green-white or orange-gold of onions and clusters of grapes providing a note of clear, pale moonlight green or deep aubergine purple.

Any local product usually is, or should be, given first place. For instance in the parish church of Tenterden, England, bowers of hop garlands decorate the pillars or provide special decoration for the harvest festival scheme. In most churches there is a stack of corn as well as baskets of eggs.

The idea of decorating the font for a christening seems to me a very charming one. It is so simple to do that it is quite unnecessary to have any particular knowledge of flower decoration, and a good effect can be achieved with only a few flowers.

Whatever the decoration, simplicity should be the keynote. Small flowers seem to be more in keeping and seem to make the best decorations. After all, the most important person present is usually still rather small, and probably, if we only knew, prefers small things. The same applies to the containers for the flowers. The area to be covered is not very large, and anything big or clumsy might look out of proportion, apart from probably getting knocked over.

Some churches have a semi-circular tin tray for flowers which fits their own font, but this, I have found, is not usual. (The idea of flowers for the font seems to come from the parents and is usually carried out by them.)

Containers can vary from small porcelain troughs to egg cups. I have seen, and used myself, small branches of wood scooped out to hold water and flowers. These seem to fit in rather well in a country church. Silver egg cups filled with snowdrops and interlaced with branches of shining ivy leaves made another decoration, slightly more formal. Rosemary played an important part on another occasion. Only two troughs were used this time, but the small collection of spring flowers, yellow, white and pale green, were given greater width and importance by sprigs of rosemary, which have a most attractive and rather sprightly shape.

Perhaps the only special point to remember about decorating a font for a christening is that space must be left for the clergyman to approach close to the font with the infant in his arms and lean over into it. Anyone who has been present at a christening will appreciate this necessity, having probably noticed the often generous sweeps of drapery involved in the process of pouring the water on the baby's forehead. A flower decoration which is too pretentious might well prove restricting.

Equipment for doing the flowers for church vases depends on how well the vestry is organised, but the following may be helpful: scissors or secateurs are essential, as well as large mesh wire netting. (In most altar vases, however narrow, I have found it helps to have some kind of anchorage, and crushed wire netting provides this.) Also a dust sheet to spread out close to the vase with the fresh flowers laid out on it, so that you can see exactly what material you have available.

Fill up the vases with fresh water to within two inches of the top and fix in your wire netting. Spread out the dust sheet, so that you can arrange the vase in position without fear of spilling or making any mess which might spoil the vestments. If you are using foliage, it seems sensible to arrange it in the vase first. This will help to get the height and outline necessary to take in the flowers.

When you have finished, and before removing everything, go to the back of the church to see how the flowers show up from a distance. Finally fill up the vases to the very top from your narrow spouted jug, then clear away the dust sheets, watering can, etc., (these may all be left, by arrangement with the verger, in a cupboard for the next time.)

Now there is the problem of trying to keep the flowers looking tidy during the week and, most important of all the clearing away of the old flowers before the next Sunday when the vase will be arranged by someone else – usually there is a compost heap in a corner of the churchyard where the old flowers should be taken – and leaving the vase clean and empty and in position. if this is convenient. In some churches, if the vases to be arranged are of great value, they may be locked safely away in the vestry while not actually in use. In one of the big London churches the altar vases are screwed down in position and only the container inside each vase holding the water can be taken away to clean and re-fill.

Right, A harvest festival arrangement including leek heads, golden rod, small white Michaelmas daisies, dahlias, Zéphirine Drouhin rose, yellow achillea, pampas grass, clematis, berberis, golden privet, rose hips and snow berries.

Bottom, A large group of mixed summer flowers arranged in a Chinese urn on a pedestal. The summer jasmine and curving periwinkle stems are arranged in a green enamel holder, fixed to the upright pillar with wire. At the foot of the pillar is a narrow green trough filled with shorter stemmed flowers and foliage.

Clematis

Clematis are invaluable for decoration on account of the long lasting qualities of certain varieties, the beauty of the individual flowers, the shape and arrangement of the leaves, and the curving stems and tendrils.

There was a time, only a few years ago, when many gardens boasted one clematis–a deep purple one–but usually only one. In these days many more clematis are being grown in gardens and so the nurseries are putting more on the market, more is being written about clematis, and therefore knowledge of how to grow this plant successfully is probably more general than it has ever been before.

It is now well known that clematis can be grown in many countries. They will also flower almost throughout the year–beginning with *C. calycina* in early spring (with fern like evergreen leaves and small cream flowers) and rounding off in the late autumn with the lovely soft lilac coloured Comtesse de Bouchard. In between these two there are many varieties, some, small-flowered like most of the montanas which come out in the early summer months, others with large single flowers in white, red, mauve with a pink stripe, or deep purple.

Three examples which do not quite fit into either of the above categories are the medium-sized Etoile Violette, with a small deep purple flower and a wonderfully rampageous growth; *C. chrysocoma,* with soft pink flowers and rather hairy wine coloured leaves (there is one growing to an immense size and height in the Savill Gardens,

Windsor Great Park); and *C. flammula* with small, star like, creamy white, scented flowers.

There are also yellow clematis, e.g. *C. tangutica,* and a deep red Ernest Markham. Once they are established and have grown past the dreaded 'wilt' stage one can be sure of a regular and varied supply for arrangement.

The charm of the curving sprays may best be seen, either when they are arranged in a tall narrow necked container, such as a wine bottle, decanter, or an old glass scent bottle (when the shape gives ample support to the stems), or else on a flat dish or plate.

In the former case care must be taken to keep the neck of the container well filled up to the brim, as clematis are thirsty plants, and in the case of the latter the water supply must also be watched and carefully checked.

Clematis make particularly attractive dining table arrangements, when arranged so that one is able to look down into their flowers and to trace clearly the curves of their stems and tendrils. One method of holding them in position that I have found suitable for dinner or lunch party arrangements (they only had to last in that particular arrangement for a few hours)–was to have two or three stems held together in a thimble. The clematis was Comtesse de Bouchard whose soft lilac and pink colouring I have already mentioned. The flowers were arranged on a long, flat pale purple dish so that the curving stems lay across it. The thimble fixed in position at one side in lilac coloured Plasticine held enough water for the three thin stems.

Some people feel that clematis may be difficult to deal with in the garden because of the different times for the pruning of some varieties. But this is not as complicated as it sounds, and there are, in fact, certain clematis which need very little pruning apart from the usual tidying up and training of the new shoots.

I have found that most clematis will climb up a framework of string or strong netting between posts but that, on the whole, they are not usually happy on wire netting. (There may well be cases where this is not so, and I only make this comment in a general sense and write of my own experience.) And then there is the question of situation–clematis will grow facing most aspects, often doing reasonably well on a north or north east wall, but they do resent, more than anything, even in the most promising situations, a draught. Like most plants clematis will stand up to winds of gale force strength as long as it only blows against them and not through them.

Once clematis have their backs safely supported by a solid wall, or are trained between tall posts and form a thick pillar of growth, all will be well, but they should not be so far away from their support that the draughts can blow up between the gaps.

It is not necessary to have a large amount of garden space to grow a clematis. One of my most successful results was with an old favourite, the Comtesse de Bouchard, which I had to grow in a very small London garden, so small that to find room for it we had to take up a slab of concrete against a wall close to the gate. Here my clematis flourished year after year, giving me valuable flowers from late June until early November.

For those with no garden space at all, or for those requiring an upright growth of clematis, it is possible to buy special oak tubs with an upright framework attached to them through which the plant can climb.

There is also another point worth mentioning, and that is clematis sometimes disappear for a year or two and then, when one has nearly given up hope of seeing them, come to life again. They may put out fresh leaves and shoots and behave altogether as though there had been no interim period in their development. I have myself 'lost' one clematis for five years in this way, but it eventually put in an appearance again.

I should like here to include a plea for the wild clematis, known as old man's beard. Anyone who has used it in decorations will know its possibilities, but to those who are still to be converted I should like to stress its enchanting qualities and to suggest they try it when they have a chance. (Old man's beard likes a chalky soil and grows on the chalk ridges wherever they come in the countryside.)

Its greatest charm, I think, lies in the seedheads and tendrils remaining when it has finished flowering before they have reached the completely furry stage, although I have seen these used to good effect for Christmas decorations with silver honesty.

The seedheads of many garden clematis are often attractive, soft grey-green whorls of methodical tangle, and when this is so they can either provide an unusual addition to an arrangement, or can be the focal point of interest from which the arrangement develops. Seedheads are surprisingly beautiful earlier on while still silky in texture, although the later, fluffy stage also has its attractions–contrary to expectation, the fluffy stage lasts well when cut for decoration and does not, as one might think, fall quickly or blow about the room–it is, in fact, remarkably tough.

How pleasant it is to sit by a warm fire on a cold winter evening poring over catalogues illustrated with tempting photographs or to read again favourite gardening books full of fascinating descriptions and pictures of plants and flowers. Ideas come and go as one turns the pages and even if only a few of these materialise there is the pleasure

The charm of clematis depends on the buds, leaves and curving stems; therefore it is better to cut these together with the flowers. Clematis is a valuable and long lasting plant for flower arrangement – these in the photograph lasted for almost a fortnight.

Right, Clematis is a particularly suitable plant for a table arrangement The Comtesse de Bouchard is a reliable one to grow for this purpose as it has a long flowering period, from the end of May to November, and is not too fussy as to conditions in the garden.

of planning and making selections. Amongst the most exciting catalogues to include in such a collection is, I think, one on clematis. Only recently have the opportunities for using clematis in flower arrangements been thoroughly explored and, even now, there are still gardening enthusiasts who have not planted more than two or three clematis plants.

Varied in colouring, size of bloom and time of flowering, some of these clematis are long lasting for cutting. I have known some of the deep purple *jackmanii* clematis last for over a fortnight in water. Since they are difficult to have on sale in a florist's shop, owing to their manner of growth, it is essential to put some into the garden.

And so, get out the catalogues and make a selection at once with cutting for the house in mind.

51

Colour in flower arrangements

The question of colour at any time seems to me
to be so bound up with painting, as to make it
almost impossible to discuss one without the other.
There is so much to say that it is difficult to know
just where to begin. Generally one starts with
the study of colour charts (which, of course, we all
did at school) learning that the three basic colours
are red, blue and yellow, and that the opposite of
each colour is composed of the two remaining
ones mixed together. This explains why yellow
goes well with purple, blue with orange, and red
with green.

Flowers (i.e. colour in the garden) like a box of
water colours or oils (i.e. colour in painting) come
in so many shades of colour, and in such varied
tones that their possible blending of colours when
mixed are endless.

There is for instance, the basic difference between gamboge, raw sienna and chrome yellow but
all are termed variants of 'yellow'. Another point
is that no two people see colour alike (what appears
to be a clear cobalt blue to one person takes on
the semblance of a greeny-blue to another, and so
on). This makes the description of colour schemes
precarious, but adds to the excitement and chal-
lenge of arranging flowers. It is important to
remember that colour can either be used to emphasise other colours or detract from them. For
example imagine say a grey and primrose yellow
room, a flower arrangement in it might be of

53

Far right, Here is an example of different tones of red blended together. These colours all come in the same flower and in each of them there is a little of the tone of the flower next to it —
a peach coloured ranunculus next to a fiery orange one catches some of the peach glow, without clashing.

Bottom, Now comes an example of different colours and different flowers arranged together.
The cluster of soft pink bergenia flowers towards the centre of the group contrasts with the violets.
This soft pink is introduced again in the *Rhododendron praecox* and in the freesias. The lilac coloured freesia provides a link between this soft pink and the more purple shades of the anemones. The colour of the deepest purple anemone is picked up by the violets.

primrose and lilac which would tend to blend in and to emphasise the yellow of the room. On the other hand, a strong chrome yellow would surely clash with the primrose and drain the colour away.

A large hotel laid out its small garden this year, at what must have been a vast financial outlay, with one border full of crimson geraniums, and a row of the purple-pink variety at a little distance behind. It produced neither the surprise of a good startling clash of colour nor any suggestion of harmony, and seemed to be a good example of opportunity wasted. On the other hand, a white washed cottage with a deep leaf green door (a real Robin Hood green), and a harmonious border of

white peonies, with rich dark foliage, white Iceberg roses and the chalk plant (gypsophila), is a delight to the eye and an opportunity used to the full.

Perhaps one wall of a North facing room may be painted in a warm colour (red, orange, yellow etc.) immediately giving the feeling that the room is a smaller, warmer place. (An orange or red flower arrangement would have the same effect, obviously). Imagine again a room painted in grey, white or green, when thinking in terms of a cool effect. A flower arrangement in these colours would give a similar feeling.

However, one can only make suggestions, very tentatively, and leave the rest to personal taste, selection, and experiment. With that proviso, here are some ideas for arrangements—using various flowers of one colour. This is formed by a list of colour combinations which I have found interesting. (These are groups which were all collected during the months of July to September).

ONE-COLOUR ARRANGEMENTS
GREEN: sorrel; spurge; large horseradish leaves; a spray of green blackberries; scabious buds; hedge privet, with some of the leaf cut to show the green berries; hop flowers; mignonette; pale green heads of hydrangea.
WHITE: gladioli; white scabious; chalk plant

Top, Two or three sprays of mimosa are arranged here on a pin holder (which is concealed by moss) in a green and yellow porcelain dish. The shape of the leaves and the grouping of the small flowers is seen more clearly if only a little material is arranged.

Bottom, The colours available in snapdragons are as numerous as those of the rainbow. Snapdragons can be used in conjunction with almost any colour scheme, either as a mixed collection of colour or in varying shades of one colour.

(Gypsophila); lilies; love-in-a-mist; Shasta daisies; pinks; carnations; phlox; white cornflowers; green grasses.

PINK: larkspur; carnations; hydrangea; dianthus; antirrhinums; cornflowers; bouncing Bet; asters; gladioli; geraniums; roses.

BLUE: delphiniums; larkspur; African lily *(Agapanthus)*; globe thistle; flax; cornflowers; hydrangea; Canterbury bells; sea holly *(Eryngium)*; love-in-a-mist; monkshood; scabious.

RED: geranium; gladioli; bergamot; corn lilies *(Ixias)*; roses; godetias; snapdragons.

GREY: lamb's ear *(Stachys lanata)*; lavender foliage; cotton lavender; rosemary foliage; verbascum leaves; garden ragwort foliage; plume poppy foliage. (To these were added three large white clematis flowers and white geraniums.)

YELLOW: yarrow *(Achillea)*; golden rod; marigolds; montbretia; pansies; nasturtiums; dahlias; snapdragons.

PURPLE: larkspur; lavender; asters; Michaelmas daisies; hydrangea; monkshood; sweet peas; gladioli.

COMBINATION-COLOUR GROUPS

Phormium leaves with green leek heads, poppy heads and dianthus foliage.

The deep green and tan leaves of the cucumber tree

Bottom, The beauty, colouring, shape and scent of pansies cannot be overrated.
Here they are arranged on a flat dish so that the face of each can be seen. A few sprays of tradescantia provide a suitably light and delicate background.

Top, An arrangement of bright red anemones; there is a red and white one in the group which picks up the white of the vase.
The sweet scented geranium leaves give a covering for the rather bare anemone stems.

Left, In this photograph colour is illustrated by the contrast of the mauve and orange in the strelitzia — a contrast which is worked out again by the rest of the material in the arrangement and the shells.

Right, Red, like the other primary colours has an an enormous range of tones. When using a primary colour in an arrangement it is helpful to introduce a little of an opposite colour. In the photograph green is introduced by using geranium and rose leaves and by arranging the group in a green dish.

White lilac, mauve lilac, broccoli with purple heads on it (some of them breaking into a pale yellow flower), Queen Anne's lace, whitebeam flower, hollyhock leaves.

Blue-green heads of hydrangea with eucalyptus.

Curving branches of the white shrub spiraea with white lilac (cut short) and white bluebells.

Green love-lies-bleeding with white African lily (Agapanthus).

Green tulips with deep cerise dianthus.

Lamb's ear (Stachys lanata) with white sweet peas, white roses, and rosemary foliage.

Pink mauve clematis (Comtesse de Bouchard) with periwinkle.

Grey green buds of mullein with mignonette and deep wine hydrangea flowers.

White summer jasmine with everlasting pea, catmint, and two or three Ophelia roses.

Regal lilies, delphiniums, and Paul's Scarlet roses.

Buff coloured fox-tail lilies (Eremurus) with pale and dark delphiniums with deep rose peonies, blue cornflowers, and pink Canterbury bells.

White fox-tail lilies, allium heads, longiflorum lilies, and white peonies.

Elder flowers before they are quite out, with most leaves taken off, and deep yellow roses.

White foxgloves, Queen Anne's lace, and mock orange (Philadelphus).

Curving branches of rosemary in flower with the bright yellow cluster of berberis flowers.

Yellow columbines with hare's-tail grasses and cow-parsnip flowers.

Red polyantha roses with tradescantia foliage.

Red bergamot with blue love-in-a-mist.

Feverfew with evening primrose.

Globe artichoke heads–rich purple–poppy heads, green grasses, and small bulrushes (lesser reed mace).

Blue green heads of hydrangea with drying bear's breeches (Acanthus) and carnation foliage.

(Magnolia acuminata) with buff Japanese chrysanthemums.

Solomon's seal with guelder rose, green tulips, and longiflorum lilies.

Purple lilac, pink stocks, and purple sprouting broccoli.

White rhododendrons with whitebeam foliage and flame coloured tulips.

Chinese Lanterns (Physalis alkekengii) with their leaves, two or three sprays of spurge and a bunch of marigolds.

Containers

Jugs and baskets provide more vases for flower arrangement than any other kind of container. It is important that something of the handle and spout of the jug or basket handle should be seen wherever possible, so that its character is not lost.

Vases for flowers have been found in England since the middle of the eighteenth century when some of the first Wedgwood 'bough pots' made their appearance and the Leeds factory produced wall brackets. They were not made in any great quantity, as far as we know, but there were enough to give proof that flowers or branches were cut, brought into the house and put into containers.

Two hundred years in which to perfect designs, create new shapes or copy old ones–how much has been accomplished and what are now the most attractive, suitable and widely used types of container? It is an interesting question to consider when looking through one's collection of vases, searching, perhaps, for something for a table arrangement, for a pedestal or just a small vase for a few roses. And it is interesting, too, to try to decide which is the most important factor governing the selection of a container–shape, texture, or colour.

One certain fact emerges from such research and that is the usefulness of a pedestal. By a pedestal I do not mean a tall column supporting a large vase for church decoration, but just a small base, and sometimes it is only very slight, to give extra height. Several containers which achieve this height include:

A wicker basket with an almost exaggerated pedestal. (Flowers here would have a lift of a few inches from the base.)

Here is a collection of containers of which
only three were originally designed to hold flowers.
They include a soup tureen, a Wedgwood coffee pot,
a candlestick holder, a sauce boat, a glass tazza for fruit,
a champagne glass, a mug and two ginger jars.

This collection of containers includes a decanter,
two jugs, a shell, an oval pedestal cake dish,
a waste paper basket, a cup and saucer, candlestick holder
and an early sherry glass. The small stand on the
second row from the bottom was originally a clock stand.

An early glass tazza which has to have a shallow bowl to hold the water. This, too, has a high pedestal. A champagne glass has a small stem, and a porcelain dish has short feet which give it extra height.

An early glass bowl with a small base.

A sauce boat produces a raised effect.

A Wedgwood coffee jug and a wine glass in quite different ways give a pedestal effect and an alabaster ornament which at one time held a clock face. This latter is not a big vase, as it will take only a small shallow dish for water in the top, but what is put in it will be shown off well.

A Staffordshire vase with the conventional pedestal of the time.

A porcelain shell, has a small, flat base, and a Worcester cake stand also has a low, solid stem which gives the flowers arranged in it extra importance.

Using any of these, a certain type and shape of arrangement would be suggested by the container. The relation of the container to the flower is of paramount importance. Too many flowers in too small a vase, or too few in a big one; tall flowers in a short vase, or short ones in a tall container—all can counteract the results of time and trouble. Probably the shape is as important as the colour, although clashing colours, or dark colours with dark flowers, can equally spoil an effect, and the character of the container to suit the character of

61

the flowers is almost as important as the shape.

In my own experience, some of the most suitable containers have been glass or porcelain jars or jugs which were never made for flower arrangements at all. For example, old glass scent bottles and decanters make wonderful containers for tall sprays of flowers or for slender branches, the narrow neck giving excellent support where it is most needed. A tea-pot which may have lost its lid over the years and be difficult to fit with another one, can have a new usefulness in life as a container for flowers. A porcelain cake stand with a round painted cake tin to hold the water is one of the most successful containers to use for spreading arrangements, particularly for the table. Old sauce boats and gravy dishes are interesting to use with flowers, and an early porcelain soup tureen is one of my favourites for a big arrangement. I've also enjoyed doing flowers in an early glass bell jar—originally intended to hold a candle—and a Dutch glass decanter is another special favourite. My own miscellaneous collection of containers includes baskets, painted cake tins, cake stands, little bits of Victorian nonsense, early scent bottles, a fantastic Victorian shell in porcelain, a large genuine shell, and an ebony jardinière inlaid with brass. None of these was initially intended for flower arrangement, but happened to be the right texture, colour, and shape for certain occasions and certain flowers.

It is not necessary for these rather interesting types of containers to be expensive. Most of my own have been found—after some searching, it's true—in secondhand shops or on market stalls.

In compensation for the growing shortage of antique containers there is much good contemporary material that is being produced at very reasonable prices. Every possible kind of taste is catered for, both in containers and in holders for flowers. To many people these holders are as important as the containers, and they appear in great variety. There are heavy glass ones with holes in them, there are flat pads with needle-like points sticking up from them made of metal and rubber, and there are wire ones made in a double framework rather like a small two layered toasting tray, only circular. My usual method of securing flowers is to use a piece of large mesh wire netting crumpled up into three layers.

The Wedgwood factory is producing some containers of excellent shapes and colours, some of them plain and others decorated in the style of the original jasper ware. They are very reasonably priced and would fit well into almost any furnishing scheme. The Wedgwood factory have had, among others, Anna Zinkeisen and John Skeaping modelling for them.

George Monro & Co., of Covent Garden, have lately introduced a series of bowls and containers for plants and flowers, the plainer ones of which are suitable for contemporary settings.

The work of Stephen Sykes is well known for its originality and particular application to plants. Fritz Lampel designs glass containers suitable to hold only one or two flowers—an encouraging idea from the point of view of arrangement when so many vases are made to hold far too many. Lucie Rie, working with Hans Coper, produces pottery and stoneware which are described as 'original, sometimes bold and striking, sometimes delicate, with a graceful application to use'.

Constance Spry has a comprehensive range of all shapes and sizes of containers produced for the most part in white. (These can then be dyed in soft leaf greens, apricots, greys and dirty mauves if required.) A very lovely chalice shape comes in a dark aubergine colour.

A green wine bottle is a simple container, and, is particularly suitable because of its long neck, for arranging a few branches.

A ginger jar has special virtues as a container. It is a good shape, will hold plenty of water and the small opening at the neck provides support for stems and branches. Ginger jars come in attractive soft shades, cheerful patterns and sometimes with figures and landscapes painted on them.

In the Italian magazine *Domus* there were photographs of the work of Ettore Sottsass, Jnr. He has made many experiments with plexiglass and brass wire, and is one of the few designers who express a free and contemporary feeling for flower holders.

The Rosenthal Porcelain Company have called in well known American and European designers and have held interesting exhibitions of porcelain, including unusual contemporary flower containers. When selecting a container it is well to remember whereabouts it is to go in one's room, the comparative heights of the objects near to it and, of course, the colouring most suitable to the furnishings.

It is the greatest help to have one 'foolproof' vase. I like to describe it like that, because if it is a favourite vase that is almost what it finally becomes. It is selected because it is a good, easy shape in which to arrange. It is a vase which will hold a reasonable number of flowers, but does not look ridiculous with a smaller quantity. It becomes the vase which one uses most frequently and which, in time, one can almost arrange with one's eyes shut. The flowers usually look graceful in it, and the colour—most important—will go with anything.

Once such a vase has been selected, installed and become a favourite one, then any others which are collected are useful, or fun to use, or specially good for branches, or better still for dried arrangements; but none of them is as necessary or as dependable as this particular one. This is not in any way to minimise the delight one can have in trying out different containers, or in finding exciting vases or bowls which may only be suitable for certain occasions or flowers—a friend of mine brings out of her porcelain cupboard a special treasure which is only used for Christmas roses, as it suits them so perfectly. Experimenting with kitchen dishes, baking tins, and different types of baskets can all be most stimulating, and the more variety one can have, the more chance of trying out new ideas there will be.

Design can be varied within the same shape of container. A flat dish can provide a base for two or three large flowers with foliage, or it may be used quite differently for a cluster of smaller flowers. This contrast of outline gives many opportunities for trying out various sizes and types of flowers, although the general shape of the container remains the same.

A further variation is obtained by using containers made of different materials. Sometimes a plain white porcelain one will give the desired effect, sometimes glass is the answer, and sometimes wood. Copper often provides a suitable background, especially with bronze and yellow

The plates and oval dish in this photograph are deep green in colour; everything else is white or white and gold. This particular shade of green is most attractive with red ranunculus, orange, red and yellow nasturtiums or red gladioli. The small Victorian pieces in white offer many possibilities for arranging a few flowers. In some of these the water level has to be watched as even when they are filled, they hold only a little.

coloured flowers such as nasturtiums, dahlias, and chrysanthemums; and old Bristol glass, if it can be tracked down, in its inimitable deep blue, makes a satisfying colour scheme with the crimson and cerise found in certain zinnias.

A great deal can be done to enhance the effect of a handful of flowers by setting them off in a good contrasting colour: blue and orange crocus in a small black jug, or bright yellow mimosa in a blue glass vase, or the clear red of ranunculas against the rather deep green of a Wedgwood dish.

It seems to me well worthwhile—and not necessarily extravagant—to select a container suitable only for certain colours if the vase is attractive in itself. It is stimulating to think out something new to go well with it, and you may discover material that

you had not thought of using before. An example of this was a sauce boat, or gravy dish, in cream porcelain with a decoration round the rim and round the base in brown and yellow. This might reasonably be considered restricting, but in fact this dish looked enchanting with Mermaid roses and bronze Korean chrysanthemums in the autumn, and in the summer it was well suited to buttercups, creamy-yellow honeysuckle, and sprays of *Rosa hugonis*.

This is an obvious case of the container dictating not only the shape of the arrangement but also the colour.

Now let us stake the claims of a white vase. Apart from taking any coloured flowers, including white, it will fit in with almost any surroundings and look just as good either with soft colours or strong ones.

A favourite arrangement combines grey foliage with white flowers, such as *Santolina maritima*, or *Senecio laxifolius* with sprigs of white sweet rocket (cut quite short) or white bluebells, or sprays of the floribunda rose Prosperity or one or two clear white, golden centred marguerites cut very short. White freesias would be especially lovely.

On the other hand bright colours show well against a white vase: a mixed bunch of clear red anemones, yellow freesias or wallflowers, mist blue grape hyacinths or one or two deep purple anemones, and a small cluster of primroses and violets would all bring colour, which may be spread out in the garden, with concentrated effect into the house. Almost any roses look attractive in a white vase. The softer tones of aquilegia, love-in-a-mist, and mignonette, will show equally as well against a white vase as the deeper jewel colours of wallflowers, antirrhinums and zinnias.

It is well known that white introduced into a mixed group acts as an interval between colours that might otherwise clash. A white vase has the same effect.

Then there is the question of whether containers should be transparent or not. If they are of porcelain obviously the stalks will not be seen. Sometimes this is a good thing, but at times a glass container becomes an important factor in an arrangement. This is especially the case with some of the spurges, whose lower leaves have a fascinating escalator-like formation, as do also some kinds of veronica. However, an advantage of porcelain is that if the water is discoloured it will not show, whereas with glass it may have to be changed instead of just being topped up from time to time.

A practical point about cleaning a decanter or narrow-necked glass bottle might, perhaps, be helpful, for such a container may present something of a problem unless one is familiar with it. I use newspaper or stiff tissue paper—soft paper

The use of a coloured plate can make an interesting container for a small group of material.
The flowers and leaves are arranged on a pin holder; the white of the plate border is repeated in the shells and the petals of the flowers — the yellow of the plate is picked up by the small yellow frill of the perianth.

One of the most attractive materials to hold flowers is a vase made from alabaster. It is soft in colouring and usually attractive in design. The one in the photograph takes to pieces and can be used in at least four different ways. A vase of this kind may seem an extravagance, but in the long run will turn out to be an economy.

tissues are too soft and crumple up too quickly either pulled into small pieces or left in long, tight rolls and pushed gently into the bottle when it is three quarters full of water. The paper should be allowed to stand in the water for an hour or so, and then the bottle should be shaken firmly and the water swished round and round. Sometimes gritty sand is recommended or cold tea leaves. In every case it is essential to have the glass only three parts filled with water so that whatever is used will produce friction. Too much water prevents this happening.

The mention of cleanliness of glass, of course, applies to all other textures of containers. Most porcelain vases, for instance,—unless they are badly cracked or have been repaired with a kind of glue

which will not stand up to heat—are all the better for an occasional complete soaking in really hot soapy water. Brass, copper, and silver containers must be kept bright and shining and cornucopias, on account of their narrowing shape, should frequently have a good rinsing out, preferably under a running tap. (Vases for large arrangements, for use usually on special occasions, such as weddings, receptions, etc. are mentioned elsewhere.)

Reverting again to the question of the suggestion of a shape being made by the container, it is interesting to notice the different types of vases and containers selected by different schools of flower arrangement, perhaps in different countries. In the Far East many baskets are used, some of them hanging, made out of bamboo. Other containers suspended from the ceiling may be constructed from bronze, to provide an opportunity for using curving branches as a decoration. Sometimes a vessel is made from a gourd or a lobster basket, or the flowers are arranged on a flat antique mirror. This may be raised up on a low platform called a 'Kwadai' or 'Shiki-its', to give extra importance and height. Then there is the use of a shallow dish where an expanse of water is left clear so that the flowers or foliage look as if they are growing out of it.

American arrangements may be dependent on small ornaments (often figures), a swathe of curtain material or a cluster of fruit. The use of wall brackets is popular and their value appreciated for parties or special occasions. Dried arrangements are sometimes composed round a suitable piece of bark and may stand on another. Pedes-

tals are valued for the additional height they will give and quite small groups sometimes stand on a plinth or specially constructed base.

This also applies to many Australian arrangements and, again, there is emphasis on the use of fruit and accessories.

Right, A variety of containers need not be an expensive outlay. Most of those in this photograph are homely ones — an old mahogany tea caddy with its lid open, a sauce boat, a small copper saucepan and a couple of jugs.

Below, The container in this photograph is a cake or fruit stand from an early tea or dessert service. The pedestal gives additional height and importance to flowers arranged in it.

Top, A group of spring flowers arranged in moss, with a background of bark, including narcissi, sprays of blossom, daffodils, clumps of primroses, primulas and branches of pussy willow.

Right, Narcissi, freesias and Roman hyacinths arranged in a large champagne glass. Narcissi are sometimes difficult to arrange and a group of this kind takes time, but the flowers will eventually fit into place.

Daffodils and Narcissi

Daffodils and narcissi include many varieties and types of flower, and have been so much 'improved' during the last fifty years, that when they are mentioned today they no longer conjure up two distinct pictures in the mind – one of a yellow flower with a frilled trumpet, and the other of flat white rounded petals with a bright orange perianth in the centre. To illustrate this point I would like to quote from a lecture given to the Royal Horticultural Society by Mr. J.S.B. Lea on *The Modern Daffodil* in April, 1962:

"In a book on modern daffodils written in 1910 by the Rev. Joseph Bacon, the recommended list of the twelve best exhibition varieties contains only two names that would be generally known today. They are White Star and King Alfred."

What does all this mean to the flower arranger? How much does it matter whether the daffodils to be arranged are the latest 'two colour' combination or one of the newest 'pinks'? To my mind this seems of little importance. (There is, perhaps, one daffodil which is not suitable for flower arrangement and that is the double one. My personal inclination would not be for this daffodil in any case, and the extra weight of the heads, especially after rain, makes them difficult to support on the slender stems – and they are inclined to look shaggy and untidy rather quickly.)

Daffodils and narcissi look best when they are growing in clumps naturally in grass, and this applies in much the same way when they are cut for an arrangement.

I have found Pheasant-eye narcissus, Cheerfulness, the early wild daffodils and some of the miniature hybrid daffodils, especially suitable for arrangements, but the conditions under which they are arranged are important.

Most flowers dislike a draught or an abrupt change in temperature more than anything else. They will even stand up to a certain amount of neglect, but put them in the way of an open door and window, then add hot air from a radiator blowing up underneath the vase, and they will soon droop. This applies more to daffodils and narcissi than almost any other flower. So one of the most important conditions for keeping them alive is, as far as possible, an even temperature and no draughts.

Another condition is that the flowers must be fresh and the base of the stems snipped off before arranging. Even if cut from the garden it is advisable to do this – only about an eighth of an inch is necessary. If any one of the narcissus family is left out of water for any length of time the end of the hollow stem will soon seal over, and obviously if the tip of the stem is not cut off it will be difficult for the flower to get a good supply of water.

This is only a small point and may seem almost too elementary to mention, but it is of so much importance to the life of a flower that I think it should be emphasised. Another point on the 'taking in' of water is sometimes overlooked.

Daffodils and narcissi are flowers which not only drink up their stems, but through them, so if possible have these flowers standing in some depth of water, – it is not necessary for the water to reach all the way up the stems. Finally, if lasting properties are important, arrange them in a container capable of holding plenty of water.

I find it difficult to get the full effect of these flowers without a good deal of patience. They are not easy to arrange naturally, although they look so straightforward. The bareness of their stems can be part of their attraction, but to give them a softer line they often need something with them. A shrub of rosemary will provide charming grey-green spikes throughout the year. Camellia foliage, dark green and shining, is another most attractive evergreen, as are branches of the paler and smaller-leaved parchment bark *(Pittosporum)*.

To enable each flower to be seen separately the flowers are cut into different lengths – a very simple but fundamental rule of flower arrangement. Another, possibly derived from the Japanese school, is that of using an uneven number of flowers whenever possible.

This is a point which can only be proved by personal experience, and let me add hastily that it does not, of course, apply to smaller flowers which look better in bunches. (No one is expected to count primroses, violets, polyanthus or daffodils if used in any quantity.) But I have found when arranging a few flowers of any size that an even number gives a square effect and that it is worth leaving out one of a dozen to get a better balance. The twelfth flower can look most attractive in a small specimen vase made to hold just one stem. This shows off the clear beauty of the single bloom's petals and the perianth frill to perfection.

All types of daffodils and narcissi are excellent flowers for lightening a furnishing scheme. They bring into the house a radiance and brightness invaluable on cold spring days and are especially suitable for giving a feeling of warmth and sunshine to a north facing room.

Either the yellow or white of these flowers is good in any colour scheme, though best of all against a blue or a pale green background. The boldness of the daffodils will stand up against deeper colours, but the clear and delicate white of many of the narcissi, such as Pheasant-eye, or the more creamy white of Cheerfulness, seem to require a more gentle shade of background.

Not to be forgotten too is the pleasure of the perfume belonging to the stronger smelling narcissi, quite different from the fresh, rather woody smell of the daffodils.

Below, Narcissi are sometimes condemned for not lasting well, but if they are cut when they first come out and are given a long deep drink before arranging, they will last reasonably well. In the photograph they are arranged with sprays of rosemary which is also long lasting.

Right, Daffodils and narcissi immediately bring a feeling of sunshine into the house. They are arranged here with wild arum leaves, cowslips and grape hyacinths. The shallow flower pot is filled with moss which has jars of water hidden in it, in which the flowers are arranged.

Whatever the surroundings, a bowl of the first daffodils or narcissi will bring into the house a feeling of spring which can only be equalled by the first snowdrops or a bunch of Easter primroses.

Perhaps here I might be forgiven for mentioning something which seems to me to be of the greatest importance – the protection of wild bulbs and plants. It seems a reflection on the diminishing numbers of wild daffodils, for instance, when a well known nursery has to list them as more expensive than the bigger naturalised ones, and then has some difficulty in getting them. This may be a question of supply and demand, but it seems a pity that the wild ones should disappear, particularly as they are most suitable for small arrangements and in many ways much more appealing.

Mention of the wild daffodil brings one's mind back to the large numbers of cultivated varieties that have developed during the last fifty or sixty years. It is a long way from the early days of the little Welsh lily to that of its more modern counterparts, and it would be a pity, I think, to lose the colour, shape and size of the original. To quote Mr. Lea again: '. . . there seems a danger that we are getting away from the essential character of the daffodil; you will all, no doubt, have seen in the Hall today extreme examples of this where the flower is no longer recognisable as a daffodil and only resembles some unhappy malformed streak of nature. I am told, however, that they have one advantage; they can be crammed into a box and sent on a rough train journey arriving at Covent Garden looking much the same as when they were picked'.

The one condition I would like to impose is that these flowers should at least resemble a daffodil or narcissus as one used to remember them.

Dahlias now come in such a variety of colours that it is possible to incorporate them into any colour scheme. Here white, cream and apricot colours are arranged in an off white Staffordshire jug with two deep tangerine dahlias to give emphasis towards the centre of the group.

Dahlias

Top, Pompon dahlias often come with interesting
curving stems and have a sturdiness of growth
which is not always found in the larger flowering types.
The flame coloured flowers with their opulent foliage,
are arranged on a pin holder, in a dish of water,
in a deep green Wedgwood dish;
the pin holder is concealed by the leaves.

Dahlias are popular flowers for arrangements
and come in a great variety of colour, types, and
sizes – but I write of them with some diffidence as
I never feel absolutely certain of their lasting
qualities. There are some occasions when it is
possible to use flowers which may or may not let
you down, and I know that there are many dahlias
which are completely dependable, but all the same
I'm afraid I still have this feeling of uncertainty,
although I have found the smaller pompon type
of dahlia to last well when arranged on a pin holder.

I would prefer, for instance, if doing a large wedding group or altar vases in church, to depend on
something else to provide an important colour note.

This may seem unjust to a noble, widely loved
flower, but one must write from personal experience
and mine, with dahlias, has not always been fortunate. I hasten, in fairness, to add that I understand
that in official flower arrangement circles this is
not the general concensus of opinion.

Dahlias come into the category of flowers that
can be arranged alone and yet provide a variety of
colour in the same way as zinnias, carnations,
some sweet peas and some roses do. The colours
range from pure white, clear lemon yellow and
fiery orange, through shades of apricot, tangerine
and burnt sienna to deep copper, bronze, and
dark red, not to mention the various tones of pink
and mauve also available.

Constance Spry expressed an affection for dahlias, but also mentioned the fact that certain species
are sometimes found to be unreliable for cutting.
It seems that some nurseries provide two lists, one
of special cut-flower varieties and another of
special garden varieties. This should make the
problem of selection easier when thinking in terms
of flower arrangements. Mrs. Spry grew many
different dahlias with various colour schemes
already in her mind, and so it seems sensible to
profit by her experience and I am grateful for
permission to quote from her book *Flowers in
House and Garden* in which she writes about the
different varieties she herself found to be most
useful: 'I grow for arrangements (with tawny
colourings) Trentonian, old gold and copper;
Isabel McElney, salmon pink and pale copper,
difficult to describe but beautiful; Fancy Free, a new
buff and crimson variety from Messrs. Riding of
Chingford. These three belong to the decorative
section. Of the cactus type I find the amber pink

Left, In this group of brightly coloured dahlias,
ranging from dark ruby red to palest pink,
a rather 'shaggy' effect is produced. For this type of
arrangement in a glass jug, only a few flowers are needed.

of Schiller and Pin Spiral are not too pink to use in beige and amber mixtures. Chancellor, from Carter Page, is a remarkable single, the petals are best described as salmon red, with a bright chestnut zone round the centre.'

'Of pale yellow, for green and yellow arrangements, I have the clear yellow Frau O. Bracht, a semi-cactus, and Lady Moyra Ponsonby, a pale yellow flower with pointed petals...'

'For red groups and purples I grow F.T.D., a rosy mauve and purple; Charles G. Read, burgundy purple; Weltruf, a camellia shaped flower of clear cherry red; and of the small decoratives, Glorious, with raspberry red flowers borne in profusion, and Goldrose, one of the best dahlias for artificial light...'

'No dahlias last better as cut flowers than the small pompons. I have Macbeth, white, edged with bright pink; Dewdrop, white with a lavender edge; Tommy Laing, maroon tipped with white; Darkest of All, blackish red; Chamois, buff; Clarissa, pale primrose; and Basra, deep plum.'

Dahlias are like zinnias in their variety of colour (only not, to my mind, of such depth and intensity of shade and tone). They also come from Mexico. There are many categories in garden varieties, some of them called star dahlias, others anemone-flowered dahlias, while others include cactus dahlias, pompon dahlias, peony-flowered dahlias and decorative dahlias. Having made a selection from pages of nurserymens' lists, it is then important to discover the conditions they prefer and to have instructions for lifting them in the late autumn.

Dahlias are rich feeders and like a deep, moist soil, well drained, and preferably not under trees, for despite the fact they are often recommended for growing in contrast against dark leaved shrubs, they do not like to be over shadowed by branches. Here, again, they are similar to zinnias, and do best in a sunny position. If the soil is naturally light and inclined to dry out liquid manure must be added and watering is essential when the young plants are first put out into the garden during May.

In case of danger from late frosts, after planting, the young dahlias may be protected by upturned flower pots at night. Owing to the weight of the flowers and the quantity of heavy foliage, buds, and stems, the plants are likely to need individual staking, so that when strong winds come they will be ready for them. To ensure that the soil is kept moist they should be well mulched once they are established, but it is of great importance that if and when this is done, the soil underneath is not allowed to become dry. One of the best ways of keeping the soil in a suitable condition is to go over the bed lightly with a hoe, so as not to injure the roots. About a week after planting, the central bud should be removed in order to improve the quality and quantity of later flowers. It is always important, too, to keep a sharp look out for marauding slugs, which seem to find young dahlias especially delectable.

Then comes the question of raising the tubers and keeping them dry throughout the worst of winter. They can remain in the garden until the leaves are blackened by frost, but if sharp frosts occur which are followed by heavy rain, they should then be lifted at once. Storing is sometimes a problem according to the amount of space one can spare. A cool greenhouse, as long as it is frost proof, or a similar shed, would be suitable, but there must be a small amount of ventilation or else the tubers will go mouldy. On the other hand, they will shrivel up if the temperature is too high.

Before storing, the soil should be removed from the tubers and then they should be allowed to dry off in the sun.

All this care and trouble may well be worthwhile, but if one is unable, for various reasons, to deal with dahlias in the garden, there are always quantities available in the shops, coming in at the end of July and going on into the late autumn.

A few dahlias arranged with buddleia and montbretia in a cornucopia.
This is a good shape for a small quantity of flowers, showing them off to their best advantage.

Yellow dahlias arranged against two or three sprays of caper spurge, a cluster of globe artichokes just turning brown and dahlia foliage. A few stems of early winter jasmine carry on the yellow theme.
The arrangement is on a pin holder in a dish of water concealed by the dahlia foliage.

The bright clear blue of these delphiniums arranged with the soft leaf green of hosta foliage is a combination of colours which were suggested by a painting—the Van Eyck of the 'Arnolfini Wedding Group' in which the woman wears a green and blue dress. This is an example of an idea taken from studying a painting.

Delphiniums

In a mixed arrangement of heavy foliage such as bergenia, lupin and scarlet oak, pale blue delphinium spikes give a light touch.

There is no doubt that delphiniums are some of the most valued of all flowers for tall arrangements either in their many shades of blue, or in white. I understand that there is some expectation of breeding red, orange and yellow delphiniums for the public market. Although these may be beautiful when they appear and make splendid contributions to a flower group it seems to me that the blue delphiniums, ranging as they do from the palest to the deepest blue, some of them with mauve petals intermixed with blue, some of them with large black centres, others in a light sky blue with white, will be hard to surpass. The white delphiniums are also lovely, again coming in a variety of types of flowers, and are especially useful for decorating on regal occasions, for weddings, church festivals, etc.

To grow delphiniums in the garden is not a difficult matter once they have got well established. They will adapt to most conditions, as long as they are kept well fed and reasonably damp in hot weather. The same applies if they are growing in a sandy soil which will not hold the moisture. Delphiniums will grow equally well in the border amongst other herbaceous plants, or they will thrive amongst shrubs if it is made sure that they get the sun, and that the shrubs are not too closely packed together. If the centre stems are cut down immediately after flowering they will usually send out side shoots which in turn will flower later on in the season, producing that welcome touch of blue or white at a time when the border is beginning to show up in terms of autumn reds and yellows. This second crop can be most helpful for flower arrangers.

A colour note from Miss Jekyll in her book *Home and Garden* seems of relevance here, and might suggest other ideas when one thinks of all the various shades of blue that are available in delphiniums. She remarks that as far as her own colour requirements of flowers went, 'It was better to treat blues with contrasts rather than with harmonies And I had observed, when at one point, from a little distance, I could see in company the pure deep orange of the herring lilies *(Lilium croceum)* with the brilliant blue of some full blue delphiniums, how splendid, although audacious, the mixture was, and immediately noted it, so as to take full advantage of the observation when planting-time came. In the autumn two of the large patches of lilies were therefore taken up and grouped in front of, and partly among, the delphiniums; and even though neither had come to anything like full strength in the past summer (the first year after removal), yet I could see already how grandly they went together, and how well worth doing and recommending such a mixture was. The delphiniums should be of a full deep blue colour, not perhaps the very darkest,

A few tall delphiniums with their leaves arranged in an upright narrow jug make a useful decoration against panelling. If they are cut with some of their spikes still in bud these will come into flower and prolong the life of the arrangement.

and not any with a purple shade'.

This seems to be such an excellent planting idea, capable of being carried out in a flower arrangement, that it is worth quoting in full, especially noting the shades of blue indicated to make a good foil to the deep orange lily.

So much for the blue, and now some suggestions, either for planting or arranging the white. There is a grey and white garden in the well known garden at Sissinghurst Castle, Kent, England, and anyone who has seen this during the summer will immediately realise how beautiful the white delphiniums can be in such surroundings. Grey, white and cream are the chief colours of this garden and the result is very lovely. For flower arrangements this leads one to think in terms of white flowers, such as white delphiniums, with grey foliage plants, white roses, mullein, white clematis, mock orange *(Philadelphus)*, white daisies, alliums (green and white) and rosemary. The charms of such a mixture are difficult to define, and, of course, it is not necessary to have all those mentioned in the group at the same time. (Perhaps they might not all be out at once.) But the idea is there, to be carried out by each person as their preference indicates.

Apart from their use for tall arrangements, delphiniums have great usefulness in dried flower groups. They dry almost without any trouble at all. I usually hang my bunches in as cool an airing cupboard as possible – I deliberately leave the door open a little to ensure that there is not too much heat (as this sometimes happens on a hot day) but try not to leave them in a day too long for they will soon bleach and lose their lovely tones of colouring if they have too much heat. The minute they feel slightly like paper to the touch it is time to take them out. Some people hang them up on an open landing or passage where they get sun (too much sun also causes fading), and others hang them in a cool greenhouse. As with all dried flower materials they must be in good condition when they are dried. It is no good cutting delphiniums which are beginning to drop. After cutting, or buying them from the florist, it is helpful to give the delphiniums a good deep drink of water in a bucket or tall jug, before plunging them into their drying operations.

Delphiniums in the garden often get slaughtered by slugs, and though there are well known chemical applications for these, it is important to keep a watch out for invaders. Grit or small bits of broken slate are also recommended for encircling the plants, and yet another idea is to sow a ring of mustard seed, but I have no personal experience of this suggestion and so cannot vouch for it. Constance Spry emphasises this problem when writing about delphiniums and relates the success of Mr. Norman Hadden, of Porlock, in his wholesale conquest of slugs. He mixed crushed meta (this is a chemical compound of carbide often substituted for methylated spirits) with bran, and the results were enviable.

Mrs. Spry also mentions some of her favourite delphiniums, both for growing and for arrangement, a few of which are listed here:
Lady Belinda, a tall white, with most handsome spikes.
Dawn, a grey blue and pale lilac with a coppery centre.
Blue Gown, an ultramarine blue.
Duchess of Portland, an ultramarine blue.
Magic Moon, almost opalescent.
Princess Margaret, a delicate lavender and blue.
Queen of Delphiniums, a lightish mauve, double.
Here is a selection from a well known nurseryman's recent list:
Kitty, a pure gentian blue, $4\frac{1}{2}$ ft.
Colonel F.R. Durham, a gentian blue, about $5\frac{1}{2}$ ft.
Crystal, a sky blue with a white eye.
Father Thames, a gentian blue, flushed violet rose, 5 ft.
Laura Fairbrother, mauve with a white eye, semi-double, exceptionally tall and fine. $7\frac{1}{2}$ ft.
Mrs. Tippetts, a rich violet purple, semi-double, 5 ft.
Sonata, sky blue, with a white eye, about 5 ft.
Betty Hay, purest sky blue, $5\frac{1}{2}$ ft., late flowering.
Ann Page, a cornflower blue, about 5 ft.

In the *belladonna* section, described as having the 'light and branching habit' can be found:
Belladonna semi-plena, light azure blue, semi-double, 2-3 ft.
Blue Bees, rich blue, single, 3 ft. early flowering.
Pink Sensation, light rose pink, single about 4 ft. keeps up a continuous show of flowers from June to September.
Moerheimii, a pure white, about 4 ft. single.
Wendy, a dark blue, about 5 ft. single, midseason flowering.

There is a wide selection and one can think of few sights finer in the garden than a collection of different blue delphiniums, perhaps with white lilies, or as suggested by Miss Jekyll, with orange lilies against the specially selected blue of certain delphiniums. Again, a group of tall white spires would be effective, especially against a dark background such as yew, box or lonicera. The same ideas apply to flower arrangement, and a mixture of blue delphiniums with white lilies or roses or carnations and, perhaps, a touch of scarlet or crimson, such as a Zéphirine Drouhin rose, would make a wonderful display – or, again, a group of white delphiniums against an olive green wallpaper. Although they are mentioned earlier in connection with weddings it is almost impossible to overemphasise the value of white ones in a large group of mixed white flowers.

A few short stemmed delphiniums make an unusual contrast with yellow, red and pink garden roses. Delphiniums are now available in many different tones of blue and purple.

Delphiniums arranged with their leaves in a dark green glass jar in order to carry on the depth of the green colour.

Dried flowers

Left, A dried group of wild grasses including reed mace, branched bur-reed, plumed rushes, hare's tail grasses, figwort, cotton lavender, leek heads and sea holly.

Top right, A dried group emphasising dark brown, orange and pale green, arranged in a flat bread basket. The material includes the rich brown of globe artichokes, lily and poppy seedheads, sprays of love-lies-bleeding and *Iris foetidissima* seed pods, showing the bright orange berries.

Right, This group of a few dahlias in a pewter mug is enlarged by the addition of dried sweetcorn. This is a valuable material on account of its interesting shape and soft buff colouring, which fits into most colour schemes.

Victorian young ladies (when walking in the country) were encouraged by their governesses to make collections of wild flowers and leaves. The bunches were brought home, sorted out, and then dried or pressed between the pages of heavy books. When quite ready they were arranged artistically and with infinite care on a background of white satin or round the border of a picture. If the dried flowers were to form a complete picture on their own, they would be framed and hung on the parlour wall. Very often the frames were made of deep and solid wood.

Plants and ferns were carried from the greenhouse and flower collecting expeditions in the country lanes were organised. The assembling of the flowers and plants promoted botanical instruction, and their arrangement proved a useful pastime for a wet afternoon. There were also isolated instances of dried flowers being used for cutting. Gertrude Jekyll in *Home and Garden* published in 1900, remarks about the sea holly *(Eryngium giganteum)* that it 'is a handsome object if kept dry, lasting well for several months, and losing but little of its form and lustre'. Mrs. Earle in *'Pot-pourri from a Surrey Garden'* published around the same time, speaks of having 'two bright green olive jars into which are stuck large bunches of the white seed vessels of honesty and some flowers of everlastings (immortelle)'.

Dried flowers are not accurately described as 'dead' and they are very far from being artificial. They are flowers, leaves, and seedheads which have been preserved, as far as possible, in their natural state.

Whether the use of dried flowers for interior decoration has been stimulated by the present social and economic situation is difficult to say. Certainly the dried arrangement is an economy during the two or three winter months when flowers are most expensive to buy, and certainly their beauty is undiminished by the central heating in modern blocks of flats, which will kill most fresh flowers on sight.

But their value is not purely practical; it is also aesthetic. Perhaps one should say it is aesthetic only so long as the beauty and softness of their colouring is recognised, appreciated, and not in any way altered. Immediately they are made 'artificial' by dyeing they are no longer true 'dried' flowers, and most of their charm is gone. 'There has been invented also a method of tinting the lily, thanks to the taste of mankind for monstrous productions'. What Pliny wrote in his *Natural History* in A.D. 77 applies just as much today. It is quite unnecessary to colour, dye, or stain dried flowers in any way. They are much more beautiful in their natural colours.

By the process of drying it is possible to preserve deep and even bright colours, but the general impression of a dried arrangement is usually a much gentler one than that of a bowl of fresh flowers. Sometimes there are strong browns, blues, and pinks, and even yellows, but still the overall impression is of something delicate rather than forceful, of pastel shades rather than vigorous ones.

A single concession, however, one would ask for dried flowers is that they should always be taken down before the new green shoots are breaking into leaf. There is nothing, after all, which can compete with the freshness of the first spring flowers or branches of blossom. It should be remembered that dried flowers are a part of the autumn and the end of the year, and that their beauty and delicacy is appropriate to their season.

Dried flowers, if carefully packed, can travel any distance and the length of the journey will not affect them, as they are not, of course, dependent any more on moisture. (I have known them make long excursions by train in England very successfully, and they are now being sent abroad). Their lasting properties are indisputable, but, even so, too much should not be expected of them.

People who live in the country can collect their own materials, and probably do some extra planting in the garden of things which will be useful for drying. Those living in a large town or city without a garden have to pay both for the arrangement and for the material.

The flowers, leaves, and seedheads all have to be located, cut at the right time, treated appropriately, and finally arranged. Dried flowers are infinitely more precarious to deal with in their early stages owing to their uncertainty of reaction, in many cases, to the same treatment. All this must be remembered, but set against this is the saving of money once the flowers are arranged.

So much of the material will last perfectly from one winter to another if carefully packed away, and it comes out surprisingly fresh and still retaining its colour.

Collecting the material for a dried arrangement is exciting and often surprising. There are few flowers, grasses, and leaves which do not dry at some stage or other – if not the flower then the seedheads

are attractive, and there is no reason at all why anything one particularly likes should not be tried. The whole business of drying can best be described as capricious. There seem to be no very definite rules, and flowers picked and dried in similar circumstances two years running have been known to be successful on one occasion and sad failures on the other.

People interested in this subject have sometimes written asking how to dry flowers, and which flowers and leaves are suitable. This is the most difficult question to answer because, however helpful one would wish to be, there is still very little proved information to impart.

There are some plants which almost dry in spite of themselves; that is to say that it is impossible to make a mistake with them. We have all known for many years that the seedheads of honesty can be a very beautiful decoration, for one example, and all one has to do is to cut it from the garden when it is ready. The same applies to sea holly (*Eryngium*). It is foolproof and has also been known for years. But there are comparatively few flowers and leaves which are as easy as these two.

Some flowers have to be cut just as they are coming into flower and put straight into an evenly warm temperature. If the heat is too great they will become brittle and probably lose their colour. If it is not hot enough they will merely go limp. Some will dry successfully, or others not at all. Some should be simply hung in an indoor room, others should be laid out in the hot sun. Some dry better by being left in a bowl of water and being allowed to drink until they can't drink any more, then they dry off still remaining in the water; others are completely ruined if there is any kind of dampness anywhere near them.

It is obvious that this branch of flower work is fraught with uncertainty; there are vagaries of temperature, different methods of drying, discovering exactly the right moment for cutting the material, and the right temperatures for drying. It can only be by patient experimentation that any definite results can be achieved. This means that there is usually a lapse of a year if something fails, as, by the time it has been tried out and the results watched anxiously, it is too late to try again with that particular plant until it flowers once more in a year's time.

Here are some ideas about drying flowers, grasses, seedheads, flowers, leaves etc., which I have tried myself with various results.

A collection of dried materials arranged in a Staffordshire jug, including ferns, figwort, eucalyptus, lyme grass, yellow achillea and brown achillea seedhead, delphinium, larkspur, rose hips, love-in-a-mist, hydrangeas, lesser reed mace and water reed.
Some of the eucalyptus has been preserved with a mixture of glycerine and water, which has turned it a wine colour.

The most usual method of drying is gentle heat. An airing cupboard is suitable for this purpose. Some of the larger flowers are laid on shelves, e.g. delphiniums, golden rod; smaller ones are hung in bunches, e.g. larkspur, cornflowers, globe thistle. It is important that the heat should be temperate but, on the other hand, when loose flowers like delphiniums are first put in to dry it should be a little warmer than usual so that the flowers will not go limp. The heat can be regulated by leaving the door open a little, or wide, or by shutting it altogether. Too much heat is inclined to bleach the flowers. The outside temperature also, of course, affects the flowers, and has to be taken into consideration.

Someone I know has a large, wide cupboard taking up the whole length of a room. Into this she throws bundles of leaves, grasses, etc. with carefree abandon. It is possible to be too nervous and finicky, it seems, though a certain amount of care can be very rewarding. However, the element of luck probably counts in this more than any other branch of flower work.

Some flowers like to remain in water and to 'dry off' themselves. This again can only be discovered by experiment. Those I have found to be successful include globe artichokes, yarrow *(Achillea)* and bear's breeches *(Acanthus)*. Hydrangeas seem to fall into two groups – those that dry and those that don't. Those that dry, dry very well indeed, but there is no way of telling which will be successful. Dried in this way the flowers may be used in an arrangement, in the usual amount of cold water, which should not be added to or changed.

Sea lavender *(Limonium)* and everlastings *(Immortelle)* prefer to be hung in an ordinary room temperature, also Chinese lanterns *(Physalis alkekengii)*. Seedheads, too, hung in bunches ask only to be kept dry.

The actual locating of material is, of course, simple in a garden but much more complicated and interesting in the countryside. Most of the deep colours come from the garden, and probably delphiniums and larkspur are two of the easiest and prettiest. Delphiniums come in all shades of blue, and the larkspurs provide mauves, purples, pinks, and white. All these come in most usefully in arrangements where something spiky is required, and, quite apart from providing colour, produce an elegance of shape which is often valuable.

My own success with roses has been rather limited, but a friend dried dark red polyantha roses quite beautifully, sometimes with heat and sometimes by allowing them just to dry off naturally.

Lamb's ear *(Stachys lanata)* contributes its soft pearl grey leaves and purple flowers, and is one of the most useful and attractive of all flowers to dry.

Hollyhocks, chalk plant *(Gypsophila)*, love-lies-bleeding, mullein, and yarrow *(Achillea)* all dry quite well, though usually only the spikes in bud of the hollyhock and mullein can be depended upon. Hollyhock spikes after flowering can be most attractive. As these are tall, they can give dignity and height to a large arrangement.

Globe artichoke, bear's breeches *(Acanthus)* and corn cob flowers are tall and decorative. The architectural beauty of the artichoke is particularly fine, and if the bear's breeches can be persuaded to dry with its little white florets still intact it is one of the most attractive of all dried flowers.

Seedheads provide one of the largest contributions to dried flower arangements. They should be cut when ready, tied into bunches, and kept in a dry atmosphere. The following seedheads of garden flowers dry without any trouble: iris, Regal lily, butterfly bush *(Buddleia)* love-in-a-mist, sweet rocket, poppy, leek, smoke tree *(Cotinus coggygria)*, broom. Marigold dries sometimes but it is not reliable.

Globe thistle *(Echinops)* and sea holly *(Eryngium)* are invaluable with their soft blue colouring and star like quality.

Sea lavender, immortelle, honesty and Chinese lanterns *(Physalis alkekengii)* are all so well known that it seems hardly necessary to mention them, but perhaps a little unjust to leave them out. Added, a few in number, to an arrangement of seedheads and leaves of soft colours, they can give an accent to almost any effect that is required. Honesty arranged with silvered branches at Christmas can look quite beautiful, particularly if it has a light shining through behind it, and Chinese lanterns mixed in with pressed leaves of autumn colourings and stout, dark brown seedheads, can achieve distinction.

Stonecrop *(Sedum spectabile)* and golden rod both dry well, and bird of paradise *(Strelitzia)* can give an original touch to a mixed group, but it is, unfortunately, temperamental. Zinnias, with their many varied and beautiful colours are a great acquisition.

The real feeling of treasure trove, perhaps, comes with the discovery of wild flowers. Their locations are more varied and their seasons are shorter. There are the grass verges where the little white bladder campion may be found, but it must be tracked down before the road man scythes the first crop of hay. Angelica, burdock, common sorrel, and persicaria are others to be found there.

Nipplewort, one of the most useful, and the greater plantain *(Plantago major)* are both to be found on waste ground or edges of fields. The borders of cornfields are often rich in odd clusters of barley, wheat or oats, which can be taken without too much of a feeling of guilt.

The teasels and great reeds of the Kentish dykes,

Top, Branches of dried hop flowers arranged
with dark brown teasels. If possible catch the hop flowers
while they are still green—they very quickly turn to a
buff brown colour. If kept for another year they may turn
to a deep tan colour which is particularly attractive.

Top right, A dried group in grey and dark brown arranged
in a plain grey earthenware jar.
The leek heads are grey-white against an outline of
chocolate brown dock and copper coloured sorrel.

Right, A few dried magnolia leaves make an interesting
background for dried poppy heads and teasels.
The colour of the leaves varies from the tan of the
underleaf to the olive green of its surface.
The poppies come in soft buff, blue-grey
and brown colourings. The teasels cut short towards the
centre of the group, give an emphasis of deeper brown.

together with the dock family, form another
valuable contribution. The number of subtle
shades in which the dock can be dried, from pale
peach to deep chocolate, is most surprising. The
majestic plumes of the great reeds are exceptionally
impressive. Teasels are almost equally useful,
dried green or brown.

Ponds are another valuable source of material.
The branched bur-reed, figwort and water plantain
are special delights as are the lesser reed mace.

Traveller's joy *(Clematis vitalba)* so well known,
is one of the most charming and delightful of all
roadside flowers and in its dried state has the great
quality of lasting power belied by its fragile appearance. If the long stems seem difficult to arrange,
they can be intertwined with something tall and of
sturdier growth, such as a stalwart stem of angelica.

The arrangement of dried flowers follows much
the same pattern as that of fresh flowers.

A basket of dried materials in green, blue-grey, brown and purple. The green is provided by the hop flowers, bells of Ireland and phlomis seedheads. Also included in the arrangement is the delicate brown of nipplewort, the richer brown of dark sorrel and spiraea and the deep mahagony brown of globe artichoke seedheads; purple is provided by *Rodgersia pinnata* seedheads. The small daisy-like anaphalis give a touch of white and the lamb's ears and sea holly produce grey.

Dried flowers and seedheads from the border, produce, in this arrangement,
a blue and silver group with a touch of soft yellow. The arrangement includes deep blue
delphiniums with paler blue and blue-grey poppy seedheads, steely grey sea holly,
buff coloured seedheads of bells of Ireland, the yellow of dried lady's mantle together with nipplewort.

Equipment

If accessories, such as shells, fir cones or pieces of wood are needed for flower arrangement,
it is helpful to have these at hand and to collect them whenever an opportunity
arises. It is also helpful to have a collection of small pots, dishes and lids to hold water;
these can be kept in a trug basket with scissors, string, wire netting and a dust sheet.

Whilst it isn't necessary to have large numbers of vases or complicated equipment to arrange flowers, there are a few accessories which would be helpful: scissors, wire netting, pin holders, 'Florapak', 'Oasis', Plasticine, sand, as well as disguises for them – leaves, moss, bark, stones, shells – watering can with long, thin spout and dust sheet.

STUB SCISSORS Like any other kind of scissors, have a habit of disappearing – they sometimes get lost amongst the stalks and leaves that are cut away from the flowers. It is more than likely that many pairs find their way into dustbins or rust their lives away on compost heaps. Once put down on a table for a minute, when one is doing the flowers, in no time at all they get tidied up and lost for ever. For this reason I try to have at least one spare pair and when that pair is brought into service, get another in their place.

The point about using stub scissors is that they are strong and, unlike ordinary kitchen scissors, will also cut wire (the small crescent in one of the blades is for this purpose). Thus they have a double purpose.

PIN HOLDERS, WIRE NETTING, 'FLORAPAK' OR 'OASIS' AND PLASTICINE These are all suitable methods of anchoring flowers under various conditions (sometimes one is appropriate, at other times another). If wire netting is used, it should be large mesh in three layers. This provides an efficient anchorage for flowers without too much restraint. The wire netting must be fixed firmly in position, for if it slides about at the beginning, all is lost. It is hopeless to trust to the weight of the flowers to hold the wire netting down. This never seems to happen.

In large pedestal groups (the weight of the tall stems often tends to lever the wire netting out of the vase, especially if the group happens to stand against a wall and most of the flowers are leaning forward) it sometimes helps to weight the wire netting down with either a small bag of sand or of lead shot.

Ordinary chicken wire is less obvious if painted a soft green. It can also be bought, at extra cost, covered in plastic.

PIN HOLDERS These come in different forms.

They are made either of metal – solid and heavy, with sharp needles, or of plastic – softer and not quite as sharp, or they may have a plastic base which acts on the principle of suction. (It should be realised that certain flowers just will not survive on pin holders – these include forget-me-nots, anchusa, lilies-of-the-valley and love-in-a-mist.) Pin holders are often obtainable in a reasonably good leaf green, which I think most preferable to the glaring unpainted metallic ones which show so unpleasantly, catching and reflecting any gleams of sunlight or electric light.

Pin holders, like wire netting, must be fixed firmly in position before the arrangement is begun, and one of the best methods of doing this is to wedge them down with pieces of Plasticine. This must, of course, be done before any water is poured into the container, otherwise the Plasticine will simply slide about and lose all its usefulness as an anchorage. A soft pliable Plasticine is essential and green is a good colour when there are any leaves in the arrangement.

Another essential factor when using a pin holder is to make sure that the water comes well over the top of its base – so that the stems are in no danger of being without water. This sounds simple enough, but it is sometimes difficult to see exactly where the level of the water is.

'FLORAPAK' or 'OASIS' are both used a great deal for certain types of arrangements. For instance when the container is porous (as in the case of sea shells), or, in a basket of flowers (already arranged) if one is taking them to a patient in

It is advisable to cut flowers for a large arrangement the day before they are needed. They should be given a good drink overnight in deep buckets or jugs of water It is helpful to tie the different types or sizes of flowers in separate bunches.

Stub scissors with
a crescent shaped gap
in the blade are a necessity
for cutting stems
in different lengths,
removing damaged leaves
and cutting wire netting.

hospital, to eliminate the possibility of spilling water *en route*.

WATERING CAN A small watering can with a long and narrow spout is invaluable for topping up the water supply where flowers have been already arranged. This does its job efficiently and without disturbing the flowers.

The point of using a dust sheet is obvious, but it becomes even more essential if one is bold enough to do the flowers in the position where they will stand finally.

Leaves are the obvious method of disguising pin holders etc. in most arrangements, but it is important that they become an integral part of the group and are not just pushed in at the last minute. Some of the most useful leaves are those of bergenia, cyclamen, geranium and ivy. Moss and bark are both usually available in copses or woodland and it is wise, whenever one is in the country to look out for suitable pieces and shapes of bark (two or three attractively shaped pieces are useful to have as a standby when they are needed) or clumps of velvety moss. (The moss can

be kept damp when it is brought home.) It is often difficult to find either of these at a moment's notice.

Stones and shells are, of course, usually to be found beside the sea, and any expedition to the seashore can be an excuse for collecting suitable stones or shells, quite apart from the fun of finding them. (I like to have a dish in which I keep some of the prettiest and most clearly marked of these which we have found on our expeditions.)

While still at the seashore it may be as well to look out for a suitable piece of driftwood (this can sometimes be an asset to an arrangement, but it can be difficult to find the correct shape, and when found it should be used with discretion).

At a flower lecture being given in a private house I heard the hostess offering to lend the demonstrator any of her own containers or equipment. 'You may borrow anything at all which will be useful', she said, 'that is, anything except my piece of driftwood'. Having once found an attractive shape after a good deal of seaching I can understand how she felt.

It is necessary to have various sized jugs for filling up vases.
A small watering can with a long spout is essential for topping up the vases once the flowers have been arranged.

Left, Most eremuri are tall and dignified
and need a sizeable container to hold them.
Here they are arranged in a large cider flagon,
with a narrow neck, which provides a support
for the thick stems; the *Fatsia japonica* leaves in the
arrangement make a dramatic contrast with the eremuri.

Top, Eremuri arranged with sprigs of rosemary.
Eremuri leaves are not, on the whole, suitable to use in
arrangements and if foliage is required
some from another plant is used. The material is fixed
on a pin holder, kept in position by two or three stones.

Top right, Eremuri are invaluable for use in a wedding
group on account of their height, delicate colouring
and long lasting properties.
The stems of the larger variety are heavy and solid
and special care is needed to keep them firmly in position.

Eremurus

The cremurus or fox-tail lily (sometimes called the giant asphodel), is one of the most useful plants for tall arrangements, equally suitable for weddings, pedestal vases and also for a corner vase in the house.

There are some problems connected with them, and perhaps one should mention these first and then make suggestions for overcoming them.

Anyone who has ever seen eremuri growing or handled them from the florist will know, especially with the largest ones (*Eremurus robustus*) the enormous size and weight of their stems. When they are being used in a large group these have to be treated with respect and fixed firmly in position before much of the material is put into place. *E. robustus* grows to a height of about seven or eight feet and has a stem with a girth almost the size of a young cherry tree, but not, of course, with a bark. The difficulty of fixing such a stem in position can be imagined.

First, there should be available some extra anchorage inside the base of the container – thickly folded wire netting or even pieces of brick or stone, over which there should be extra layers of the wire netting. It is essential that these layers should be formed from a large mesh wire netting or else one will be up against a further problem, that of the spaces between the wires being too narrow to take in the enormous width of stem.

The pieces of stone or brick or solid wire netting act as wedges to keep the base of the stem from wobbling about and these may be further supple-mented by shrubby branches which would also help to act as anchorage.

These rather formidable measures are only necessary with the largest eremuri. The smaller ones are no more difficult than tall delphiniums, lilies or gladioli, and are excellent pointers in a large arrangement where outline is concerned. Carefully placed they can delineate the arrangement and form positions between which the other flowers and branches can be fitted in.

Eremuri come in soft colourings of pink, peach, lemon, off white and cream. *E. robustus* has pink flowers as has *E. olgae,* which is one of the later flowering ones. The first to flower in May is *E. himalaicus,* which grows to a height of about six feet. There are two forms of *E. elwesii* (which flowers at the end of May or the beginning of June), a white and a pink.

Usually when cut for arrangement they should just be coming out at the base of the flower stalk and still in bud most of the way up, unless they are needed for an immediate special occasion. In the house they will last for about a fortnight if they are cut as I suggest, and it is interesting to see the small flowers opening up along the stem day by day.

There are one or two points to consider when first purchasing eremuri for planting in the garden – they are more expensive to buy than many other plants. But when one considers their dramatic appearance and beauty, the fact that they will come up again and again, and that their cost is not much more than forty cigarettes, it seems to me that they are worth their weight in gold. (A few years ago I paid 10/6d each for Shelford hybrids which come in a great variety of colours and are sturdy in growth.) There may not be any dramatic results for the first two years, although encouraging clusters of green lily like leaves are likely to appear in the spring. This does not mean to say that the plant is going to flower, but if it does, so much the better, especially as it is likely to go on year after year and may even seed itself generously as has happened in a garden in Chilham, Kent, England

When the plant is first put into the soil on arrival from the nursery it should be treated with the greatest care. Eremurus should be moved in the early autumn and not allowed to remain out of the ground a moment longer than is absolutely neces-sary. Its root system is easily damaged as it is brittle, large and spreading in growth, and easily bruised or broken. Once this happens the plant may not recover. But, on the other hand, once it is established it should go well ahead.

Rather like clematis, it may not appear at all when it is first planted and it might be thought to have died. But, again, like clematis, it may appear two or three years later and forge ahead. And so do not despair if there is no sign of life for a year

Right, Three spikes of yellow eremuri cut quite short and arranged with wide bergenia leaves in a large brass candlestick holder. A group of this kind will last well, especially if the lower flowers of the eremuri are cut off as they die, allowing the buds at the top of the stem to come out.

Left, Eremuri are the most dependable of all flowers for tall arrangements. They last well as it takes some time for the small buds to come into flower all the way up the stem. Eremuri come in white, pale lemon, yellow, peach and soft pink.

or two, or even if there are leaves and still no flower. It may just be settling itself in and liking taking some time about doing so.

The mention of cost comes up again when these flowers have to be bought in some quantity. They are expensive to buy, and it must be remembered that not only do they take time to get established but that there may only be one spike on each plant for some time to come.

From the point of view of decoration eremuri are valuable not only because of their height and delightful colouring, but also because of their dependability. They are completely reliable and if, for instance, it is more convenient to cut them two or three days before they are required for some special occasion, this can safely be done, as long as they are not fully out. They can be kept in the same condition in a closed box for a good many hours. They will also keep in water, but of course they will open out as if they were growing.

When being ordered from Covent Garden it is wise to hand in one's requirements some time before they are needed, as supplies are not yet coming in frequently and for a special order might have to be brought from some distance and made sure of in advance. Eremuri do not come into the market at the same rate as lilies or carnations and once one has tried to grow them one will understand why this is so.

Miss Sackville-West has in her book *In your Garden* a useful suggestion on how to decide what plants to put next to each other, with reference to the eremurus. This applies just as much, as she points out to flower arrangement. She suggests cutting a flower in part of the garden and standing it against a flowering shrub or plant in quite another part to see what the effect of the colour will be. "Rather in the way that one makes a flower arrangement in the house, sticking them into the ground and then standing back to observe the harmony." In this case the suggestion refers to a tall spike of *Eremurus robustus* standing against a shrub of pale pink Tamarisk – also flowering in May – and the effect is so good that she plans to have plants of eremurus close to the Tamarisk for another year.

When using the *Eremurus robustus* for decoration it is helpful to have large leaves or branches to arrange with it, and possibilities are giant rhubarb leaves, branches of lime or tall thin Phormium leaves. Otherwise the tall stalks do look rather unadorned and the leaves of the eremurus itself are not usually helpful. Towards the front of such an arrangement a few early auratum or regale lilies might also help to counteract the bareness of stem.

As I have already mentioned the Shelford varieties of eremuri come on later and are not so massive as these earlier ones.

Evergreens

Winter is the obvious time of the year when ever-greens are essential for arrangement, though certain evergreens are invaluable throughout the year on account of their colour and shape. They also seem to have the additional attraction of lasting longer than almost any other kind of foliage.

Evergreens can either be solidly green or varie-gated and, in each case, they have a different value. For instance, I think that there is nothing like the addition of a deep green leaf such as camellia or *Fatsia japonica* towards the centre of a group to pull together the varieties of shapes and colours (green).

Nowadays, the value of a spray of variegated periwinkle or the branches of golden privet which give a touch of lightness to an arrangement are acknowledged and appreciated.

Perhaps it would be best to enumerate some of the evergreens most useful for arrangement: Christmas and Lenten roses *(Hellebores), H. corsicus, H. foetidus, H. niger* are available and valuable throughout the year and although they all belong to the same family, they are quite different. The Corsican hellebore has large, spreading, prickly leaves – blue-grey in colour. *H. foetidus* has neat, dark green, fan like leaves, many of which are long stemmed. These are invaluable, fitting attractively into many types of arrangements

with varieties of flowers. (I have a friend who uses them almost continuously for small arrangements with many of the flowers from her summer border.) Then there are the large dramatic deep green leaves of the Lenten hellebores. These usually come with long stems and so are especially useful for large arrangements. They produce an interesting outline with either a few flowers or a few differently shaped leaves. The bold, divided shape of the leaves show up extremely well against a plain background.

Often grown in the garden quite close to the *hellebores* and much the same type and size of plant is the bergenia. Its solid rounded leaves vary in colour from a clear light green in the spring to a darker green during the summer and sometimes a deep wine in the autumn and winter. The larger leaves come on long stalks which makes them also useful for large groups. Some of the smaller leaves before they are quite opened grow with a charming folded effect and so at this stage are especially suitable for use with small flowers, e.g. violets, rock plants, wind-flowers, and cowslips.

Of quite a different habit is the periwinkle with either dark or variegated leaves growing on long curving stems. Both dark and variegated leaves combine well with many different flowers and are especially useful for an arrangement which stands high off the ground, i.e. giving a pedestal effect.

The camellia (tea plant) is an evergreen of constant elegance, in the early summer when it has fresh green foliage and later on in the year when the leaves become dark green. It lasts for weeks in water and the shape and beauty of the leaves make it a perfect accompaniment for many flowers including carnations, Jerusalem sage *(Phlomis)*, chrysanthemums, white delphiniums, gladioli, white campanulas and African lilies *(Agapanthus)*. Silver berry *(Elaeagnus)* with its soft green leaves, silver backed, is yet another reliable and beautiful shrub, producing quite different effects according to whether the leaves are arranged showing the silver or the green surface.

A variegated elaeagnus *(E. pungens aureo variegata)* has the same shaped leaf but with quite a different colouring. In its way this is one of

Top, Contrast of colour, shape and texture are three important points when arranging evergreens. In this group the dark green oval-shaped leaves of the Lenten hellebore contrast with the cream edged lighter green of the variegated periwinkle. The foliage stands in a lustre jug.

Right, A few branches of berberis and periwinkle are arranged in a glass decanter with a long narrow neck. The tall neck makes a useful support for the branches but it is important to watch the water level which falls quickly, until it reaches the bowl of the decanter.

Left, An arrangement of evergreen during winter is long lasting and stands up well to central heating. There are many leaves and branches to choose from — the group in the photograph has branches of berberis, eucalyptus and some fir cones.

97

A few branches of a distinctive evergreen make an interesting arrangement during the winter when flowers are scarce. The green catkins of Garrya elliptica flourish from January to March – in the photograph they are arranged on a pin holder in a glass container of water.

the most attractive of all the variegated shrubs.

Another interesting variegated leaf belongs to *Euonymus fortunei,* this is a smaller shrub than the elaeagnus with rather abrupt, angular branches. Again these last for weeks when cut for decorations.

Holly, ivy, holm oak and Laurustinus are all useful in different ways – the first two are, perhaps, more so in their variegated forms. Laurustinus has a special charm even without its clusters of pink white flowers. The neat, pointed, dark green leaves have a cheerfulness reminiscent of myrtle. Spotted laurel *(Aucuba)* and the common laurel, rhododendron, bay, rosemary, yew all provide useful material too.

The rhododendron is a reliable standby throughout the year, providing practical and most decorative foundation for a large winter arrangement, when there is little else of this type available.

Rosemary is an especial favourite – leaves dark green backed with grey, elegant in shape, and with an elusive scent. It looks charming with many different flowers.

The spotted laurel has well shaped, patterned leaves, which can provide a distinctive foil for dark green foliage such as camellia, laurel, rhododendron, etc. But its leaves must be clean and shiny, and used with discretion. (Discretion must be applied to the arrangement of any variegated foliage.) Bay – crisp, dark and pointed, has been eulogised by Miss Jekyll in *Flower Decoration in the House.* 'Of all the lovely forms of branch and leaf, the one that may be said to be of supreme beauty – that of the sweet bay – may be enjoyed in winter. For then the whole bush, or tree as it is in the south, is at its best and glossiest'.

Yew is one of the traditional evergreens, together with holly and ivy, rosemary and bay, which has been used for church decoration since the early sixteenth century. It lasts well when it is cut, and the rather angular shape of the branches often gives an interesting outline to an arrangement. Berberis or mahonia has tall, leafy sprays varied in

Branches of laurustinus with their dark green pointed leaves and pink and white flowers arranged in an early mahogany tea caddy. Laurustinus will flower, in sheltered positions, throughout the winter. It lasts well when cut for indoor arrangements.

colour and provides good support if used with slender flower stalks.

Broad leaved laurel – the new light green leaves are useful as a contrast with darker evergreens.

Ilex – the leaves are a very good shape, though dusty grey-green in colour; at its best in winter.

The cucumber tree *(Magnolia acuminata)* – its pale yellow flower is a great delight, and the large olive coloured leaves are most attractive, the Exmouth variety having coffee-coloured backs.

Myrtle – (half hardy, except in southern England). Produces a charming, brisk spray of clear dark leaves, elegant and neat.

Portugal laurel – an interesting leaf and well shaped branch. Especially good for decoration with light pink or cream chrysanthemums.

Skimmia – good clusters of dark leaves with clumps of bright red berries in autumn in the female plant.

One of the most interesting in shape of all evergreens is the false fig *(Fatsia japonica)*. Reasonably hardy it will survive the winter, for instance, in a fairly exposed Kentish garden, but is often brought in to shelter from the worst of the frosts. There are substantial clumps of these growing in the gardens at South Kensington Underground Station, London, and I know of one in a London garden which is well over ten feet high with a spread that is of almost equal size. It would be well worth the trouble to have a plant of such distinction for cutting and with such long lasting properties.

As with all woody stemmed plants the branches of the above mentioned shrubs need a good supply of water. The base of their stems should be crushed, split or smashed to expedite the supply, and in some cases should be trimmed of their lower leaves.

Note Perhaps the right to include variegated leaves with evergreens might be questioned and one should, in this case, classify evergreens as non-deciduous shrubs or trees.

99

Everlasting flowers

One of the most important things to remember about everlasting flowers is that, *above all*, they should be used sparingly and with discretion. This applies especially to immortelle and sea lavender *(Limonium)*, bunches of which are often to be seen for sale hanging in profusion with cape gooseberries *(Physalis)* and honesty. (These are the true everlastings, all valuable in their own way if introduced in small quantities among other dried flowers.)

Sometimes the temptation to buy bunches of these for 'filling up' is too great and very quickly the suggestion of 'arty-craftiness' creeps in (on about the same level as artificial beams, perma-

nently varnished brasses, and dyed bulrushes or grasses).

Immortelle *(Helichrysum)* come in a great variety of shades from white (usually with clear yellow centres) through palest pink (one of the most attractive of these is a soft double pink) to dark wine red (some of which have black centres). The enormous colour range can either pick up and emphasise colours and shades used in the flower arrangement or those used in the furnishing scheme of the room.

Immortelle shows incredible versatility, for it can be used as a contrast, say of a cluster of white immortelle against dark brown dried seedheads,

Right, Certain types of limonium, when arranged
with fresh flowers, mix with and emphasise their colours.
In this arrangement the limonium comes in deep purple,
mauve and pale pink; only a few sprays of it are necessary
to emphasise the lilac-mauve carnations.

Bottom left, Sea lavender is a most decorative
accompaniment to other dried flowers and seedheads, and
as long as it is not allowed to spoil the outline of the group,
its delicate, feathery stems help to lighten heavier material.

Bottom, The large round daisy-like flowers (helichrysums)
and the clusters of small daisy-like flowers (anaphalis)
are the everlastings in this dried group.
The white, pale pink and yellow (helichrysums) together
with the bright lemon yellow of the anaphalis
introduce a note of colour into the arrangement.
(When white, anaphalis has been bleached).

In this dried group the everlastings give the
splashes of colour. The yellow gnaphaliums,
the white daisy-like anaphalis and the pinkish white
helichrysums towards the centre of the arrangement
provide an emphasis on the softer colours of the heather,
globe artichokes and achillea.

Right, A few everlasting flowers arranged with other
dried material give a good touch of colour.
In this group yellow, cream and orange helichrysums and
sea lavender emphasise the colour of the
dried mimosa and white larkspur.

or as a complement, e.g. in the case of yellows and
oranges it can tone in with other autumn colours.

Sea lavender *(Limonium)* comes not only in the
well known shades of mauve and purple but also
in off white and a clear yellow. Both these colours
can be usefully incorporated into certain decorative
schemes, composed of the dark browns, reds and
yellows of autumn seedheads, and leaves and
flowers.

Everlastings are reasonably easy to grow and
almost dry as they are growing. For the actual
drying, they require little extra care or attention,
though they are usually more successful if they are
not dried in layers but laid out, for preference on a
layer of wire netting, so that the air can circulate
underneath as well as above them.

Give them plenty of air, but not a draught, and
very little heat. Space is essential for if they are
too crowded together either in a damp atmosphere
or an over heated one, a kind of thick mould may
develop, especially amongst the limonium flowers.

After these general comments on everlasting or
immortelle flowers, let us consider them separately:

Immortelle originally came from the Antipodes.
The hardy annual, *H. bracteatum* is probably the
best known, and the most generally grown.

Others come from Africa and from the Mediterranean, and, like many other plants indigenous
to these warm regions, they may be grown successfully in cooler climates if they are sown in
well drained soil in a sunny position. The first
flowers may appear early on in the summer. They
should be cut for drying as soon as they are fully
out, and before they are dashed by heavy rain.
If they do get soaked, they *must* be allowed to
dry out well before cutting.

Helipterum, yet another 'straw' daisy of some
charm, also comes from the Antipodes and is
known generally as the 'Australian everlasting'.
It usually comes in soft pink and white colouring,
but when grown in England produces smaller
flowers than the *helichrysums.* I understand that
when grown in their native country they produce
much larger sized flowers in a deeper pink or a
purer white.

Helipterum roseum produces one flower per
stalk, and, as with *H. bracteatum* the weight of
this single flower on the rather thin stalk does

encourage the stem to bend over at the top. This
makes these flowers difficult to arrange when dried
and so, if they can be cut as they come out (before
the stem has time to develop this curve), and hung
upside down to dry, one may be fortunate enough
to get a well formed flower on a straight stalk.

Helipterum manglesii is a still smaller 'straw'
daisy whose flowers tend to grow in clusters.
They should be cut when the first flower opens
fully. This means that others in the cluster will
still only be in bud. These buds are usually deeper
in colour than the fully opened flower and so provide, at one and the same time, variations in size
and shape and colour.

When they are dried the leaves of both the helichrysums and the helipterums shrivel up and look
untidy. They must, of course, be removed and
it is relatively easy to do this without damaging
the rather attractive small buds or side-branches.
After this is done, the cluster of flowers and buds
show to their best advantage.

Sea lavender *(Statice* or *Limonium)*. A family whose various members offer flowers in a variety of sizes and colours, the most colourful of which probably come under the family name of *S.* or *L. sinuatum*. They range in colour from blue, mauve, purple, pink, buff to white. The seeds of *L. sinuatum* may be bought in separate colours, or in a mixed packet. Unless one intends to have a good many dried arrangements, I would recommend the latter way of buying them, as this particular packet will produce enough for the usual demands of one largish group.

L. bonduellii in a clear sulphur yellow is a valuable colour to introduce into groups during the winter. This yellow with white is perhaps the most adaptable colour of all, for unlike the blues and mauves, it shows up well and cheerfully in artificial light, and as mentioned earlier on, also combines well with the usual browns and oranges of autumn colourings.

Now we come to the 'true' sea lavenders – two of which will suffice for most domestic requirements. *L. latifolium* is the very small flowered lavender coloured plant which grows into quite a sturdy bush, up to three feet in height. The other is *L. incanum* with a much stockier growth, the creamy white flowers growing in flattish pannicles. This sea lavender dries almost as it grows, and hardly needs to be cut and hung in bunches or laid flat on shelves like the others.

These last two 'everlastings' are, perhaps, the most useful of all, for however attractive and useful the helichrysums and limoniums may be, if they are used in too great a quantity they are inclined to impose an alien atmosphere of slight artificiality into a dried arrangement. This is certainly not true of the sea lavenders, whose natural, branching habit of growth, and soft colouring are of great value. It is easy to put too much into one arrangement, but used with discretion, the sea lavenders can be most attractive and effective.

Exhibition work for charity

Many of us enjoy working with flowers, either growing or arranging them, or we may simply like to see them in a flower shop, garden, or hedgerow. Some of us may collect flower books and have a special one which can be taken to the seaside or into a country district so that we have the fun of identifying wild and garden flowers.

If we also press the flowers we collect, we may then take down our notebooks on a winter's evening and perhaps be reminded of open moorland with curlews crying overhead, or of pounding waves on the seashore and small flowers growing among the shingle.

At first sight, this may seem to have little connection with flower arrangement societies, but it has more than one would think. The societies, most of them formed comparatively recently, have confirmed or promoted ideas which often existed but were not always apparent.

The first of these is to help members of societies to use various types of flowers and foliage and to encourage them to try to grow special plants for their decorative work, however small their gardens might be.

The second is to give pleasure to the sick and elderly by regularly arranging flowers in hospitals, and also to help charities by organising exhibitions and competitions.

The National Association of Flower Arranging Societies was constituted in 1959 under the auspices of the Royal Horticultural Society, when it had become evident that a central organisation was necessary to bind together the numerous flower clubs, some of which had been in existence for nearly ten years.

There are 564 clubs in the association and Mrs. Cecil Pope, of Dorchester, Dorset, England, is its Founder President. The membership is well over 52,000.

This association is a splendid example of an organisation where the individual talents of the members are used (through the medium of the flower clubs) for the benefit of others. Money has been raised for charitable causes, both at area level and by individual societies.

The home of Earl Mountbatten was decorated by the Wessex area and as a result of this £1,500 was contributed to the Edwina Mountbatten Memorial Home. In the same way, Blenheim Palace was decorated by the Berkshire, Buckinghamshire and Oxfordshire areas and £2,000 was raised for OXFAM.

Many churches have had repair funds supplemented by flower festivals and National Trust houses have benefitted financially as a result of special flower decorations. A donation was given to the Lady Hoare Thalidomide Fund from the proceeds of the raffle held in connection with the Buxton Festival.

Left, This is an example of the work done for an exhibition by Mrs Cecil Pope, Chairman of the National Association of Flower Arrangement Societies of Great Britain.
This association has organised many exhibitions for charity and raised substantial sums of money.

Bottom, This is a typical floral group arranged for charity. Such a group needs to stand out well and consist of flowers which will last for some days without replenishment; the water level needs to be kept up to the brim of the container.

Bottom right. Flower displays for charity are usually arranged in a large private house or a 'Stately Home' which has been taken over by the National Trust. The flowers are especially chosen to fit into the surroundings.

Top, This is one of the arrangements at an exhibition held in aid of the World Commonwealth Society for the Blind at Longleat, the Wiltshire home of Lord Bath, in September, 1965. The exhibition had been planned for 18 months by 34 West of England Floral Arrangement Societies; their objective was to buy a mobile eye clinic for Sierra Leone.

Right, At the Flower Arrangement Exhibition held at Longleat, Wiltshire in September, 1965, flowers were arranged which had come, carefully packed, from all over the world. Seventeen Commonwealth countries contributed flowers and one arrangement was made up of buds from Ceylon, Nigeria, Trinidad, Australia, Singapore, St. Vincent, and Granada.

The following taken from a recent copy of *The Flower Arranger* illustrate this work for charity: 'Two more new clubs, Plympton in South Devon and Looe in Cornwall, have become affiliated to the ever growing South West area. We read of the vast sums gathered in from other parts of Great Britain for some worthy cause and we would like to add our praise for the clubs of this county, for in the last twelve months they have collected no less than £1,150. Exeter itself raised over £100 for the British Empire Cancer Campaign with an exhibition ...'

'Lady Ann Waldegrave opened Wells and District's Exhibition in the Undercroft of the Bishop's Palace; Mrs. Dunscombe Bindley judged the competitive classes. Donations were afterwards given to the Friends of Wells Cathedral and to a fund for the upkeep of the Undercroft ....'

'Melksham in Wiltshire, decorated its Parish Church to aid the Freedom from Hunger Campaign. Bristol Flower Decoration Society has decorated the Cathedral regularly for several years.' This is greatly appreciated judging by the following extract from a letter sent by the Dean to the Society: 'The flowers in the Cathedral today were so lovely that I thought I must write to thank you for your kindness in arranging them, especially on a Saturday. They were, and are, a great joy, a perfect expression of the meaning of Easter and I am immensely grateful'. Bridgewater, Taunton and Minehead Clubs combined their work with an exhibition of paintings by Somerset artists at the end of June. This took place at Halsway Manor, once Henry VIII's hunting lodge, by kind permission of Miss Frances Gair Wilkinson. From the proceeds £100 was given to the Church of England Children's Society...' 'Bournemouth Society's spring show 'A Rainbow of Flowers' also provided a sum of money for Doctor Barnardo's Homes...'

'Members of Portsmouth Society are endeavouring to raise enough funds to buy a dog for a blind person and a great deal of the required amount was raised..'

'At the end of June the area held its combined exhibition at Eastnor Castle, Ledbury. The castle looked its best and each room contained arrangements harmonizing with tapestries and pictures. A donation was given to the Freedom from Hunger Campaign. The same charity was supported by Cardiff Society whose members carried out decorations for an art exhibition. They also hope to help the Red Cross in its centenary year by decorating a house and supplying about fifty flower arrangements for same...'

'The Gloucester Society has been busy with exhibitions at Sheephouse, Tuffley, Glos., in aid of the Oak Bank Swimming Pool; at Standish Park to help to raise money for the restoration of the choir stalls in Standish Church and at Conigree Court, Newent, Gloucestershire, in aid of Old Peoples' Welfare'.

And so we have the best of both worlds. Stimulation of interest in members is provided by competition (and the committee emphasises that new names for the awards appear each year) and this intensifies the obvious development of an interest which was known only to a few a hundred years ago. Secondly, there is the practical benefit that it can bring to those in need of help and financial aid. This seems to me perhaps the greatest claim that the association can make.

Escallonia is one of the most valuable flowering shrubs either to have in the garden or for cutting. As an evergreen its dark green small shining leaves are useful during the winter; when it is covered in mid summer with pink or pink and white flowers it is a sight to be seen.

Flowering shrubs and fruit blossom

Thanks to pioneers, numerous flowering shrubs and trees are now available for use in arrangements. Blossom is usually white, white flushed with pink, or pink, as in the case of cherry, pear and apple respectively. These three are the old established fruit trees which today have been supplemented by ornamental cherries, prunus and so on. Colour in azaleas and rhododendrons is so varied as to defy description.

Early summer is the time for azaleas and rhododendrons and now there is a wide variety of these two valuable shrubs. What an addition to an arrangement a cluster of rhododendron or a few

Mauve, purple or white lilac is a valuable flowering tree for large flower arrangements. It is best to cut it when still in bud, split or crush the stems and give them a deep drink before arranging. The white lilac is especially useful for wedding groups.

sprays of azalea can make, especially when a certain colour effect is needed. Both these shrubs are reliable for cutting, and so I think it is worth trying to grow at least one or two examples of each, even if it means replacing some soil with extra peat and leaf-mould.

Perhaps the most delightful azaleas for cutting are those with a delicious honey scent. With such a wealth of choice it is often a good idea at this time of the year to go to a nursery garden which specialises in these shrubs and decide from the ones that are in bloom. Another suggestion is to pay a visit to the Savill Gardens in Windsor Great Park, and in particular to the Kurume Punch Bowl, where the shrubs are at their best during the first fortnight in May.

Here is one of the greatest shows of colour in the British Isles with every possible colour and shade of azalea.

The rules for treating branches of blossom or shrubs are similar to those for other wooded stems. The base of the branch must be smashed, hammered or split up, and the leaves must be in good condition, any that are eaten or torn must be cut away. Lastly, the branches should have a long, deep drink before being arranged.

Mock orange *(Philadelphus)* is one of the loveliest of all flowering shrubs. The flowers are a pure white and their scent is strong enough to fill the average sized room. In England the earliest variety usually comes out in the last week of May, that is if it is grown in a sheltered position with plenty of sun. It will thrive on chalky soil and should be pruned after flowering, since it is important to cut out the branches which have flowered. Mock orange is one of the few examples in flower arrangement where the leaves should almost be stripped off to allow the flowers to last longer and to be seen.

A valid criticism of mock orange is that it drops quickly, but if cut when still in bud it will come out in water and last quite well. Again as with all woody stemmed flowers, it must have the base of its stalks smashed, or well slit up, to allow a greater intake of water. Philadelphus is especially associated with weddings and is very popular in bridal bouquets and church decorations.

Thinking in terms of using fruit blossom – cherry, pear, apple, quince, japonica – for arrangements one sometimes comes across two points of argument. The first is that cutting fruit blossom is wasteful and may also be detrimental to the shape of the tree. The second is that blossom drops quickly and is not, in any case, worth the trouble of arranging.

The answer to the first argument must be settled by personal opinion. Surely two or three branches cut from a well grown apple or quince will not greatly diminish the amount of fruit to come later on in the year, and if the shape of the tree is studied and a few branches taken where they can best be spared, judicious cutting can be as effective as good pruning.

The second point is of more importance from the flower arranging point of view. To answer it adequately I shall later quote from *The Flowers of Japan* and *The Art of Floral Arrangement* by Sir Josiah Conder. For blossom has a special significance for the Japanese.

In Japan there are blossom festivals. Trips are organised to visit orchards and gardens where there are fruit trees – especially cherries and plums. These trees have been planted extensively over hundreds of years, and in early records mention is made of the plum even before the cherry (this, in fact, is not mentioned before the reign of the Emperor Richiu, in the fifth century).

Sir Josiah Conder wrote: 'The plum blossom being the earliest flower of the year, is held in high esteem for floral arrangements. The hardiness of the plum tree, the duration of its blossom, its sweet perfume, as well as the austere type of its beauty, all help to make it even a greater favourite for flower composition than its more showy rival the cherry tree'.

It must be admitted that fruit blossom does on the whole drop quickly. However, there are, as with most flowers, a few simple rules which help it to last long enough to make it worth while cutting.

First blossom should be cut whenever possible while the flowers are still in tight bud at a cool time of day. It can even be cut in the early weeks of spring when there is little sign of the flowers and leaves to come and brought on rapidly in a warm room. (This method is especially successful with forsythia.) In this way I have used early cherry blossom for church decoration at Easter, which only had to be tidied up later on in the week, and I also prolonged the life of long branches of japonica in a large pedestal arrangement. This particular group lasted nearly three weeks, but the water level had to be watched carefully and the container frequently filled up to the brim. Also, when flowers died they were cut off and the remaining buds came on in their place. As in the case of all branches bearing blossom, the arrangement should not stand in a draught.

Reverting to the Japanese outlook on flower decoration one realises that special emphasis is placed on the shape and line of the arrangement to be composed of the blossom; the branches to be selected are studied with care before any cutting takes place. Branches must lean in the required direction or take on a certain shape, since the whole design of the group is thought out beforehand and a clear picture of it is in the arranger's mind.

The finished arrangement must look as though the branches are actually growing.

Since blossom is so often found on beautifully curving branches only two or three sprays are needed for certain types of arrangement. (This applies especially to a wall bracket or a group standing against a mirror.) Too many branches spoil the outline and give a muddled effect.

Most branches are heavy and must be anchored firmly at the outset. They will lose all their dignity and beauty if they wobble about. Should wire netting be used for this purpose it must be fixed in position before starting to insert the branches. If using a pin holder it must be heavy in itself, anchored with Plasticine, and also held in place with a double layer of wire netting which could clip down over the sides of the vase.

To return to some of the other flowering shrubs. Berberis, so well known, and grown in most gardens, is reliable and uncritical of its situation, it obliges by growing sturdily almost anywhere.

Camellia is rather a different matter, although it is more hardy than was thought previously. William Robinson, writing in the late nineteenth century, remarked even then that he did not consider it difficult, its greatest enemy being a fierce wind 'which beats it about'. A camellia can sometimes be quite conveniently grown in a tub, but as it seems to catch the wind where the main stem goes into the soil, it is helpful either to wrap a piece of sacking or to tie bracken round the base of the stem to keep the frost out. Apart from this the idea of a camellia growing in a tub in a small area of garden, perhaps in a town garden, is a most attractive one. The foliage, which lasts well, is a great asset both in winter and in spring decorations. (If branches are cut which have small flower buds in the leaf axils there is the possibility of flowers coming out later on in the warm temperature of a room.)

The usual pink flowering currant, *Ribes sanguineum* is covered first with fresh green leaves, which are pleasant in colour but are sometimes too heavily scented to have indoors. Then the racemes of deep pink appear (a difficult pink for flower arrangement) still accompanied by the rather stuffy smell. But if bare twigs are cut in late January, brought indoors, put preferably into a dark cupboard, and then stood in water, it is like waving a wand and getting rid of both the overpowering scent and the difficult pink. Then there is no noticeable smell and the flowers come out early in a beautiful creamy white. This is a valuable idea which comes from the late Miss Victoria Sackville-West.

So if you were thinking of digging up your rather despised flowering currant bush, do try this idea first and perhaps you may feel that it is worth keeping after all.

It does seem ungrateful to write about flowering shrubs without mentioning three very old friends, so old that they may almost be taken for granted amongst so many new introductions. These are lilac, laburnum, and bridal wreath (*Spiraea arguta*). 'But they don't last' I can hear you reply. 'They drop all over the place'.

Well, I would like to contest this point of view. Lilac, I must agree, is liable to fade quickly. The only hope of prolonging its life is to cut it just as it is coming out, for the ends of its woody stems to be smashed and some of its foliage stripped. But I think it is worth the trouble, not only for the reward of its exotic smell and soft, rich colouring (the simple charm of the pale single lilac, like that of an old fashioned sunbonnet print—or the beauty of the white, Marie Lemoine), but also for the beautifully shaped leaf, especially in the autumn when it turns and becomes like copper and bronze valentines.

Laburnum is another matter. Given the same

Escallonia provides a wealth of material either with its dark foliage or when it is in flower. Sometimes the flowers are pink and white, sometimes pink and sometimes rosy red. They are all useful and delightful, growing on curving branches, which are a gift for flower arranging.

treatment as prescribed for lilac, I have found it lasts reasonably well. And it is hard to get the same effect of two or three slender branches, with their pendulous pale yellow flowers, in any other material.

The bridal wreath shrub has thin arching branches which look almost as though they are constructed of black wire. In the spring, usually a stage or two ahead of laburnum and lilac, these branches are almost covered with clusters of small white flowers and fresh green leaves. This is a hardy shrub and will grow in most ordinary soils, though it does rather enjoy a good feed of manure either in the autumn or early spring, before flowering. Once it gets going bridal wreath will develop into quite a large bush and should, if possible, be given a position where the curving branches can spread themselves, perhaps at the corner of a bed or at the back of a rock garden. In either case the branches will not be squashed up against other shrubs but will stand out and show off their charming white sprays to perfection. Sometimes, the tips of the branches may droop a little when cut

if they are not immediately put into water. When this happens, the usual treatment of a long drink (having first had their stems snipped and crushed at the base), should put the matter right.

One of the loveliest plants to be introduced to England is the Chilean gum box *(Escallonia)* so called after a botanist named Escallon (a pupil of Mutis, chief of the botanical expedition to New Granada). It comes from the mountainous part of Chile and now seems to be quite hardy, at any rate in more southerly gardens. (There are, in fact, situations where they are planted as a wind break.) It flourishes in a mixture of loam and peat, and when in season usually flowers profusely, sometimes breaking out into bloom again later on in late summer. Part of its attraction is the curving line of the branches and the way that the shining leaves are arranged along the stem. The Chilean gum box will form spreading bushes although they will also grow against a wall or form a hedge. Some need protection against frost, but only a little extra care is called for in special cases or in more exposed situations in a colder climate.

Flowers and furnishings

During this century throughout Western Europe and America there has evolved an increased appreciation of the importance of flower arrangement in the home although, compared with the Far East, where flower decoration has been considered an art since the sixth century, this is a relatively late development. This fact may account for a certain lack of discrimination on our part, the inclination to use too much material where a smaller quantity would be twice as effective. (Mr. Christmas Humphreys, in his excellent history of Buddhism sums it up by saying 'The Japanese have *par excellence* what the scriptures of Zen in China sometimes advised in vain: a knowledge of where to stop. In their gardens as in their architecture, in the arrangement of flowers as in their dress, the minimum is expressed and the maximum left for the beholder to supply'.) Flower arrangements, however beautiful they are in themselves, can never look at their best when placed in a room at random without due consideration of the existing colour scheme or furnishings. Consider your flower arrangement in the same way as you would a good painting. Both need all the light and space they can get to show them off to their best advantage, and both are integral parts of furnishings – they are, in other words, 'functional'.

We have established that there are three basic factors to take into consideration:

The relationship between the colour of the furnishings and colour of the arrangement. One may wish to accentuate something rather special, say, a painting, and an arrangement which picks up two or three colours in a painting gives just the right kind of emphasis.

A good example of this is an arrangement I once linked up with a lithograph by Barnett Freedman. The lithograph was in his typical colouring: warm coppery red, blue-green, clear yellow and deep dark aubergine shadows, whilst the arrangement with it consisted of blue green hydrangeas, copper coloured branches and purple berberis.

The type of furniture used in the room, and finally the size of the room, its light and the remaining decorations in it (e.g. paintings, ornaments) will determine where you place your arrangement (obviously no one will put the flowers in the way of a draught and it is as well to remember that with small children about, flowers are safer out of reach). The next consideration must be the choice of container which may be determined by the choice of flowers; or the container, if it is perfect for its position, can determine the choice of flowers. Having said this, I think that plain vases are a safe selection and most generally used, although some of the earlier porcelain bowls and vases, such as Rockingham or Chelsea, produce delightful results. The period of the container is important where a room is completely furnished either in contemporary taste or in that of any one particular period.

The selection and arrangement of the flowers is, naturally, very much a matter of personal taste. In most creative work a great deal of care and thought are needed to produce the best effects, and this applies equally to flower arrangements.

The essentials having been studied it is then important for the results to be as natural as possible. Over formality and affectation immediately reduce flower arrangement from a natural art to a clever but artificial medium of expression. The real test of a good flower arrangement is whether you can live with it and grow to like it more and more every day. Like a good painting or a piece of poetry, new facets ought to reveal themselves all the time. This form of unity can only be termed 'harmony.'

Once this is achieved, flower decoration will really have fulfilled its purpose and come into its own. It might then be described as taking its place as an art in the same way that Japanese flower arranging is an art.

Right, To fulfil its function a flower or foliage arrangement must link up with furnishing schemes,
without being too obtrusive. This applies to colour,
texture and position in the room. A plain background
is suitable to show up the outline of foliage and branches,
but the heavier leaves of camellia
are solid enough to stand out against the curtain
and provide the link with the furnishings.

Overleaf, Azaleas and rhododendrons are amongst the most valuable of flowering shrubs for house decoration. They come in a large variety of colours and,
if cut when still in bud will last well.
Two or three sprays of rhododendron leaves are arranged here with some azaleas and their foliage.
Such a group will drink a good quantity of water
therefore it is essential to arrange them in a large container.

Foliage arrangements

The appreciation of foliage seems to depend very much on two things, first the value of green as a colour (the consideration of the various tones and shades which are possible within this colour), and secondly on the importance of design.

In the past the Western demand for colour has often been interpreted by something vivid and bright and even garish. We have chosen bright flowers for our gardens-beds—Siberian wall-flowers, lobelia, slipper flowers *(Calceolaria)* and marigolds, and arranged our flowers to give a massed and colourful effect. The design of the garden generally or the line of the flower arrangement have often come as an afterthought.

The Victorians dallied with the idea of using green, but only as something subsidiary to an arrangement. 'Green is essential in all bouquets',

writes a gardening editor of the period. 'Feathery and plumy green adds grace to all arrangements of flowers, and variegated foliage is exceedingly pretty for bordering baskets and flat dishes'. This attitude suggests some, though rather limited, appreciation of leaves and ferns for use with flowers, but does not give any hint that they might aspire to being the main decorative feature.

In complete contrast are books on Japanese flower-work, where much space is devoted to illustrations of camellia leaves, bamboo canes, and branches of maple, cedar, pine, and willow. As Josiah Conder says in his *The Theory of Japanese Flower Arrangement:* 'The foliage of flowers and evergreens and other trees is much used in *floral* composition, the arrangement often being without a single blossom'. Mary Averill goes still further

Left, Evergreen foliage often provides a suitable background
for a few brightly coloured flowers.
In this case the dark skimmia leaves
show up the clear colours of the carnations.

Short sprays of berberis with their oval shaped leaves
are arranged, towards the centre of a pedestal cake stand,
with longer, curving branches of rosemary.
The rosemary is beautiful on both sides,
either showing its deep blue-green colouring or
silver grey on the reverse side of the leaves.

in her book *Japanese Flower Arrangement* and says: 'Branches are much used . . . . they consider them as flowers and use them for their most important arrangements'.

Writing at the turn of the century, William Robinson remarks on lessons already learnt from the Japanese in appreciation of form and line 'in a single twig or branch, with its natural habit shown, apart from any beauty and form or colour of its flowers'. This coincides with the ideas of Gertrude Jekyll at the time, but then they were both pioneers in simplicity and the appreciation of the truth of natural things–ahead of their own time and, it seems, in many ways of ours too. The final word must rest with Jason Hill, who, in *The Contemplative Gardener* says '. . . . . . there is a great deal of beauty . . . . if only we do not insist upon flowers and if we are willing to regard green and brown as colours'.

The possibilities of using foliage in this country are only now being discovered, and exploring them extends the field of floral decoration.

The two most important factors in the use of foliage are the development of line arrangements, and the contrasts possible between the different shapes, textures and colours of leaves. In the latter case it is as though one type of leaf takes the place of the flower in the group, and the other acts as a background or as a setting for it by virtue of its distinctive shape or colour. The development of line in connection with branches is obvious, and striking silhouette effects can be obtained.

Many branches are, in themselves, dramatic and graceful in shape and line. If they are arranged as far as possible in their natural position (the way in which they were growing) they will be shown off to their best advantage. It is usually quite unnecessary to bend or twist them or to try to improve in any way on their normal growth. There are two exceptions where one may be forgiven for using the leaves back to front. The beautiful tan coloured backs of magnolia leaves look very effective if arranged against their own dark green fronts, and the soft silver grey of rosemary branches

can only be seen effectively when used the wrong way round.

It is most important that leaves should have a clean, shining appearance, and this is possible even if they are cut from a town garden, as they can actually be washed. They should also be in very good condition, not having been eaten or broken in any way, as they depend so much on their shape for effect. All woody stems should be crushed or split up well to allow for a greater intake of water.

On branches where there are many leaves, it is sometimes advisable to remove a few of them, as this may give the branch itself a longer life; but it has to be done judiciously as the whole shape can very quickly be spoilt. The weight of heavy branches often makes them difficult to secure, and it is important to be quite sure that they are firm and immobile and in position before anything else is added to the arrangement.

The actual container used is a matter for personal selection, but tall, thin, branches show off well in a narrow necked vase or jug and are much easier to arrange in something which has height. It is imperative to remember that most foliage likes a large amount of water to drink, and if the container is kept filled to the brim, time and patience will be well repaid. Some ideas for foliage arrangements include: Branches of silver grey sea buckthorn with two or three giant horseradish leaves, arranged in a baking tin.
Branches of cotoneaster forming a pattern as if they were growing, with the flat, shiny leaves of laurel, in a cooking dish.
Branches of Chilean gum box *(Escallonia)* spreading sideways in feathery sweeps, with bold stems of large leafed ivy interlaced through the centre and coming down to the front of the bowl.
The leaves of the globe artichoke, (with enough size and shape to lend distinction to any group) a sprig of ling heather, branches of St. John's Wort, and a cluster of acorns.
Broom arranged with leaves of summer jasmine.
Pine used alone in a line arrangement.
Globe artichoke leaves, golden privet, variegated periwinkle, and one pale sprig of a climbing rose foliage to make a green and yellow colour scheme.
A collection of autumn foliage, including almost everything that is available at this time of the year.

It is difficult to know where to begin to enumerate the different leaves and branches particularly suitable for decoration. Perhaps it would be as well to go through the seasons of the year.

In winter there are long sprays of periwinkle—dark and shiny or variegated—branches of holm oak, sweet bay, Portugal laurel, camellia, grevillea, variegated holly, eucalyptus, deep red branches of dogwood, holly, ivy, clusters of 'pale green, fairy mistletoe', and bergenia.

In the spring all the fruit tree branches are coming into bud and a particularly beautiful one, if it can be spared, is a branch of quince. There are wild arum leaves, berberis in fresh green shoots, flowering currant, budding viburnum, pussy willow and catkins, alder catkins, larch, silver shoots of whitebeam, Corsican hellebore and the dark fan like clusters of *Pieris japonica* foliage. A branch of budding chestnut is, of course, one of the most dramatic additions to an arrangement that it is possible to find. Purple sprouting broccoli and the rather knobbly, brown branches of sea buck-

119

Bottom, One of the most beautifully marked of all leaves are those of the cyclamen. Here, a few are arranged towards the centre of a small bunch of heather. This photograph shows a different shape and style of arrangement from the colour group of violets and mimosa, using a French bread holder.

Contrast of colour and shape of leaves is shown here by the long curving branches of grey-green eucalyptus with, towards the centre of the arrangement a cluster of *Euonymus fortunei.* A long lasting group such as this needs a good supply of water which is provided by the Swedish jug.

thorn before it comes into leaf make an exciting contrast.

Summer time is overflowing with suggestions, and one can only mention a few possibilities. Lamb's ear *(Stachys lanata)*, garden ragwort, giant cow-parsnip, globe artichoke, *Hostas,* privet, fennel, hart's-tongue fern, vine, everlasting pea, summer jasmine, lungwort, horseradish and iris; these all come to mind amongst many others. (This list is given, of course, only with reference to the foliage and not to the flowers.)

In the autumn there is a surprising selection Forsythia and azalea both achieve very beautiful autumn colourings. The foliage of beech is well known and there are also scarlet oaks, varied bergenia, clematis, fig, *Garrya elliptica* with its grey green catkins, polypody fern, broom and golden privet, tradescantia, magnolia and ivy, rosemary and deep-toned berberis. Having listed various leaves in their seasons, I suggest taking one from each, (e.g. winter – holly,) in some detail.
EUCALYPTUS: one of the most attractive, long

In this group a clump of purple broccoli with its soft pink mauve young leaves and the blue-green of its larger leaves edged with a deep purple frill, form the centre of this arrangement.
They contrast in shape, texture and colouring with the oval, pointed eucalyptus leaves.

Bottom, Any thin branches of evergreen such as certain berberis, escallonia, winter jasmine, or evergreen ceanothus contrast with the flat wide shaped ivy leaves. This is a group which must stand against a plain background.

lasting and unusual of foliage plants or trees to grow for arrangement. Coming as it does from Australia, it has settled down in certain parts of England as though it really belonged here. It must be admitted that it may also be capricious, and that even, having once got it going it may die back again. If one has had a young tree for two or three years and it seems to be going well ahead and then to die back do not despair. It is possible that before long young shoots may appear round the base of the stem, just above the soil level. If this happens, cut out the dead wood above, keep the young leaves supplied with water, as their roots may be short, and wait patiently. In time, the eucalyptus may get going happily again, providing a useful supply of its blue-green-grey leaves for indoor decoration throughout the year. It is surprising, in some ways, that there are extensive plantations of the eucalyptus in parts of Scotland, but these are, of course, in Western Scotland. However, I have known it to thrive in exposed parts of the east of England with little or no protection. *WILD ARUM LEAVES:* the plant of the wild arum as a whole is not an attractive one. The flower is greedy and sucks in insects and the bright orange-red berries, coming later in the summer, have rather a sinister quality about them. But the leaves are fresh and green, charming in shape, coming early in the spring when there are few others out. (They are like miniatures of the large arum leaf, but are still bigger than most leaves of wild flowers.) They may be found in hedgerows or ditches, some of them growing in small clusters with each leaf about three to four inches from tip to base, while others belonging to much larger plants have individual leaves which may be from eight to ten inches in size. The value of these leaves, in early spring, cannot be over estimated. They are such a fresh green and last so well and are so attractive with many different types of flowers, e.g. anemones, scillas, grape hyacinths, wallflowers, certain daffodils and narcissi, and are especially useful with the pink and blue flowers of 'soldiers and sailors' or lungwort, which appear before their own leaves are fully developed. *PRIVET:* this is a shrub which I have often championed. It is despised as being 'ordinary' and only useful for hedging, where it is kept tightly trimmed

Top, In foliage arrangements the interest depends on different shades of green and different shapes of leaf. The photograph shows the narrow serrated foliage of hellebores which contrasts with the round bergenia leaves; the tall thin ladder fern shows up the lightness in colour and shape of the mimosa foliage.

Right, Lenten hellebore foliage is available throughout the year. It is distinctive in shape and colouring whether cut when a clear dark green or when it has turned to a dark olive and wine colour.

with no opportunity for developing its long, decorative branches and its panicles of creamy-white flowers. However, for flower arrangement it must be grown freely and allowed to achieve its natural height and its natural shrubbiness. It flowers usually in mid-summer, at a time when there are not always many long-stemmed plants for cutting. I have personally found it invaluable. This is not its only attraction: its leaves are a good shape, (a point which is often overlooked), not unlike those of the myrtle, its berries are first green and later a deep purple-black, both these colours are useful for foliage arrangements. (When they are green they combine well with the blue-grey of poppy leaves, certain hellebore foliage, variegated hosta and garden ragwort, showing the darker side of its leaf.) When the berries are black, they come at about the same time as honesty seedpods are turning to silver, and they look most dramatic arranged together.

Variegated privet (although not an ever-green) does keep some of its leaves throughout the winter. *FORSYTHIA:* this is best known for its wonderful splash of golden yellow in the spring, but the foliage can be of great value and have a charm of colouring which is almost unexpected,

in the autumn. It usually has, in its growth, some lovely curving branches, and it is the leaves on these which may turn anything from a pale, rather faded yellow, to a deep wine. Sometimes the leaf is variegated in effect, having both colours at one time. For arrangements of any size, these curving branches with exotic autumn tones and shades, are a gift. (They will last quite well, but, of course, should be cut before they are beginning to drop, like any other autumn foliage.)

There must be many more, and as I write I think all the time of yet another addition; but quite half the delight and enjoyment is to discover interesting and exciting shapes and colours of leaves for oneself, and so I will be content with an incomplete list.

'In the night of the chestnut, by the chestnut candles
Burning, red and white, upon the lowest boughs;
We will lie and listen for a god to come.
What is that glitter from the ilex-trees,
For the leaves flash like armour in a torch-lit night:
What is this sweetness from the myrtle-wood?'

From *Canons of Giant Art* by Sacheverell Sitwell.

Gardening for flower arrangement

Ideas carried out in the garden, either in the contrast or combination of colours in a border or in the way in which they grow together can often give ideas for using these same colours or plants when they are cut for indoor decoration.

This seems to me to be another excellent reason for visiting gardens that are open to the public, either through the National Trust or for various charities. So often when wandering round such gardens one comes across a bit of planting which arrests the attention.

Perhaps it is a certain clematis climbing into a rose; a sowing of mignonette beside a clump of lamb's ears *(Stachys lanata)*, white bluebells coming up against forget-me-nots; a good, red polyantha rose against a deep blue delphinium, love-

in-a-mist growing close to a cherry-red Sweet William; tall spires of wine-red bergamot in a mist of *Alchemilla mollis*; *Euphorbia epithymoides* growing near to grape hyacinths.

Then there is the fascination of contrasting shapes in foliage and interest of a tall, spiky iris or gladiolus leaf against rounded bergenia, oval hosta or pointed false fig *(Fatsia japonica)* leaves.

I myself have found certain ideas emerging from gardens of this kind which provided the basis for many other flower arrangements–not just the one which comes to mind immediately. I saw for instance, in at least two or three gardens a white flower planted close to dark, evergreen leaves. In another garden there was a planting of the white form of *Cyclamen neapolitanum* under a walnut tree, this in turn was interplanted with green leaved forms of ivy which the white flowers showed up before their own leaves put in an appearance, and in yet another garden a white rose, *Rosa moschata alba* climbing over a well grown dark green holly. (The white cascade through the dark leaves could almost give an impression of a waterfall.) Then again there was the white rose, *Rosa filipes* clambering through the dark branches of a well established oak, and flaunting long white streamers through the thick foliage of the tree.

All these varied plantings in different gardens lead to the same idea, that of using white with dark green. For flower arrangement this may be interpreted in many ways–snowdrops with ivy leaves, *candidum* lilies with camellia foliage, Iceberg roses with the shining green oval leaves of laurel, white delphiniums with branches of the evergreen Californian lilac *(Ceanothus)*.

A different idea for using white comes from the grey and white gardens to be seen at Nymans, Sussex, and at Sissinghurst Castle in Kent, England. Here, white is used with grey or silver-grey foliage and this in turn opens up vistas of possibilities, such as white pinks with *Helichrysum splendidum* or white border carnations with garden ragwort *(Senecio laxifolius)* or the pure white roses of Virgo or Iceberg with sprays of *Senecio cineraria*.

Then we come to ideas for using different shades of one colour, sometimes in one flower, as in the planting of gentians.

In one garden there are various clumps of gentians and among the *Gentiana sino-ornata* and *G. acaulis* there is also planted a light Cambridge blue strain which is called Drake's strain. This is followed by the usage of one colour to highlight

Left, There are some flowers which seem simple enough to have in the garden, but are invaluable for cutting for the house—one of these is the marguerite, which flowers, on and off, throughout the summer. With its clear white petals and golden centres, it is excellent to use alone or as a foil to brighter colours. It is long lasting, valuable for wedding arrangements and shows up well when arranged against its own dark foliage.

another as in the case of blue with yellow. The pale yellow of *Thalictrum glaucum* with certain shades of blue delphiniums is a colour scheme that is worth remembering.

Such schemes can also be used in a garden if vivid colours are wanted, but perhaps would be more suitable for a flower arrangement (which can, after all, be changed often.) In some gardens, where the softer tones of harmonising colours are preferred, vivid contrasts of planting must be omitted.

One of the most usual arrangements of garden flowers might well be described as the 'mixed

Above, The colour and variety of material which can be grown in a small space can be surprising. These few roses, catmint, London pride and everlasting sweet pea came from a London garden made out of an area previously paved with concrete.

Bottom, This small group of garden flowers and grasses includes the sweet rocket, which comes in soft lilac shades or in white. There are tree peony flowers and leaves, sprays of single mock orange, two or three columbines and elder flowers, both in bud and fully out. The two large lungwort leaves, flecked with grey, have a velvety texture.

Left, Here is a collection of flowers and shrubs, which with the possible exception of the scarlet nerines, towards the centre of the group, are invaluable for flower arrangement and easy to grow in the garden. Tall branches of broom and peony leaves, sprays of rosemary, fuchsia and berberis are arranged with roses, garden privet and chrysanthemums. A little wild clematis is included in the arrangement as it is so decorative.

Right, Foliage plants and wild flowers make a contribution with garden flowers and it is often helpful to have some of both planted for cutting. In this arrangement the grey of the lamb's ears and the cream bordered hosta leaves together with hedge parsley and meadow sweet help to emphasise a green, white and yellow colour scheme built up round yellow roses and sprays of mock orange.

bunch'. There is a great deal of charm about a mixed garden bunch, arranged as naturally as possible. I have often heard it said at flower group meetings and discussions that what really gives the greatest pleasure is a bunch of flowers from the garden arranged as if they were picked in a basket. This does not necessarily mean that it must be a large arrangement, using a great quantity of flowers –far from it. But it does mean that the foliage of the garden is brought into the house and in this way a mixed bunch helps to forge a link between gardening and flower arrangement. It is, after all, almost impossible to cut for the house what is in season without getting to know about such things as habitat, flowering time, lasting qualities, and structure of the plant as a whole. All this is of the greatest value when arranging flowers, because respect for the material becomes more important than a dramatic effect.

This brings us automatically to the question of foliage, and here are one or two selections of leaves for foliage arrangements which it is possible to produce from a garden of no great size and of reasonably small upkeep.

First of all there are rosemary and berberis. These two are valuable and, I should say, essential in any garden. The same could be said of periwinkle, both plain and variegated. For lightness, I choose the ever useful lavender cotton *(Santolina)*. Then there are two kinds of hellebore which give excellent contrast of shape whilst the hosta leaves provide a good broad outline at the base of any one arrangement.

An alternative in the way of something solid would be bergenia, the good old-fashioned plant often used in Victorian gardens as a border or edging, and effective when grown in clumps in front of shrubs.

Next come three plants which are rather more special either because as shrubs they are half-hardy or because they are more expensive to buy. These are skimmia, *Eucalyptus gunnii* and the elegant clearly shaped leaves of *Pieris forrestii*. The last two are not found growing frequently or very generally in England but once established they will amply reward the trouble or expense spent on them.

Eucalyptus will grow in a fairly exposed garden and is a treasure for flower arrangement. The *skimmia* provides bright scarlet berries in quantity, which makes it particularly useful at Christmas time. It once was necessary to have two shrubs, male and female, but now there is a new form, *Skimmia foremanii*, which provides both.

The *Pieris forrestii* is a most exciting addition to a garden, producing bright red, new leaves which are both decorative and unusual. These have all the qualities of a poinsettia flower, pointed and fiery red. The flowers themselves are creamy white and hang in clusters, appearing in the spring. This shrub may seem almost too exotic to try in the uncertain climate of England but as long as it is protected from frost in the winter and spring by a packing of straw or bracken, and given lime free soil, it will flourish as well and as heartily as some of the better known hardy shrubs.

Naturally each garden will produce different material, but the fundamentals of an arrangement should be the same: a varied selection of colour, shade and especially of shape. In this way one will have an interesting and economical decoration at any time of the year. During the winter evenings ideas for the introduction of different material, either in the garden or the arrangements, are provided by the countless tempting catalogues prepared for our enjoyment.

Geraniums

Geraniums and pelargoniums – it is a botanist's work to decide which name to apply under what circumstances. For the purpose of arrangement I think it is best to use the one term of geranium. The flowers are charming, invaluable for decoration and come in a great variety of colours – white, palest pink, salmon-pink, rose-pink, scarlet, deep red, carmine, cerise, pale mauve, crimson, etc., and the foliage is a most attractive shape and comes in many colourings from the plain green leaf to the more marked zonal plants, with circles of white, yellow or bronze, according to the type.

Just as there are experts on lilies, roses, hydrangeas and rhododendrons, so there are experts on geraniums. Books are written about them and whole nurseries, as with clematis, are given up entirely to growing them. It would be impertinent to discuss geraniums in too much detail without this expert knowledge but anyone seriously interested in propagating them should get in touch with a nursery garden or go to a good library or bookshop and ask for books on this subject. (There is, for enthusiasts, a geranium society.)

Let us take the colours of the geranium flowers first, and see how they may be utilised in an arrangement. It has always seemed to me that the value of white geraniums has been under-rated. For an all white group, perhaps a table decoration, there can be few more suitable flowers to arrange, in a white container with two or three buds of Iceberg or Virgo roses and short sprays of tradescantia. White geraniums usually have plain green leaves, but if one has a zonal plant with the white edged green foliage, these leaves look most attractive with the white flowers.

There is perhaps not enough contrast in shape or colour for white geraniums to be used with white carnations as a wedding table decoration, but white garden pinks would make a contrast, I think, if kept on longish stems with the geranium flowers cut quite short.

If the flowers are taken off as they begin to fall it will be found that the surrounding buds open out and the arrangement will have a long life. I have known a similar group of white geraniums and coloured geranium leaves to last for nearly a fortnight, with only this small amount of tidying being necessary.

The ivy leaf geranium which has the soft rosy-lilac coloured flowers is of great value, either arranged alone or with other pinks and purples, or as a contrast to creamy-white. The leaves often come on quite long stems or else in charming small clusters close to the flowers, and if the whole stem can be spared this may almost make a decoration in itself, suitable for a plate or dish on a dining table in much the same way as a spray of clematis. The ivy shaped leaves, valuable in their own right with the rather light green of their usual colouring, combine well with yellow or orange roses such as the sweet scented bouffant Gloire de Dijon or Emily Gray. They are also useful as a contrast with darker foliage like a spray of camellia or the neat pointed leaves of myrtle.

Flowers of the ivy leaf geranium are fun to use with clashing reds and pinks, and a collection of these cut from different geraniums can be most exciting and colourful. The green of a Wedgwood plate is a good background colour for such a group, and although it may be an unorthodox colour scheme, it can also be exhilarating when used occasionally.

During the winter one cannot say too much in praise of the usefulness of a pot or two of geraniums. They should, I suppose, be cast away into a dry attic or garden shed once the cuttings have been taken. But I always keep two or three, especially those with marked or variegated foliage, in a small jardinière which I try to have indoors throughout these months. Sometimes there are one or two flowers (I know of plants which flourish in bright and gay colourings in the sunny cottage window of a certain village street) and these can make a completely satisfying group arranged with differently marked leaves with the addition of perhaps a spray of scented geranium foliage.

The serrated leaves of this scented geranium plant often come on longish stems, like the ivy leaf geranium, which is especially useful when a little extra height or width is needed for a table arrangement. These leaves are charming in themselves and seem to flourish when kept in the house, providing a constant supply of useful material at a time when they are most needed.

A group of geraniums can look attractive, as I have mentioned, on a flat Wedgwood plate, and they will also gain added importance from being arranged in a shallow dish with a low pedestal. This shape gives an opportunity for more spreading branches and if the plants are doing well a larger spray might be spared with the added attraction of clusters of new unfolded leaves. But for white geraniums a white container is, I think, especially suited.

129

Contrasts in colour can be obtained by using a red geranium, i.e. Pillar-box, with certain purple blue anemones, or with one spike of yellow gladiolus where each floret is cut off the stem and arranged low down on a flat dish. The bright red is also, of course, valuable for Christmas decorations. A toning colour effect may be obtained by using the true purple of anemones, especially one or two of the clear, lighter shades, with the rose-lilac flowers of the ivy leaf geranium.

Geraniums seem to prefer being rather more dry than damp, but contrary to some ideas, they do repay extra care and treatment. It is a mistake to keep them in large pots – they seem to prefer for their roots the cosiness of a small one. Geraniums, unlike so many indoor plants, do not like to have their feet standing in a damp saucer or on wet shingle. On the other hand, their soil must not be allowed to get dry and hard. Whether the idea of watering them with cold tea is an old wives' tale I could not say, but personally I have often done so and it seems to suit them.

Perhaps geraniums can be described as an 'architectural' plant almost as much as other more obvious ones, such as acanthus or globe artichoke, both of which are well-known for the structure and

shape of their flowers and leaves. (The acanthus leaf, especially, is one which has often featured in wood carvings, sculpture, etc.) But the sturdiness of the geranium stem, the arrangement and shape of its leaves and the general 'bunchiness' of many of the flowers all contribute to a certain type of group when the flowers and leaves are arranged together and not with other flowers or foliage.

This is something important to remember as it means that a definite outline is almost sure to emerge when using geraniums which may be quite unobtainable in any other material. It is so often the colour of the flowers which first catches the attention when, in fact, the whole structure of the plant may be its most important contribution to an arrangement.

Eucalyptus leaves look as though they come from a hot house or are half hardy.
In fact they can be grown out of doors in fairly exposed positions.
They are valuable for flower arrangement on account of their colour, shape and long lasting qualities. If treated in the autumn, they will turn a deep wine colour.

Green arrangements

The helleboro family provides plenty of interesting
evergreen foliage — It is reliable for cutting
and elegant in shape and colouring.
These few stems with a cluster of pale green flowers
stand on a pin holder in a dish of water (concealed by stones
and branches) on a grey and white contemporary dish.

In this green-arrangement the two spear-like
phormium leaves come in green bordered with cream,
the poppy heads are a blue-green and the leek heads
a pale leaf green and white. The soft grey-green carnation
foliage links these various shades of green together.

The idea of using green by itself for an arrangement is almost contemporary. Perhaps it is
only recently that people are beginning to see its
possibilities (leaves can range from pale lime green
and a soft grey-green to the darkest blue-black
green of the camellia or holly leaf).

One of the most important factors in the use
of green materials is the contrast possible between
the different shapes, textures, and colour of the
leaves.

The rounded shape and soft colouring of angelica
contrasts well with the curves and variegated
colouring of *Hosta undulata* and *H. variegata* and
the thin, dark foliage of *Helleborus foetidus*. An
arrangement using this kind of material not only

has the advantage of looking cool during hot
weather, but will also last for two or three weeks,
as long as it is kept well supplied with water.

Angelica is a most obliging plant to grow in the
garden as it flourishes almost anywhere, but grows
especially well in part shade and in rather moist
conditions. If it has the benefit of a stream or
pond close at hand, it will show its appreciation
and grow to great size. The kind usually cultivated is *A. archangelica* (its medicinal virtues are
said to have been revealed by an angel during a
time of plague).

All types of hostas, or plantain lilies, are useful
for green arrangements, lasting well and providing different kinds and colours of leaves which

133

dark silver-grey-green leaves of *Convolvulus cneorum* look charming with carnation foliage.

Camellia leaves, sprays of the new light green foliage contrast beautifully with lavender and *Cineraria maritima.*

False fig (Fatsia japonica) the new light green foliage contrasts well with the rock sedum and the blue grey of eucalyptus.

Golden *privet* and *holly.*

Variegated periwinkle with dark green camellia foliage.

Hart's-tongue fern along with small leaved ivy.

Garden ragwort, Senecio laxifolius, lungwort and tufts of fennel with dark tree peony leaves.

Another useful ingredient in green arrangements are materials not connected with foliage. These include some flowers either when they are fully out or before they are completely open and some seedheads before they turn brown (in the interim stage between drying as a flower and becoming a seedhead). At first sight there may not seem to be many of these, but it is interesting to realise that, in fact, a good many exist which are not only unusual but come in a great variety of greens. Here are some of them:

Poppy heads – when the flowers have fallen and before the seedheads turn to grey-blue or coffee colour.

Guelder rose flowers – before they are fully out.

Honesty seedheads – after the flowers have died and before the seed capsules have begun to turn to their later brown or buff colourings which eventually become silver.

Love-in-a-mist seedheads – after the flowers have died before they turn to their eventual dried colourings of buff or brown. Some of these are especially attractive.

Angelica–grows wild in damp ditches and is an attractive addition to the herb garden.

Astrantia–a green and white flower of great charm lasting from early May until August.

Mignonette–a sweetly scented flower of coppery brown with green.

Bells of Ireland–before these are dried they are a bright, fresh green.

Fennel–if cut before the flowers are fully out they

vary in size and sometimes in shape. (Some are much broader than others and can be ribbed, plain or variegated.) Hostas, on the whole, prefer semi shade in the garden, although *H. crispula* and *H. lancifolia* both grow well in rather dry, sunny positions. Unhappily the young shoots, coming up in April, seem to be particularly attractive to slugs and snails.

Hellebores also produce a variety of flowers and foliage, and the large dramatic leaves of the Lenten hellebores are especially useful for arrangement. They are available throughout the year and incredibly valuable when there is only a small supply of material for cutting. I have been more than grateful to cut their shining dark green leaves after a heavy fall of snow when they seemed to acquire an extra lustre. They like a fairly heavy soil, usually in a rather shady position although I have known *Helleborus foetidus* to flourish in full sun in a garden with a slightly acid, clay soil.

Contrasts in tones of green and shapes of foliage come in the following suggestions:

Rue with blue-green foliage, fits into many flower groups providing fullness if it is needed, contrasts well with bergenia.

Rosemary gives a lightness to solid material, especially gladioli, wild arum leaves or roses. The

give an impression of a soft green.

Bluebell – spikes of seedheads immediately after the flowers have died.

Ivy berries (as soon as the flowers have fallen) before they blacken.

Privet berries (as soon as the flowers have fallen) before they blacken.

Dock – when the seedheads have just formed before they turn to a deep copper or chocolate.

Teasels – when they first come into flower (with small rings of purple) and before they begin to turn brown.

Hop flowers fresh and also dried later.

Helleborus corsicus – pale green flowers.

Garrya elliptica – grey green catkins.

Leek (Allium) – green and white flower heads fresh, will dry later.

Spurge (Euphorbia species) – green flowers, some with touches of brown or burnt orange and yellow. These include *E. wulfenii* and *E. epithymoides*.

A note about the Euphorbia family as a whole might be helpful here. There are many members, but the three mentioned here are outstanding for green arrangements. *E. wulfenii* is large in comparison to the others, growing to a height of four to five feet. It keeps its foliage throughout the year and is useful at all three stages when the flower is first coming into bud, while it is fully out, and after it is over. *E. griffithii* has vivid bright orange and red bracts, but is immensely useful when these are not quite so bright. *E. epithymoides* gives an overall impression of green and yellow when it is in flower, but more green than yellow I should say.

Grey
and
silver
foliaged
plants

Top. Two favourites amongst grey foliaged plants
are lavender and rosemary which are available
throughout the year. In this arrangement lavender flowers
are combined with sprays of rosemary
and hydrangeas in colourings of wine and green.

Top left, Silver-grey foliage is often decorative
for arrangement without any other material.
Here the silver and feathery Centaurea falls like a fountain
from a Victorian vase. The delicate design of the leaf
needs a plain background and should be used sparingly,
otherwise it becomes too fussy.

Left, Two of the best known silver-grey foliage plants
come from the senecio family. The large lace-like leaves
of the *Senecio cineraria,* which gives the outline
to this group, are particularly decorative
and a few are usually enough for a small arrangement.
Towards the centre with the lilies-of-the-valley
are a few short stemmed sprays of *Senecio laxifolius,*
also known as garden ragwort.

It would be difficult to over estimate the value of
these plants for indoor decoration, either used on
their own, or in contrast to other foliage or with
flowers. The main assets are: their beauty, unusual shape, colour, their long lasting qualities—
most of them will last literally for two to three
weeks without any trouble or coaxing—and their
availability throughout most months of the year,

and often at a time when deciduous shrubs and
plants are losing their leaves and it is important
to have something else to take their place.

Two or three essential factors in growing grey
foliaged plants which one should perhaps mention
before concentrating on the different varieties
suitable for use in flower arrangement are, firstly
that under no circumstances, and at no time of the
year, will they tolerate their roots being waterlogged. Secondly, they dislike extremely bitter
winds or draught. It is interesting in this context,
I think, to notice the original homes of some of
the most attractive of these white leaved plants.
For example, many of them come from the Mediterranean—*Artemesia splendens,* known as the wire
netting artemesia on account of its deeply cut
leaves, is to be found growing at the foot of cliffs
at heights varying up to 5,000 ft. high in Persia
and the Caucasus, whilst others come from North
America. Many helichrysums grow indigenously
in South Africa and Australia, and some of the
best of the senecios in New Zealand.

Most of the situations where they are to be
found growing naturally are dry, sunny and well
drained. Sharp sand and good root drainage,
sometimes with richer soil and compost to a depth
of nine to ten inches (as in the case of *Convolvulus cneorum* this seems to be essential; *Senecio
leucostachys* is one of those which does not require
compost—it thrives and keeps its colour better on
a starvation diet).

Many of the grey foliaged plants have yellow
flowers, and if these are cut off when still in bud
most of them will grow into sturdier plants. An
exception is the white flowered pearly everlasting
(*Anaphalis*) which has charming, small daisy like
flowers which dry on the plant and make valuable
contributions for dried arrangements.

In spite of suggesting that the yellow flowers
should usually be cut off I would like to put in
a special plea for one or two which are particularly
attractive. For instance, the clear yellow of garden ragwort (*Senecio laxifolius*) is such a good
colour, especially when used in contrast with deep
blue delphiniums or to lighten the rather harsh
orange of marigolds, that I always leave a few
sprays to come out. I also like to see the tight
white buds with other white flowers, especially
campanulas. The soft indefinite yellow of the
curry plant (*Helichrysum angustifolium*) before
it is fully out also makes a useful contribution to
certain colour schemes.

One of the dangers of using grey foliaged plants
is to use too much material at one time. It is so
easy to overcrowd an arrangement and to end up
with a bunchy effect, resulting in a loss of shape
and outline. Given breathing space and used
sparingly very beautiful effects can be obtained.

Mulleins might also be included in the grey

Garden ragwort foliage, with its white backed leaves contrasting with the olive-grey surface, is invaluable for flower arrangements and available for cutting most of the year. The pink gerberas in the photograph pick up some of the different shades in the begonia leaves.

foliaged section, although they are so different in size, habit, and shape of leaf, from any of the plants already mentioned. The smaller leaves sometimes resemble those of foxgloves in their definite shape and soft colouring, and can provide a useful contrast to the lacy effect of the grey foliaged plants.

Now let us mention some specific plants that are suitable and reliable for use in flower arrangement.

Perhaps the best known are the cotton (sea) lavenders, or santolinas, which make sturdy groups in the border, provide abundant material on quite a small bush, and are among the hardiest of all grey foliage plants. From an arrangement point of view (perhaps a word of warning might be forgiven) the formation of the leaves and small interlaced stems may easily give the bushy appearance I mentioned earlier if the longer, thinner stems are not cut. In all other respects this is an excellent plant, literally lasting for weeks and eventually drying off.

A variation of garden ragwort, *Senecio cineraria* (*Cineraria maritima*) is a popular dramatically decorative bedding plant used where spectacular effects are required. With its silver-white foliage

cut and patterned like old lace, a little goes a long way. It is generally considered to be half hardy, but given good drainage and a sunny, sheltered position and protection from frost it will usually come through the winter. (Bracken is most satisfactory for this purpose.) One of the best of the *Senecio cinerarias*, White Diamond has especially opulent foliage.

Senecio laxifolius (or *greyii*) is familiar to many people as garden ragwort. This is a valuable plant indeed, and if suitably trimmed will grow into a well shaped sturdy bush. The foliage on one side is a beautiful dark grey and on the reverse almost a chalk-white. Stems and buds are also white, and the latter, growing in decorative clusters, are especially attractive in an arrangement.

As already mentioned they will eventually break out into clear yellow daisy-flowers. Garden ragwort can grow into a sizeable shrub and keeps its foliage throughout the year.

Immortelle is another dramatic grey and chalk-white plant, but with quite a different growth and habit to the other two. Its branches are spiky in character and the small leaves grow in tufts rather than in any definite order. However,

The large serrated silver grey leaves of *Senecio cineraria* are arranged with spiky silver-grey *Helichrysum splendidum* sprays. There are two or three branches of *Senecio laxifolius*, which, with the other foliage emphasise the gentians in the arrangement.

it does have yellow flowers (rather small) which should be cut off in bud if a sturdy bushy plant is required.

Lamb's ears *(Stachys lanata)* is so widely grown that it seems hardly necessary to include it in this list, but I wonder whether its uses as a dried flower are equally well known. If cut at the appropriate moment, on a fine day when it has been well baked in hot sunshine, and hung in bunches in a warm, sunny position, *Stachys lanata* will provide an interesting addition to a group of dried flowers and a good foil for dark colours.

Lastly, there are two more plants, quite different in shape, colour and texture of leaf, different from each other and from the previously mentioned plants. These are yarrow *(Achillea)* with grey green foliage, long, narrow and serrated, and rue with clover like blue-green leaves which produce a few small yellow flowers. The rue, especially, provides a delicate and valuable accompaniment to small winter flower arrangements.

Having already said 'lastly', I still want to mention two more plants which officially do not quite come into the silver-grey category. These are lavender and rosemary, two of the best loved of all flowering shrubs for gardens or for cutting. They do have a certain claim to being grey foliaged, although they do not have any silver in their colouring.

Rosemary is known for its rather spiky habit of growth and enchanting dark green leaves lined with grey, to say nothing of its soft blue flowers in the spring. But for arrangement it is the foliage that is so important and so valuable throughout the year.

Lavender makes charming clumps in the garden, and there is little to equal the beauty of a good lavender hedge. The leaves, a soft grey-green, can be so useful for arrangement, but the flower spikes themselves are perhaps even more important. Used in bulk they can give an effective outline to a group, or can provide a contrast with more bulky material, such as hydrangea flowers, dahlias, zinnias, etc.

Finally, there is the added attraction of the subtle scent of a few spikes of lavender in a flower arrangement. These can bring their gentle perfume into a room in such a discreet fashion that it would be impossible to realise where it comes from.

139

Herbaceous plants

There are still certain gardens which are expressly designed to have a herbaceous border as their focal point, but today in England the number is decreasing. The reason for this may be that most gardens have to be run more economically and herbaceous plants do require an extra amount of care in the matter of weeding, feeding, staking and cutting back. This, however, applies only to the conventional herbaceous planting, which need no longer be carried out to the letter. It is quite possible now to include many other types of plants in a border which are not strictly herbaceous.

Let us read what Miss Jekyll had to say on this subject over sixty years ago in her books *Wood and Garden* and *Colour Schemes for the Flower Garden*: 'I have a large mixed border of hardy flowers. It is not quite so hopelessly mixed as one generally sees and the flowers are not all hardy ...' Later she mentions the difficulty, if not the impossibility of keeping 'it in beauty throughout the summer'

One notices that Miss Jekyll did not in any way restrict her planting in the 'mixed' border only to

herbaceous plants, but included a variety of shrubs and flowers such as half hardy lilies (sunk into the ground in their pots to fill up disastrous gaps which appear even in the best regulated borders), golden privet, hydrangeas and foxgloves. There is no doubt that, from the cutting point of view, it is valuable if one has a garden to put in some herbaceous plants for use during the summer months. Shrubs grown amongst herbaceous material will give it support, keep out the draughts, and keep down the weeds. In this way quite a lot of useful cutting plants can be grown together in a smallish space.

Perhaps the first herbaceous material that springs to mind for cutting is the delphinium. These are now available in magnificent colours and for state occasions there is an elegant white. Growing close to the blue delphiniums I always like to think of the yellow meadow rue *(Thalictrum)* and the pale lemon cephalaria.

There are those who regard both the meadow rue and the delphinium with suspicion from the cutting point of view. Both will drop, certainly,

after a period of time and unless they are cut while still in bud may drop the day after they have been arranged. Try cutting them before they show much colour and then have the pleasure of watching them come out in water, appreciating the fact that one does not have to clear away thousands of yellow stamens or hundreds of blue petals. For tall arrangements, when either of these colours are required – in the case of delphiniums, also white – there is little to compare with them for beauty.

Cephalarias (giant scabious) are useful for bringing the rounded shape and appearance of the scabious into a group in a soft yellow colouring.

Sage *(Salvia)* comes in many colours and types, and one of the prettiest is perhaps *Salvia turkestanica,* with pale lilac grey spires. This is magnificent for tall arrangements but it does have one drawback and that is its scent. There are people who dislike it intensely, and so, like other flowers with debatable perfumes, sage should be used in large arrangements at some distance from the public where it can give the least offence. Blanket flowers *(Gaillardias),* cone flowers *(Rudbeckias)* and the yellow daisy flower *(Anthemis tinctoria)* are all good growers, they last well for cutting, are daisy like in shape and come into the yellow flower group.

The clear yellow of the last named is especially useful for colour contrasts. It flourishes not only through the summer months but also well into the autumn.

Phlox are herbaceous plants, but apart from growing in a border they like having their roots in damp soil and so they also thrive near a stream or in partial shade where the soil does not get sun-baked. These again are sometimes regarded suspiciously on account of dropping quickly, but, again, if they are cut while still in bud and if one has the patience and time to take off any of the small flowers from the cluster when they have died, one will find that the buds come out and the general lasting qualities of the plant are lengthened. There is nothing that quite introduces the same brilliant note of cerise into a mixed group as the commonly grown bright pink phlox.

Marguerites must be included in this list of herbaceous plants. Invaluable on so many occasions and with so many different flowers, they are especially good with delphiniums and dark red polyantha roses such as Frensham or Moulin Rouge, or with the clear cerise-pink of Zéphirine Drouhin. They also look enchanting cut quite short, so that one can see well into their faces, with some good green foliage such as the Lenten rose *(Helleborus orientalis)* and bergenia, or the blue green of rue. Marguerites last almost as well as their wild sisters, the ox-eye daisies, and more than that one cannot say for them.

Lupins are one of the first herbaceous plants to come out. They can add useful notes of colour to a mixed arrangement if cut when still in bud, but they do sometimes tend to curve their stems into quite opposite directions which may be confusing or attractive as one's taste goes. Finally they drop perhaps more quickly than almost any other flower.

Cornflowers are reliable, come in a good colour, and may be grown with short or long stems, according to one's requirements. Mignonette, one of the most delectable of all the flowers, lasts well, and goes on growing and developing after it is put into water, giving off its sweet perfume as a gift to the room in which it finds itself.

Top, This arrangement of herbaceous plants
is from an early September border,
where many summer flowers are still available.
The group includes copper coloured prunus,
sprays of *Achillea* The Pearl, plume poppy, snapdragons,
dahlias, gladioli, montbretia, summer jasmine,
Achillea Moonshine and roses.
Such a quantity of flowers needs to be arranged
in a container which can hold plenty of water.

Left, This arrangement includes achillea, meadow rue,
anthemis, catmint and anchusa, all from a border
in late June. Some of the meadow rue and delphiniums
are cut quite short and arranged
towards the centre of the bowl.

Alliums are another reliable flower for cutting
and also most decorative in the border, coming
in a variety of types, colourings and sizes. Michaelmas daisies are often grown in separate beds to
have a display of mauves, pinks, and blue such as
only Michaelmas daisies can provide, but a few
in the border will make a good show if the colours
are chosen carefully. For cutting they are invaluable and provide height at a time when material
for tall arrangements would be getting difficult to
find. The white Michaelmas daisies are not only
especially charming, but also useful for harvest
festival decorations where the white flowers with
their golden centres tone in well with the other
autumn colourings of yellow, red and bronze.

It is known that there was an interest in flowers and plants as far back as 3,500 B.C., and that wreaths were made in the Sumerian kingdom, that carvings of the lotus flower have been found in Egyptian tombs dating from about 2,400 B.C. and garlands of flowers (consisting of the compositac family) in tombs at Thebes dating from about 1,500 B.C. These are the early beginnings and background of flower arrangement, but the actual development seems to hang on the fancy of a dream.

In A.D. 61 the Emperor of China, Ming-ti, because of a dream that he had one night, sent two messengers to India to collect books and bring back teachers of Buddhism. As a result, Buddhism spread from India into China, and from there to Japan by way of Korea. (Few dreams can claim such realisation.) So it was that in Japan certain Chinese Buddhist priests were responsible for the first teaching of flower arrangement.

The same Buddhist doctrine which forbad the wanton sacrifice of life is said to have suggested the prolonging of life in flowers. By cutting and bringing them into their cool temples and then putting them into containers of water, the monks preserved the life of the flowers which, otherwise, would probably have died in a day owing to the intense heat of the climate. The Buddhist priests whilst being faithful to their rules of conduct were, at the same time, laying the foundations of flower arrangement, knowingly or unknowingly.

The early style of arrangements was free and flowing, without artificial bending and twisting of branches or fixing of blossoms. As has always been the case in Japanese arrangements, foliage was given importance and 'attention was paid to the bends and curves of leaves so as to reveal their front and back surfaces in a well balanced contrast'.

But it was one of the first and most important developments of flower arrangement – flowers were deliberately being put into vases for decoration.

There was then a pause and little development occurred beyond the original ideas of nearly a thousand years before.

So we can see that the various schools of Japanese floral art did not develop rapidly. Progress did not occur until, in fact, the fifteenth century when the Tea Ceremony was inaugurated. Sir J. Condoi says: 'It was mainly with the object of contributing

History of flower arrangement

Below, At the end of the Second World War when there was a return to period furnishings, flower arrangements were often overcrowded. Everything available was put into a 'bouquet' and there was little respect for the fact that a painting or a collection of porcelain should be seen clearly, as long as an impression of opulence was obtained.

This is an illustration of the art of the late Constance Spry
whose work in flower arrangement, from the late twenties until her death
in 1960, has influenced its development in Great Britain and abroad.

to the Tea Ceremonial that the first modifications
in the flower art took place, and the chief reformers
were the CHAJIN, or Professors of Tea'. The
reign of Yoshimasa (1436-1490) was a period of
cultural awakening and as the scroll picture and the
flower arrangement were the only ornaments in
a Japanese room, there came about a renewed
interest and study of this art. Mary Averill in
her book *Japanese Flower Arrangement* says:
'Yoshimasa finally abdicated the throne in order
to devote his time to the fine arts. It was he who
said that flowers offered on all ceremonial occasions
and placed as offerings before the gods should not
be offered loosely, but should represent time and
thought. Rules then began to be formulated'.

In England the first record of flower arrangement is to be seen in the painting by Holbein (about
1530) of 'The Household of Sir Thomas More',
which contains three large vases filled with flowers.
Later, in the 1633 edition of Gerard's 'Herball'
the title page is decorated with bouquets of flowers.
Then came John Ray the pioneer of modern botany
with his 'History of Plants' in 1665. (In China
in 1688 a book was published, written by a retired

government official who had apparently taken up
gardening late in life. This included a chapter
about cutting and arranging flowers, with suggestions on how to make them last well.)

Thomas Fairchild in 1722 wrote: 'I find that
most persons whose business requires them to
be constantly in town, will have something of a
garden at any rate'. He also mentioned several
of the flowering trees and shrubs then to be found
growing in London – syringa, guelder rose, and
lilac in Soho Square; a vine bearing good grapes in
Leicester Fields; figs in Chancery Lane; lily of the
valley at the back of Guild Hall. Fairchild, as
well as writing *The City Gardener*, was a member
of The Society of Gardeners, (this was a society
which met at Newhall's Coffee House in Chelsea
every month for five or six years. Each member
brought plants of his own growing and the names
and descriptions were registered).

Later in Samuel Richardson's popular novel
Pamela published in 1740, there is a reference to
flowers in the house. 'I beseech you . . . . . . to
stick me into some posy among your finer flowers
– and if you won't put me into your bosom, let

A typical Victorian table setting as might have been described in a first edition
of 'Mrs Beeton's Cookery and Household Management' (Published 1861) illustrating the use of glass and silver epergnes
equipped with quantities of small vases so that the general effect is of a profusion of flowers.

me stand in some gay flowerpot in your chimney-corner'. In 1745 some of the first wall brackets for flowers were made, and designed often in the shape of shells or cornucopias.

Towards the beginning of the nineteenth century, flower arrangement was probably stimulated not only by the appearance of vases being specifically made to hold flowers, or by the more scientific heating and ventilation of houses, but also by the number of new flowering shrubs and plants being brought back to England by explorers. The first plant of wisteria came from China in 1818, and David Douglas, according to Alicia Amherst's *A History of Gardening in England,* sent clarkias, blanket flowers *(Gaillardia)*, godetias, beard tongues *(Penstemon)*, Californian poppies, *(Eschscholtzia)* and lupins from North America and California in the 1830's.

Edward Sayers, writing in the *American Flower Garden Companion* in 1838 says that 'it is now an almost universal practice to have cut flowers in rooms as natural ornaments', adding 'some hints relative to the management of them perhaps be of service to their fair patrons'. He suggests

methods for prolonging the lives of various flowers, mentioning points still suggested today. He describes one of these in graphic terms – trimming an inch off the stems which have become 'closed with glutinous matter that had exuded from the stem when first cut'.

From now on various magazines on both sides of the Atlantic took up this latest craze with equal energy. In America Godey's *Lady's Book* was eagerly awaited month by month for details of how to care for flowers, which ones to grow and how to make fancy embroidery as a supplementary adornment with vases of cut flowers. Cassell's *Household Guide* in this country did much the same and *Mrs. Beeton's Cookery Book* carried on the good work in the matter of table decorations suitable to her groaning dining tables. 'Take two dozen eggs' meant to cookery what six dozen carnations meant to flower decoration, and 'enough was never as good as a feast'. The Victorians wanted more and more, both in delectable dishes and in the numbers of flower vases filled to overflowing with greenery and flowers from their recently constructed greenhouses.

It is worthwhile, apart from the pleasure of having
geraniums flowering out of doors in the summer,
to have a few plants growing throughout the winter months.
Invaluable for their bright colours when in flower
it is in fact their foliage in different shapes and tones
which makes an important contribution
at a difficult time of the year.

Sprays of green and white tradescantia are arranged here
with November roses.
It is worthwhile having tradescantia in the house for cutting,
quite apart from its decorative value as a house plant.
The leaves often have a touch of lilac colouring
which combines well with violets or purple anemones.
Tradescantia is easily propagated from cuttings
and will root equally well in soil or water.

Right, A few sprays of fuchsia arranged in a white vase
give a bright touch of colour. Half-hardy fuchsias can be
put in the garden during the summer; if grown indoors
they need to be well watered and kept in a cool atmosphere.

House plants

House plants are, of course, quite a different
subject from flower arrangement, growing in
pots and being decorative in themselves. They
brighten up our homes during winter months
and lighten up many a dull corner with their fresh
green leaves, either grouped together on a table
near the window, arranged in a wire container
especially designed to hold them or looking bright
and gay on shelves in a conservatory to be seen
through the sitting room window. But do they
always look 'bright and gay' and are their leaves
always a 'fresh green', and what is their immediate
connection with flower arrangement?

Perhaps one should answer the last question
first. There are certainly three different types
of plants which are reasonably easy to keep going
through the winter months and their foliage is
invaluable for the type of arrangement often made
for the home. A good example is the small

arrangement usual in a normal sized dining room,
with flowers which have little foliage of their own
and need something to conceal the pinholder
(if that is the method of fixing the flowers) or the
wire netting. Bare stemmed flowers can look
more attractive with foliage from other plants,
even if there is no fixing apparatus to conceal.

In winter especially it is not always easy to find
something suitable in the garden and there may
not be time to go off on an expedition into the
country for the sake of a few leaves. This is when
two or three pot plants are invaluable.

Thinking mainly in terms of small groups for
a dining table or a table for books and a reading
lamp, I recommend the use of geranium or pelargonium foliage, with a few flowers. The variegated
and coloured leaved geraniums are some of the
most valuable for this purpose and are most
successful with various colour schemes. For in-

stance, the charming green and white leaved geranium (this is the round lobed leaf, mostly green, but edged with white), makes a good background for two or three short buds of the Iceberg rose, arranged in a white container. Then there is the dark green leaved plant with a paler green towards the edge and a faint ring of pinky-orange about $\frac{1}{4}$-inch from the outside lobes. These leaves are almost a decoration in themselves but look charming with yellow or something in the pinky-orange line of colouring – either a few of the yellow daisy (anthemis) cut quite short, or, in the winter, a couple of pale yellow carnations. Otherwise salmon-pink carnations could be brought in to tone with that pinky band in the leaf, or a tight cluster of alum root *(Heuchera)* again cut short, or one or two salmon pink zinnias. (Unfortunately that shade of pink is a difficult one to match and sometimes the contrast of white is safer.)

The usual green leaf of a geranium is a charming shape and grows in such an interesting way that it is indispensable in itself. Sometimes a short spray cut from the parent plant will include two or three small new leaves still pleated before unfolding and these are useful indeed, especially for a flat table decoration, growing on the stem as they did on the plant. Geranium leaves last well and a good sized plant does not seem to resent having a few cut off now and then. The scented geranium has a serrated leaf and is rather a different shape, and attractive in its way. It grows sometimes in clusters which are useful as well as decorative.

There is, of course, the usual procedure with geraniums of taking cuttings and allowing the older plants to dry off and have a rest during the winter. But this all depends on whether the flowers are more important to you than the leaves. I have kept two or three plants, of which I am especially fond, through four or five winters in the house on account of their foliage, and cut from them whenever the need arose. They are not first-class exhibition plants but they are quite adequate for this purpose and revive throughout the summer when I put them outside in their pots.

Another standby is the green-and-white tradescantia. It is propagated so easily that once there is a plant in the house others follow on rapidly for there is usually a constant supply of small new ones. The foliage is almost the exact opposite in shape and habit of the geranium. A soft grey-green with white markings, it hangs or droops or spreads itself out horizontally, making valuable material for a small pedestal vase. The leaves themselves are narrow and pointed and are a good contrast with rounded flowers such as clematis or anemones.

The Rex begonias (ornamental begonias) form the third of this valuable trio and are, again, a complete contrast to the other two. They have large heart shaped pointed leaves, sometimes in silver-green or deep wine with soft green marking or deep wine with a lustrous pink veining, these leaves are dramatic in themselves, but tone in a remarkable way with various deep colours. The darker wine-toned leaves are excellent with purple anemones and the grey-green silvery leaves with white carnations. In a small group three leaves toward the centre could be the chief constituents and all that would be required to complete the arrangement might be two or three other flowers.

I think I should mention that, in my own experience, these last two plants do not care for pin holders. I have never known them to last well arranged in this way, and so I have given up using this method. Geraniums, on the other hand, seem to be reasonably happy in any form of anchorage. I have known them last for a matter of weeks when arranged loosely in wire netting, but do not think their span of life was quite as long when a pin holder was used, although to all intents and purposes, no serious damage was incurred. This was not true of the tradescantia and begonia foliage, which went into a rapid decline.

So much for the use of these three house plants for decoration. Now let us return to the original question of keeping them bright and gay with fresh green leaves. This is not as simple as it may sound. Some people have the proverbial 'green fingers' with house plants and with these people I am not concerned. I feel much more for those who say 'Oh, but I have only got to look at a plant in a pot and it curls up and dies.' This may be rather a dramatic way of putting it and, we hope, an exaggeration, but there is still the feeling of not knowing how to go about making a house plant settled and happy.

There are a few definite rules, of course, and most florists and nurserymen will be helpful and give one a few tips when plants are bought. But from my own sometimes depressing experiences I have found out a few simple points about plants which may prove helpful to a beginner. First, about geraniums, I think that on the whole they prefer to be over dry rather than over wet. When the temperature is low in very cold weather, the plant will stop growing and will not start again until the necessary rise in temperature takes place. If it is watered too much at this time the geranium is unable to take in the liquid and the roots will become sodden. Unlike some plants they do not like to have a continuous supply of moisture or to have their feet standing in water.

The opposite is true of begonias and a plant which I have not so far mentioned, but which, to a certain extent, is useful for cutting – the maidenhair fern. I keep a plant of each, usually in the bathroom, where they enjoy the steam from the hot tap and where they both stand in dishes also

containing water. People with a greenhouse may deal with them differently, of course, but this is how they enjoy being looked after in the house.

The number of house plants are, of course, endless, but from the point of view of using the leaves for flower decoration I have found the ones mentioned above particularly useful. Perhaps I should not end without mentioning the false fig (*Fatsia japonica*), which is also invaluable for large groups, but I personally prefer to see this growing in the garden whenever possible.

In this arrangement a few purple anemones reflect the colours in the *Begonia rex* leaves and the sprays of tradescantia again pick up the purple tones in the backs of the begonia leaves. Both the begonia and tradescantia are easy plants to grow in the house, the begonia prefers a slightly damp atmosphere i.e. a bathroom.

Bottom, A few sprays of maidenhair fern arranged in a small white porcelain vase, which picks up the white in the striped leaf of the spider plant. The maidenhair fern is commonly grown in a greenhouse but it will also flourish in a bathroom.

Top, Two or three hydrangea flowers are arranged here towards the centre of the group.
The container is a large natural shell with a curved edge, over which the long thin berberis branches stretch out giving added width and lightness to the arrangement.

Bottom, In this group hydrangeas are arranged with a few of their leaves against a background of veronica foliage. Hydrangeas come in a variety of colours and if allowed to dry off will make a long lasting group.

Hydrangeas

As with roses, lilies, rhododendrons, and many others, whole books have been written about hydrangeas. Mr. Michael Haworth-Booth is one of the leading experts on hydrangeas and anyone wishing to make a study of this plant should either purchase or take out of the library any of his books on the subject.

Unlike iris, lilies and some other plants, hydrangeas grow so abundantly, especially in areas close to the sea that one might think that there are no cultivation problems relating to them.

I think that generally they are easy plants to grow, especially once they have become established in a well drained soil. In the dry weather hydrangeas need extra care over their water supply, perhaps because their large green leaves need a good deal to drink. However, they seem to stand up to gales remarkably well and their flowering season means that there is no worry on account of frost.

One of the hydrangeas specially recommended is *H. paniculata grandiflora* which came originally from Japan where it grows to an immense height.

In a more temperate climate and in most small gardens its height is usually about eight feet. This plant produces flowers for at least three months varying in colour from deep pink to lilac pink and almost to green.

It is impossible to over estimate the value of hydrangeas for large flower groups, for whatever one may feel about the flowers themselves (some people prefer smaller, more individual flowers) there is nothing to compare with them when a solid mass of colour is required in a large area of space. Church decorations spring to mind immediately.

Clusters of hydrangea flowers, buds and leaves are arranged here in a Leeds basket. The natural gloss of the clear green foliage provides an interesting background for the deep colour of the flowers.

Right, Hydrangeas come in a variety of shades of pink and blue and when these various shades are grouped together the arrangement is most attractive in colouring. By using the hydrangea leaves the rather bunchy shape of the flowers is counteracted and the arrangement has a more distinctive outline.

Two or three large hydrangeas cut quite short and arranged towards the centre of a group give the necessary emphasis on colour. In this arrangement the purple flower heads carry on the deep purple of the salvia spikes and the blue of the globe thistle contrasts with the bright pink of the phlox.

Hydrangeas, like rhododendrons, are large flowers with enough splendid foliage to stand alone. They can be impressive, arranged with their own clear green, well shaped leaves, in a mixed colour group of pale pink, rose-pink, deep blue and lilac-blue, cream, white and soft green. On the other hand, if one colour only is required, they can produce enough differing tones and shades to make a splash in that colour. Hydrangeas also have amazing lasting qualities, as long as their water supply is well provided for and looked after.

They can provide the focal point of colour in a mixed arrangement – either a large group for a party or a wedding, or in a smaller one for the house. A blue colour scheme was built up around three heads of blue hydrangeas, arranged with delphiniums, scabious, globe thistles, anchusa, and love-in-a-mist, with a touch of purple in stocks and gladioli. Again, they can be used as a contrast in a mixed colour group, for example; blue hydrangeas with Ophelia roses, sweet peas of all colours from palest pink to deep purple, scabious, Dr. Van Fleet (or New Dawn) roses, summer jasmine and the silver-grey of garden ragwort.

The bunchiness of their flower heads sometimes presents a difficulty owing to their likelihood of being top heavy on the stem, especially when they are the true 'mop head' hydrangeas. It is sometimes also a problem to arrange other, smaller and more delicate flowers around them so that these

flowers are seen properly and that there is not too much contrast between the heaviness of the hydrangeas and the lightness of the other material. It helps, I think, to try to arrange the more solid flower shapes next to the hydrangeas, – for example, scabious, which is in itself a definite shape and easily seen. On the other hand the summer jasmine arranged immediately next to the hydrangeas could well be too much of a contrast.

Hydrangea foliage is useful almost throughout the year. The leaves are a good green and an excellent shape. They seldom seem to be afflicted with insects or bugs to bite or spoil them and so are usually in good condition. The leaves come in some quantity and by cutting them one is not in any way denuding the shrub or making the remaining flowers look bare or unsightly. They will often provide a solid background for a large arrangement, and the only time when one has to be careful that they do not droop at the tip is when they are still young. This is something to watch with all young shoots, especially globe artichoke leaves, peony leaves, wild arums, etc. Lupin and poppy leaves are both usually reliable soon after they appear but this is unusual and most foliage has to have time to harden up for cutting. Even then, if they are given a good drink before being arranged, they will usually strengthen and produce straight stems again.

The large mop heads can also be charming and useful for small arrangements if they are cut off into

segments, like a cauliflower, and then arranged with other small flowers. They can look enchanting when cut like this for a narrow trough-like container, or else for a low table arrangement with rosebuds, (Iceberg buds or Grootendorst flowers) silver-grey foliage of one of the artemesias (southernwood) or sprays of *Helichrysum splendidum*.

Now we come to the use of hydrangeas as dried flowers. Even if they were of no use in any other type of arrangement they would be worthwhile to grow just for drying. I do not think this is too big a claim to make for them, having seen their dried flowers used on so many different occasions and in such a great variety of colourings. (One of the big London stores completely decorated their windows one late autumn with dried hydrangeas.)

They are invaluable throughout the winter to give substance and colour to more fragile and less colourful dried material.

There are various opinions about how best to dry them. I myself have found that usually they will eventually dry themselves off if left long enough in water. (It is easy to tell when they are quite dried by touching the flower and feeling that it is brittle and not soft to the hand.) Otherwise, I am

told that they may be hung in bunches in a warm atmosphere or treated in the same way as beech leaves, that is given a mixture of glycerine and water to drink. I have not experimented with either of these methods. Usually I cut the flowers rather late, if possible, as I incline to the theory that those cut early on, without having felt the touch of frost— like celery—do not dry as successfully. Then I put them into a vase in water and leave them to drink as much as they need, after which they dry off. Nothing could be more simple, and it would be difficult to find lovelier colours than the deep wine shades, soft apple green, buff or deep rose into which they turn.

One of the most difficult of these colours is the green, which often turns to brown if left too long on the plant, and which may flop if sprays are cut off for drying. However, it is worth experimenting to get the particular sweet shade of green which they often produce. So far I have found white hydrangeas impossible to dry, but intend to go on trying as this rather creamy white shade would be useful to contrast with many other dried materials, especially dark brown dock, artichoke heads or blue and white delphiniums.

International flower arrangement

Can anything in the world be more international than flowers, trees and flowering shrubs? One has only to turn the pages of horticultural magazines, and see the articles about plant hunting, discoveries, and pioneering, to realise how world wide this interest in plants is.

To support this point one may read some of the lectures given at the Royal Horticultural Society of Great Britain, to articles written for them, or to photographs illustrating one or the other. A lecture on *Plant hunting in the Triangle, North Burma* by the late F. Kingdon-Ward, O.B.E., V.M.H., told of the discovery of rhododendrons, berberis, primulas, lilies, prunus and iris. A written account of plant hunting in New Guinea (further west still and just north of Western Australia) describes the quantities of orchids and rhododendrons to be found there. Then a description of the National Botanic Gardens of South Africa at Kirstenbosch, where there are fig plants or ice marigolds (*Mesembryanthemum*), spurges, proteas, heaths, treasure flowers (*Gazania*), dimorphothecas, nerines, gladioli, lilies etc. Photographs of another visit, this time in spring show drifts of the arum lily growing wild in the fields as well as many brightly coloured treasure flowers and Cape cowslips (*Lachenalia*).

Another account, this time about the Himalayas, Tibet and China, and the plants to be found there, which include anemones, asters, columbines (*Aquilegia*), bergenias, campanulas, orchids, gentians, delphiniums, spurges, flea-bane (*Erigeron*) and geums. (This is only part of the list.) Admiral and Mrs. Furse penetrated into Iran and Afghanistan and found not only rare plants of all kinds, including brightly coloured tulips, tall fox-tail lilies (*Eremurus*), varieties of lilies, but also the familiar wayside flowers such as clover and St. John's worts, vetches and peas, stinging nettles, thistles and members of the hedge-parsley (*Umbelliferae*) family.

Going on with this round-the-world tour, Keukenhof, in Holland, comes next and here, as one would expect, one is told about the bulbs—the carpets of daffodils, tulips, grape hyacinths, and late jonquils, which have all been heralded into flower by plantings of crocus. (The grape hyacinths are planted so extensively that in the distance they look like a sheet of water.) North America is the country now. Here various botanical gardens have been visited, they include the Morton Arboretum in Illinois, (especially famous for lilacs), the Niagara Falls Parks (which extend for thirty five miles and which produce wonderful examples of magnolias, maples and lilacs, the Royal Botanical Gardens at Hamilton where there is a newish and large rock garden, the New York Botanical Garden containing over 4,000 woody plants along the Hudson river, and the Morris Arboretum at Philadelphia where there are wayfaring trees (*Viburnum*) witch hazels (*Hamamelis*), magnolias, lilacs and azaleas.

Colour photographs illustrate a visit to Morocco in the spring and show bushes of golden broom, pink peonies, wild ox-eye daisies and blue flax amongst other more rare flowers. Many of us tend to connect gentians and blue moon wort (*Soldanellas*) with Switzerland; wisterias and oleanders with the Dordogne and the South of France; bear's breeches (*Acanthus*), myrtles and Jerusalem sage (*Phlomis*) with the Greek Islands; sheets of poppies streaking across the golden cornfields of Normandy; bird of paradise flower (*Stretlitzias*) and eucalyptus with Australia, and so on. But when you realise that eucalyptus groves flourish in the Western Highlands of Scotland, that camellias and rhododendrons thrive in the west of Ireland as well as in the west of England, that lilies from Tibet, gentians from Austria and Switzerland grow happily in gardens all over Western Europe, and that almost all these plants are grown in different areas in America, there can be no doubt about the universality of flowers.

But there are noticeable differences in the flower arrangements of various countries, depending to an extent on the flora of that country, as well as the way of life. This is what makes the spirit of international flower arrangements alive and worthwhile.

Books of typical flower arrangements from each country are fascinating for they show not only the types of local arrangement but also the flowers and foliage used.

For instance, Japanese flower arrangement is known for its simplicity of style and emphasis on ontline, and these two characteristics shine out from every page. First there is an arum lily, with curved branches of broom, or three chrysanthemums with camellia foliage. Then a different kind of arrangement showing plum blossom in a hanging bamboo basket and followed by yet another type—iris standing in a shallow trough of water with bamboo. This typifies the Japanese love of showing plants as

The arum lily grows wild in immense quantities in various parts of Africa and is one of the chief flowers used in flower arrangement. Here it is arranged with branches of horse chestnut.

158

Left, Australian flower arrangements often include various locally grown materials including strelitzias, callistemons (bottle-brush), the shrubby, hypocalymma, dryandra, proteas, banksias and eucalyptus. Some are arranged here with honesty seed pods.

A collection of garden flowers from Germany. They are arranged in a tall narrow necked vase and include most of the generally known border plants such as lupins, campanulas, erigerons, yellow sun daisies, sweet peas, ox-eye daisies and iris.

they grow. This is the essence of good flower arrangement–to be characteristic, to use the locally grown flowers and to make the most of them. (The same principles apply to good architecture.) Therefore, in England one expects and hopes to see garden flowers arranged as naturally as possible, whereas in America, there are so many different influences at work, (this is because some parts of America are much influenced by Japanese and Chinese ideas, and some show a strong Mexican influence.) New England, for example, is similar in many ways to Great Britain, where its trees and flowers are concerned and many flowers are common to both but there are other parts of America with a totally different flora and so there is a greater

variety of taste and less chance of something emerging which epitomises the United States of America as a whole.

In Holland and Belgium the love of flowers has always been pre-eminent, (the great flower paintings of the seventeenth and eighteenth centuries bear witness to this,) and contemporary flower arrangements in these countries often still show the influence of paintings of Van Huysum, Van Brussel and Jan Van Os.

French, Italian and Spanish flower decorations are inclined to depend on the use of brightly coloured flowers interspersed with pot plants, whilst the Scandinavian countries are well known for their use of indoor plants and gardens. Australian

The Oriental influence is shown in this Australian
flower arrangement in the selection of material
and the outline of the group. The camellia is one of the
most popular flowering shrubs in Japan,
but more branches are used here
than are usual in a Japanese flower arrangement.

This Austrian group consists of anthuriums arranged
with their own leaves in a distinctive vase;
the design on the vase emphasises the formality
and slightly artificial texture of the flowers.

flower arrangements often include bamboo flowers
and foliage of bird of paradise flower and curled
banana leaf. (The first two materials, though not
typical, are sometimes used in England and can be
most dramatic for certain kinds of arrangement.)

I should now like to mention an occasion which
illustrates the international aspects of flower
arrangement. The home of the Marquess of Bath
(Wiltshire, England) was decorated for an exhibition in October 1965, in aid of the Royal Commonwealth Society for the Blind. The arrangements were carried out by thirty four West of
England floral arrangement societies. One of the
leading arrangers described the arrival from various
countries of some of the flowers used in the decorations. 'It was terribly touching', she said,
'in the shipment of anthuriums, toy balloons were
filled with water and fixed on to the stems with
rubber bands, then covered with gauze and each
stem was wrapped in cotton wool. The orchids
from Ceylon came in little test tubes and the swamp
orchids from Uganda were packed in banana leaves.
Talk about the biggest aspidistra in the world—
you ought to have seen those banana leaves. They

were as big as the boxes'. Seventeen Common-
wealth countries had contributed flowers, and one
arrangement was made up of buds from Ceylon,
Nigeria, Trinidad, Australia, Singapore, Saint
Vincent, and Granada'. (*The Illustrated London
News*–October 2, 1965.)

Flower arrangement is undoubtedly an international and a universal link and so it cannot be
too much to hope that it may help to promote
understanding between the countries of the world.
There are small instances of this happening which
give one encouragement. For instance, in this
country there are gardens open to the public and
many of the visitors are from abroad. And a
contingent of Florentine gardeners are coming
over specifically to visit the Chelsea Flower Show
and are being entertained by various groups of
people who in their turn, will probably visit some
of the gardens and flower shows in Florence in
other years. Within the last three years "The
Garden History Society" has been established in
Great Britain with members from many other
countries.

The introduction of a fan in a flower arrangement immediately gives an impression of Oriental influence as well as, in this case, providing a useful background for three zinnias and a few clusters of wild clematis.

Top, Brightly coloured begonias, deep scarlet
and creamy-white make an attractive window box
in the Bavarian Alps. The luxuriant foliage
makes a good background for the rather opulent flowers.

Right, American flower arrangement embraces many types
and styles from large bouquets of the modern
mass arrangements to the simpler lines of the groups
showing Oriental influence. The Americans are conscious
of the importance of the materials and dimensions
of the arrangement being suitable for its surroundings.
(Often small figures and other accessories
stand by the container on a raised platform or dais.)
They are especially skilful in using fruit and vegetables.

Left, This South African arrangement of proteas
(a typical South African flower) includes the *Leucospernum
neutans,* commonly called pincushion, the lighter, slightly
yellow flower arranged towards the centre, the
smaller *Leucospernum reflevum* and the rather similar larger
proteas the *Barbigera,* commonly called woolly bearded protea,
one of which is placed at the base of the vase

Irises

We all know the Dutch flower paintings which include amongst them many fine examples of differently coloured irises. However, although this flower was represented in the carvings in Greek and Roman temples, and often included in medieval paintings (in the John Gerard herbal of 1599 no less than eighteen different irises were mentioned), it is only during the last hundred years or so that an enormous variety of irises have been put on the market. This has led to many gardens now having a collection of irises. 'Come and see the irises', one's host may say, as easily as he might say 'come and see the roses'. Apart from a few of the larger gardens, this remark would not have been possible some years ago.

It is possible to have a different iris out during almost every month in the year, such is the scope of variety and colouring available. In the opening sentences of his lecture on *Old and New Bearded Irises* to the Royal Horticultural Society in June, 1965, Mr. H.T. Randall, C.B.E., extols their virtues both for spring and for cutting. 'The genus *Iris* is of value and interest to the three main groups of gardeners in Britain today. First, to the great majority who wish to grow hardy plants which are not expensive, which give attractive flowers, and which do not require excessive care and attention. Secondly, to those who are keen on hybridising and the more scientific side of gardening. Thirdly,

to that ever growing body of enthusiasts who indulge in the pleasant and harmless pastime of arranging flowers in receptacles of various kinds. The genus also provides excellent plants for every type of garden from the window box of the crowded city to the damp, untenanted spots in waterlogged places: for small or large pockets in rock gardens of any size: and for public and private gardens . . .'

For arrangements there can hardly be a more picturesque flower than the iris. Quite apart from the beautiful colourings, their shape alone, dignified and elegant, is of great value especially when they are to be arranged without other flowers. Added to this is also the charm and swordlike quality of the leaves. These are especially useful for contrast with other foliage.

Perhaps one small point about the lasting properties of the iris might be mentioned here. The flower which has been out longest on the stem may die a day or two after it is arranged, but if this is cut off, the other buds will open out and the whole beauty of the flower will come alive again. (This is only a small point, but I have seen a vase of irises looking sad and faded when all they needed was to have the dead flowers removed so that the buds could break open.)

Irises are one of the flowers which seem to approve of pin holders. Like chrysanthemums, they will last for over a week arranged on these

as long as the water supply is kept well up over the base of their stems.

I have included here a list of specially recommended irises. These are known as 'intermediates' which means they grow, on the average, from about ten to twenty inches in height:

Austrian Sky, medium blue; Greenspot, white with a green spot on each fall; Lemon flare, creamy yellow; Lime grove, white with yellow edge to falls; Scintilla, pale ivory; and Small Wonder, light blue.

The following tall bearded irises have a price range from about 4s. to 12s 6d. each: (Many of them can be seen in the large collection at Kew.)

Arabi Pasha, deep cornflower blue; Belle Meade, blue plicata; Carnton, chestnut-red; Cliffs of Dover, milk-white, a great iris; Desert Song, primrose; Eleanor's Pride, powder-blue; Elleray, bright yellow, tall, branched well but needs staking; Headlines, almost white standards and purple falls; Lady Ilse, pale blue; Lady Mohr, tall oncocyclus with delicate shades; Party Dress, soft pink; Patrician, a golden centred white; Patterdale, well branched, pale blue; Sable Night, black-violet; Starshine, blend of pastel shades; Staten Island, gold standards and reddish brown falls; Tarn Hows, cedarwood brown; Total Eclipse, tall, blue-black.

For additional information I shall again quote from the Royal Horticultural Society lecture already mentioned:

'The bearded irises are the most widely grown in gardens throughout the world: in these the greatest progress has been made by hybridisers during the last hundred years; and these offer, perhaps, the greatest scope for the hybridisers of the future . . .

'No one man or country can claim the exclusive credit for introducing hybrid irises to the gardening public; but it is certain that during the nineteenth century nurseries in Western Europe were the first to grow and distribute them commercially and, what is more important, perhaps, to raise new cultivars in order to improve the genus. In France, for example, Jacques, Head Gardener at the Royal Neuilly Domaine near Paris, raised irises from seed before 1830, but he issued no catalogue and, as far as we know, gave no names to his seedlings. But in 1840 a French nurseryman named Lemon, who probably acquired some stock from Jacques, issued his first list of irises for sale . . .

'Another great event in iris history occurred towards the end of last century when American gardeners began to import plants from Barr in England and Vilmorin in France . . .

'Most of the bearded irises will do moderately well in partial shade but they all prefer full sunshine. They thrive in good soil which must, however, be well drained, and I cannot emphasize

Left, A few irises not only give extra height and importance to shorter flowers but also carry out a definite colour scheme. In this case the deep purple of the violets, the various mauves of the anemones, the sky blue of the grape hyacinths and the pale lilac of the freesias are all caught up and emphasised by the iris flowers and the grey-blue of the vase. The use of the iris leaves helps to give a definite line to the arrangement.

Right, In this large group of grasses and garden flowers arranged in an early pewter urn the main points of interest are produced by the yellow and white iris. These link up with the other material and provide a point of emphasis in their colours.

this requirement too strongly...

'The plants increase in size each year and should be dug up about every three years and divided. The divisions can then be replanted in well prepared ground and left for a further period. It is important in this country to leave the top of the rhizome (the hard body of the plant) above ground level and exposed to the sun, because the quality of the bloom each year is generally decided by the amount of ripening received by the rhizome in the previous summer. Should there be a shortage of sunshine in any summer — and this shortage has been known to afflict us in Britain! — it is a good plan to cut back iris leaves to half their length at the end of August so that the rhizomes may have a larger amount of the sunshine remaining . . .

'Whereas years ago tall bearded irises were mostly off white or variations of mauve or violet (frequently mis-called blue), or variegatas with their yellow standards and brownish-red falls, or dullish yellows, nowadays they cover every colour of the spectrum. The white ones, like clothes washed by the latest detergents, have perfect whiteness: the blues have greater clarity, and range from pale Cambridge blue to the darker shades of Oxford: a whole range of pinks can be had, again in light or dark shades: rich brown irises are becoming more widely grown, and so are the reds which, I am glad to say, do not yet rival our post boxes in vividness: very dark cultivars, loosely called black, are adding depth of colour to many a garden, and so are the purple ones. In the past few years orange coloured seedlings have been raised, and while some gardeners think that these are too bright for the iris border, I predict a great future for them. Then we have a delightful range of orchid-pink and orchid-lavender cultivars which are destined for great popularity: the amoenas, with their white standards and coloured falls, of which Whole Cloth is a notable example: the ruffled, pale orchid lavender and white irises of which Rippling Waters was the first and might still be regarded as the finest . . .

'A new race of irises, known as 'lilliputs', have been grown at Wisley and in countless other gardens throughout the world. Paul Cook's Greenspot, baria and Fairy Flax, together with Small Wonder, Lilliput and Tinker Bell by Geddes Douglas are popular everywhere because of their well formed and attractive flowers, their vigour and freedom of bloom and their reliability as garden plants'.

Japanese
and Oriental
flower arrangement

The Japanese flower arrangements are described by Sir Josiah Conder in his book *The Flowers of Japan and the Art of Floral Arrangement*. These early groups were based on a style of composition named Shin-no-hana, meaning central flower arrangement. 'Branches of blossoming trees or foliage were employed in their natural state, without artificial bending or trimming, to form a vertical central mass; and other flowers or bunches of foliage were disposed on either side in balancing groups'. Without the guidance of prints depicting the central flower arrangement, one would be inclined to imagine from this description something closely approaching the Victorian idea of profusion. But this is far from the case, and Sir Josiah's remark about a 'central mass' is obviously based on a comparison with the severity of later developments. He adds, however: 'Even in this comparatively early form of the art, the proportion which the floral composition held to the vessel which contained it, was fixed by a rule, a practice which was followed in all later arrangements'.

Left, In this group three arum lilies are arranged with a few evergreen leaves to one side of the container. The arrangement illustrates two rules of Japanese flower arrangement—cutting the stems different lengths and the use of an uneven number of flowers.

Right, A few hyacinths and bulrushes are arranged here in a contemporary George Wilson container showing in modern style Ikebana the possibilities with contemporary shapes.

Japanese dwellings have a Toko-no-ma, an ornamental alcove or recess. On the back wall of this alcove, the Kakemonos, the rolled pictures are exhibited and in front of these pictures there is usually a stand for the floral arrangement, unless a hanging decoration of flowers is used. As the flowers and scroll pictures are the only objects of size and importance in the room it is essential that they agree in character and colouring.

Primitive Japanese flower arrangements known as Shin-no-hana,
meaning central flower arrangement developed from the sixth century when Buddhism reached Japan through China.
This type of decoration was especially designed for use as an offering before shrines and tombs.
This group is an example of an early central flower arrangement.

The whole theory of Japanese flower arrangement is intermingled with Chinese philosophy and traditions. Virtues are attributed to the professors of flower arrangement themselves, and a certain goodness is said to emanate from the practice of arranging flowers, 'a religious spirit, self denial, gentleness and forgetfulness of cares'.

Male and female personalities are given to different flowers, colours and compositions. Earth, Heaven and Mankind are names given to a tri-lineal group, and wood, fire, metal, water and earth to a five-lined design. The male and female principle is also applied to colours and contrasting forms, blue, yellow and white are female and red, purple and pink are male. Sometimes a part of an arrangement will be considered male – the right hand side, and the other female – the left hand side.

Some flowers are given precedence over others, for example white flowers are always regarded as being of the highest rank, with the single exception of the yellow chrysanthemum. The evergreen of the camellia is held in very high regard because 'it is recorded that in the time of the gods, one of the gods and his consort built a palace and as a token of unchanging felicity for eight thousand years, planted a camellia tree.' This tree is still said to exist in the province of Izumo, and is called the camellia tree of eight thousand years.

Various flowers should only be used in certain positions and at certain times of the year. The morning glory, for instance, should be attached to a twig or stump 'round which it should be wound in the direction turning the flowers to the left side.'

The Peony (the king of the flowers in China) 'when used in combination with other flowers is entitled to the most important position'.

There is the charming tradition of the water diving plum. 'With regard to these special arrangements it is related that Soho upon a certain hunting expedition saw in the mountains a large plum tree, one of the branches of which bent into the stream below, the extremity again rising upwards clad with blossoms. Being struck with the effect, he applied it to artificial arrangements of plum branches in shallow water vessels'. *Theory of Japanese Flower Arrangements – J. Conder.*

The whole subject of Japanese flower arrangement is fascinating, and worthy of years of study and research. It should be treated with respect, love and interest. The people who study it do so over a long period of time.

Perhaps it was the foundations of legend and tradition, religion and philosophy which helped to make Japanese flower arrangement an art so worthy of respect and an art of such high artistic order. During the fifteenth and sixteenth centuries Japanese flower work developed through the different stages of artificialities and unnatural curves and finally emerged in its purest form, towards the end of the seventeenth century. The Nageire School supplanted the more complicated patterns of the Rikkwa School, and took over the name of Ikebana (the Japanese word for living flower arrangement).

The aim of the Japanese has always been to reproduce as far as possible the character of the plant, tree or shrub being used. Some schools would not allow the use of a flower unless the arranger knew its habit and growth. Flower arrangement is studied in Japan in the way that

An arrangement of *Hosta ventricosa (Giboshi)* with seven leaves in a bronze vase on a stand.

Top, An arrangement of chrysanthemum flowers
in a three-storey bamboo vase on stand.

Top left, An illustration of a modern Ikebana decoration
by Stella Coe consisting of dragon tails
and black and white strelitzia from South Africa
with red snapdragons. Such an arrangement
is dependent on a plain background for its effect.
It does not have the sensitivity of a group
composed of more natural material
but would combine well with a severe furnishing scheme.

Left, Branches of willow in tight bud are arranged
here at an unusual angle in a black Rosenthal container,
with two lilies and wild arum leaves.
The whole arrangement gives a feeling of movement.

Left, A contemporary Western flower arrangement
showing the use of some of the rules
in Japanese flower arrangement.
There are an uneven number of flowers with their stems
cut different lengths so that each bloom is clearly seen.
The general effect is clear and uncluttered
and stands out well against its background.

Top, The patterned vase and the brightly coloured fan
in the photograph show an Oriental influence
in this contemporary arrangement of a few irises.

other nations study music or painting – it is a
creative art, so enriching that it defies description.
Whoever is arranging the flowers is called a
'composer'.

The Japanese approach to flower arrangement
is intellectual and serious and their art has reached
its high standard through many centuries of study
and application.

Jasmine

This group shows the curving sprays
of summer jasmine arranged with
the thin stems of broom
in a Staffordshire jug.

Bottom, The long stems of summer
jasmine combine well with everlasting
sweet pea. Here they are both
arranged in a pedestal cake stand to
show off their graceful shape.
Clusters of the jasmine flower are
arranged with heads of giant wild
parsley towards the centre of the dish.

Winter and summer jasmine could hardly be more different although both are well known and probably grown in the majority of gardens.

Jasminum nudiflorum, the yellow flowering winter jasmine comes into flower often in late summer or autumn. Its long, straight or slightly curving stems are studded with small flowers (looking like the proverbial 'showers of gold'), until the worst frosts come, when the soft yellow turns transparent and the golden effect is temporarily lost. Often the flowers recover. They seem to dislike the bitter east winds of February almost more than the coldest frost.

Winter jasmine foliage is splendid in the summer – dark and rather shining, and the leaves look exactly as though they are evergreen and will remain throughout the winter. (Perhaps this is because of their dark colour and neat sturdy appearance.) In fact, they fall in the autumn like all other deciduous shrubs and climbers, leaving the bare branches to carry the splendour of the flowers.

These flowers can bring their clear yellow so reminiscent of spring to brighten the greyness of a cold winter day. It is especially heartening to cut branches with tight buds and watch them open and come out in the heat of a room. Sometimes for a table decoration a long stem can be cut into two or three short pieces and arranged in a small group, with other flowers. The feathery blue-green foliage of rue looks most attractive with the rather austere jasmine stems, and gives it a becoming lightness of shape.

The long, dark green branches with their small neat leaves make excellent material for line arrangements, and will give extra height in a tall pedestal group. The straightness and the curves of the stems make this plant suitable for many types of arrangement.

Jasminum officinale, the 'ever-welcome' white jasmine, a well deserved favourite of all time as Miss Jekyll describes it, is enchanting in both foliage and flower. The fern-like leaf grows on curving stems which are a gift to flower arrangers. (There are very few plants with such stems and such foliage.) *Jasminum officinale* is sometimes described as 'a semi-evergreen', since it keeps its charming leaves on well into the winter, when they are even more welcome than ever.

The white flowers, touched with pink, grow in small clusters with the tight and more deeply tinged buds. All are sweetly scented. In August when the flowers are out this is a wonderful plant to cut for arrangement. The stems are immensely useful either in a tall pedestal arrangement, where they curve forward, or in a smaller pedestal group, such as those arranged in a cake stand or a fairly flat dish, where they give width as well as an attractive outline. The flowers themselves can be cut short in a small bunch and arranged in a piece of white porcelain where they look quite charming. In fact they make a better show when arranged in this way as they are more clearly seen. However, when left on long branches the effect of the small rather demure flowers shining luminously through the foliage is not without its own appeal.

Later on in the year, the foliage is invaluable for contrast either in other autumnal foliage groups or alone with two or three late clematis, arranged in a narrow necked bottle or wine decanter. I find that the older jasmine foliage is inclined to last better than the new sprouting stems.

Both the winter and summer jasmine grow well against the wall of a house and although they will probably survive on a northern aspect, they prefer a sunny position. Once this is guaranteed they will repay one a thousand fold. Since both the jasmines come from more exotic lands, *Jasminum officinale* from Persia and *Jasminum nudiflorum* from China, this is understandable, and one is very grateful that they have taken so well to the weather conditions in England. Both plants grow to a height of about twelve to fifteen feet and profit by a certain amount of pruning. The winter jasmine especially, is all the better for having branches of its flowers cut, almost like sweet peas. (The new flowers do not come in the same season.)

Half hardy jasmines tempt the amateur when once they have been seen and then smelt in full

Although winter jasmine flowers from October it still gives a feeling of spring in the early months of the year. Here it is arranged with pussy willow sprays and geranium leaves.

Long curving branches of summer jasmine with its small white and pink flowers are among the most graceful and decorative of any garden plants. The leaves last better than the flowers, but when these have dropped small clusters of delicately tinted buds remain.

flower. Mrs. Spry has written about one of these, *Jasminum primulinum*, and of using long sprays of it for a successful Japanese type of arrangement in a bamboo vase. Miss Sackville-West in her book *In Your Garden Again* introduces a half hardy plant, *Jasminum polyanthum,* and feels that this choice is justified. *Jasminum polyanthum* was introduced from China in the early part of this century, it is said by Major Lawrence Johnston, maker of the fine Hidcote garden. It has flowers that are similar to the summer jasmine, but grow in greater profusion and are rather larger in size.

This jasmine flowers indoors or in a greenhouse in the middle of the winter. Although the flowers and leaves are beautiful it is the scent which is the most remarkable thing about this plant.

During the summer and autumn it is quite possible to keep it in the garden and so *Jasminum polyanthum* can be included in the same category as most geraniums (Miss Sackville-West mentions it growing outside all the year round in the famous garden of Highdown, near Goring-on-Sea, Sussex, England, where it has climbed up the side of the house to the edge of the roof).

One can say then, that in sunnier climates this jasmine is perfectly happy out of doors, but what-

Winter jasmine comes into flower as early as October and often continues until February
when the flowers may take on a transparent look and lose their bright yellow colouring.
In the arrangement in the photograph the bare branches are given interest by the rather fussy blue-grey rue foliage.
If cut when in tight bud winter jasmine will come into full flower when brought indoors.

ever the trouble one had to take over growing it in England, all would be worthwhile just to have the glory of those white scented flowers against the dark green leaves – a delight throughout winter.

I have included here one or two suggestions for yellow-toned arrangements, using the winter jasmine when it first comes out at the beginning of the autumn:

Long, rather straight, sprays amalgamate well with yellow pompon dahlias, late, fiery red zinnias, nasturtiums, and montbretias, almost giving the effect of a bright sunset such as Turner might have painted. Then there are other pos-

sibilities with the spray chrysanthemums, white or yellow, and three or four lemon carnations. Later on, in the winter, when a sheltered cluster of early primroses may obligingly appear, a few short cut sprays of jasmine will make an interesting addition to the arrangement, especially if they are grouped in a flat dish with moss to look as though they are growing. Jasmine can also look most attractive at Christmas time with variegated holly.

179

Jugs for containers

For some hundreds of years jugs of all types, shapes and sizes, have been used to hold flowers. In the early fifteenth century a painting of the Annunciation scene shows two stems of lilies in an unusually shaped jug standing on the table in the room. (This painting, by The Master of Flemalle, is now in the Brussels National Museum.) In an altar piece of the same period there are again stems of lilies but this time depicted in a metal jug or ewer.

In the still life by J.J. Treck, 1649, the jug is a pewter one, with a branch of vine leaves threaded through the handle. Coming nearer to our own time, there is the vivid painting of mixed lilies and roses in a brown and yellow jug by Suzanne Valadon, and the glorious painting from Picasso's 'blue period' of mixed flowers in a grey blue jug. (This may be seen in the Tate Gallery, London.)

A jug like a basket is valuable apart from its use as a container for flowers. This immediately makes it an asset in the house and the purchase of an extra jug (when it is bought with flower arrangement in mind) is not a luxury.

The first thing to consider about jugs is their texture. There is the jug made in elegant porcelain. (It may be in Sunderland lustreware, in cream Staffordshire with the Staffordshire knot forming the handle, in Prattware with raised patterns and glowing colours, and Wedgwood—in their various well known colours – or from other factories such as Leeds, Lowestoft, Swansea, etc.) Then there is the jug made in copper and brass (sometimes in copper with brass studs or vice versa, which have been designed to hold beer or cider. Some are even relics from the days when there was no running water and when hot water was carried upstairs for washing). These are quite original in shape, with a stumpy spout, sturdy handle, and a hinged lid–the lid stands back and gives plenty of room for the stalks of flowers or branches, and acts as a support.

There are, of course, glass jugs which could be made either of early coloured Bristol glass, of plain glass, Waterford glass, or white Swedish glass with black glass handles, (these were made originally

Left, A homely Leeds porcelain jug makes a good container for a small bunch of garden flowers.
In this arrangement the blue pattern on the jug contrasts with the brightly coloured snapdragons.
A jug of this size and shape does not usually need any anchorage for the flowers.

Top right, Pewter combines well in colouring and texture with the greyish tones of dried flowers.
The jug has a simple outline which makes a good contrast with the fussy shape of some of the dried material e.g. nipplewort, sea holly and the various grasses.

Right, A cream Staffordshire jug with the lid pushed back, holds a cluster of softly coloured dahlias.
The narrow neck and lid of the jug help to keep the material in position.

This large pewter jug is suitable for a collection of leaves
and branches as it holds a good supply of water
and the long neck provides anchorage for the stems.

to hold water, lemonade, beer, etc.). Finally
there is the larger silver jug (made at times to
hold hot water), often with a small black lid which,
again, hinges back and acts as a support for the
stems. Its companion the small silver jug (intended
to hold milk or cream – the kind of wedding present
that everyone might hope for) is only suitable for
a few flowers, but shows them off well with the
help of a pedestal base.

The next consideration must be the size and
shape of the jug in relation to the size of the flower
arrangement. This consideration will dictate the
eventual size and outline of the group to be composed. Having just mentioned the small silver
cream jug it seems sensible to begin the next paragraph discussing in detail these smaller jugs
(made either in silver, porcelain or pottery) and
their suitability in texture and colouring with
certain flowers.

The milk jugs of blue ware, with the name of the
local town or village written across it that can now
be seen everywhere in England are splendid foil
for yellow flowers, either the wild Welsh daffodils
with their rather short stems, or a bunch of primroses. Cowslips also look most attractive arranged in a natural bunch in one of these. Since
these jugs hold comfortably a half pint, or even a
pint, of milk, they can obviously contain enough
water to support an average small bunch from the
garden, including flowers like pinks, short roses,
grey foliage, snapdragons, forget-me-nots, polyanthus, bluebells (these are especially attractive

in the blue and white of the well known willow
pattern pottery).

The next size up may be the Staffordshire jugs
which hold anything from $1\frac{1}{2}$ to $2\frac{1}{2}$ pints, and as
they are usually designed with a narrowing neck
towards the spout, this makes them especially
suitable for the taller flowers which need support.
These might include zinnias, daffodils, achillea,
Korean chrysanthemums, tobacco plants, phlox,
marguerites, lupins, delphiniums and peonies.
Large groups of tall flowers will naturally drink
more and the water level should be carefully
watched if the jug is not a transparent one.

Glass jugs are attractive in their own way,
especially when something with interesting foliage
down the stem is seen through the water. This
applies particularly to the wild caper spurge, with
its architectural leaf structure down its stout stem.
Seen through water it looks even more exciting
than when it is growing.

Before talking about the largest jugs of all, I
think that we should mention the narrow necked
dark brown pottery jugs as well as the contemporary designed large bowled but narrow necked ones,
which are excellent for holding a few branches
or two or three long stemmed flowers. Summer
jasmine, with its spreading stems and branches
is especially suitable for this type of container,
as are honeysuckle, clematis and periwinkle.

Large jugs with wide necks, some of which hold
from three to four quarts of water, are obviously
suitable for a big arrangement, as there is plenty
of space for the stems, and plenty of water for them
to drink. A jug of this size is held steady and
by the weight of the water (this is valuable with
large groups which are easily inclined to become
top heavy.) These jugs are most suitable for
branches of flowering shrubs like Chilean gum box
(Escallonia), Californian lilac *(Ceanothus)* and
also the taller herbaceous plants.

An important point to think of when arranging
flowers in a jug of any size or description is that
part of the spout and the handle ought to show.
It is a great pity if they are almost or completely
hidden from view. (Practically, the spout can
be of great use for curving branches.) When
this happens the jug is no longer a jug and looks
like any other vase, but is not so well proportioned.

Anchorage for the flowers in a jug depends
very much on the shape of the spout, etc. If the
jug is a wide lipped one and holds a good deal of
material, it may help to have a small quantity of
large mesh wire netting pushed into the top with
some of it raised above the level of the brim. If the
jug is narrow necked that in itself will act as a
support and it is unlikely that any other anchorage
will be needed. In a shallow sauceboat shape of
jug, I have sometimes used a pin holder.

This contemporary lustre jug provides an interesting contrast against the clear fresh green of Solomon's seal
with its small green and white pendulous flowers and the pure white of pheasant's-eye narcissi.
The jug holds plenty of water and the branches are kept in place in a mesh of wire netting fixed well down into the jug.

Lilies

'If you have two loaves, sell one and buy a lily'. Taking this not quite literally let us turn our attention to lilies for flower arrangement. For some reason, perhaps because they are to a large extent grown as hot house plants, and provide flowers out of season, lilies are often associated with costliness and even extravagance. Though they are expensive to buy, lilies may still be more economical in the long run than other flowers because of their long lasting qualities. Once established in the garden they will prove an investment indeed.

There are, of course, many different kinds and colours of lilies, and of these there are at least four white ones which are reliable, elegant, useful for tall arrangements, and fairly easy to grow. One of these four, *Lilium longiflorum*, may need extra care and protection in certain areas, but the other three will flourish in almost any garden and most of them grow just as happily in pots or deep window boxes as they will in the border or among flowering shrubs. Two schools of thought exist on this matter of where to plant lilies in the garden.

One prefers to see them coming up against a background of flowering shrubs, providing lightness in contrast to the dark foliage when the shrubs have flowered. The other likes to see them in pots, standing on a terrace, sunk into a border, or decorating a flight of steps. One point in favour of having lilies in pots is that although they are more trouble to water, they can be easily moved about either to lighten a dark corner or to delight the nose with their delicious scent if placed near a garden seat.

The four lilies I have in mind are:
L. auratum or the gold-rayed lily of Japan. Robert Fortune describes finding this lily on one of his journeys into the mountains above Yokohama in July, 1861. 'A very beautiful new lily was met with on the hillsides in full bloom, and its roots were dug up and added to my collection'.

This fine lily, with a honey scent, is white with a yellow stripe on the inside of the petals, chocolate brown spots and bright orange stamens. The flowers are sometimes nearly ten inches across. It lasts well when cut, and flowers which are still

Left, Arum lilies are amongst the longest lasting
of all flowers. In this arrangement of eucalyptus,
ruscus, camellia and arum foliage
the three flowers make a focal point.
The pale green on the outside of the flowers is repeated
in the soft green and white of the guelder flowers.

Right, The beauty of lilies is in their buds,
leaves and stems as well as their flowers.
Two or three lilies placed in a focal position
in the room can often be more effective
than large arrangements of other flowers.

Bottom right, Two longiflorum lilies are arranged here
with branches of caper spurge.
This spurge is unusual in the arrangement of its leaves
and seedpods and needs a contrast which is provided
by the clear white of the trumpet shaped lilies.

in bud will come out in water, prolonging the life
of an arrangement by days. If the flowers appear
to be too heavy for a small arrangement they can be
cut off at the top of their stem and arranged towards
the centre of the group.

The Madonna lily *(L. candidum),* one of the oldest
cultivated lilies, has been grown in England since
the end of the sixteenth century (about 1596) and
often appears in early religious paintings.

It flourishes in many cottage gardens under
varying conditions. Sometimes it seems to like
a rich soil, sometimes to resent it. Sometimes
it likes sunshine, sometimes shade. It may well
be described as capricious. The secret of growing
the Madonna lily has not yet been completely
discovered.

A border of these white lilies can be the focal
point of a garden, and the charm of the flowers
with their sweet scent is ample repayment for any
trouble one takes to find out the conditions that
suit them best. In flower arrangements Madonna
lilies are especially connected with weddings, but
a few of them can be a worthy addition to a group
of mixed border flowers. *L. longiflorum* tall,
elegant, and cool, is sometimes almost greeny
white, in colour, and its curving foliage is an important part of the plant's attraction, together
with its sweet scent. These lilies are invaluable for
church decoration.

As older flowers die and are cut off buds open
to take their place. The species was introduced
from Japan about 1820 and is popular for forcing
because of its usefulness for ceremonial occasions.

This fine lily will grow successfully in pots and
as it is not as hardy as the other three mentioned
here, this is often a good way of growing it. *L.
longiflorum* can start life in a cool greenhouse and
then be brought out into the garden later. As it
prefers to have its roots kept moist, a shady position
with some sunshine is ideal, and the purity of the
cool white flowers (six inches long by five inches
wide is a general size) show up well against other
green shrubs.

L. regale is not a clear white like the *longiflorum*

or the Madonna lily as it is flushed with pink on the outside of the petals. However, *L. regale* is one of the prettiest and one of the easier species of this sometimes difficult family to establish.

This lily comes from Western China and usually flowers during July. It was found there in 1910 by E.H. Wilson when he was collecting plants for his American friend, Professor Sargent, for the Arnold Arboretum. Wilson had reason to remember finding this lily, for shortly after digging up quantities of its bulbs there was a severe landslide and he was thrown hundreds of feet down the hillside towards the river and one of his legs was smashed against a rock. On his return to America with the plants, his leg was saved by the skill of a surgeon, but he walked with a limp afterwards.

At this point it would be neglectful, I feel, not to mention the usefulness of the arum lily for flower arrangements, although it is not a true lily. The arum is perhaps best known for its reliability in church decoration. I have seen a large group used in Canterbury cathedral where an all round effect was needed and absolute dependability was essential. The clear and definite shape of each flower means that it can be effectively seen from every angle and its lasting qualities (often resistant to changes of temperature and even to droughts) are almost unique.

Arum leaves can be grown out of doors in many parts of England. In the south west, the Channel Islands, and the Scillies they are often to be seen, giving a slightly exotic touch to cottage gardens. However, most arums will survive as long as their bulbs are planted well down into the soil, to escape the depth of frost usually experienced during the winter. I have a friend who grows them close to the pond in his Kent garden and they are such good clumps that they are the envy of many neighbouring gardeners.

But even if arums do call for some extra trouble in their planting and care, they are worth every bit of it when one considers the value of their leaves for arrangements, quite apart from their flowers. One of the Editors of *Amateur Gardening* assures me that if they are planted in good soil (heavy clay for instance may cause the bulbs to rot), or where they are close to a depth of water which will protect them from frost, they can be regarded as reasonably hardy.

Here are some points to remember when arranging lilies: they last well if kept cool and given plenty of water to drink. They are suitable for various shapes and kinds of containers, although their regal qualities and the purity of their white flowers seem to be especially emphasised when they are arranged in glass.(I saw a tall yellow glass vase used effectively for flowers which stood beside the lectern in a church near Falmouth in Cornwall.) Try a tall glass container which will stand on the floor and still be high enough to be seen throughout the church (this would eliminate the use of a pedestal and is, I think, an idea worth remembering, especially for weddings.) A narrow neck means no other anchorage is necessary and once the flowers are fixed into position with the help of foliage or branches they will stay there.

Left, A large group of lilies arranged in a tall container can make an impressive decoration.
The two lilies *L. longiflorum* and *L. regale* are arranged with long stems and plenty of leaves
and buds to give variety of shape to the group.
As the flowers die they can be cut off,
allowing the buds to come out into flower,
ensuring a long lasting arrangement.

Right, Auratum lilies grow to anything from 5 – 10 feet and for a low arrangement they need to be cut short.
Here they are arranged with bergenia leaves
on a pin holder in a dish of water;
the foliage conceals the pin holder.

Line

I once knew someone living in the country who was fortunate enough to have a small orchard as part of her garden. Not only was it beautiful with the blossoms of the pear, cherry and apple trees in it when they were in season, but during March and the beginning of April, clumps of daffodils and narcissi burst into flower under the still bare branches of the fruit trees. Inspired by the sight of so much spring colour she would cut great bunches of flowers for the house.

But she would never take any trouble about

arranging these flowers, being inclined to regard the whole business as 'too much fuss'. Then one day she remarked to me how delighted she was with a new idea she had invented. 'I cut the narcissus stems to different lengths and the flowers really look much better and show up properly', she said, rather surprised.

These particular flowers are, to my mind, some of the most difficult to arrange, and, of course, they benefited from being seen at separate levels rather than all being at the same height. This

Left, A few branches of pine arranged in an early glass container and kept in position by large mesh wire netting. The height of the tall central branch is balanced by the heavy cluster of the short stem at the base and by the width of the longer branch towards the side of the arrangement. This is a group which must stand against a clear background.

Right, The small leaved branches of eucalyptus provide good material for a line arrangement. In this group the three curving stems are supported by a cluster of pink-orange echeverias. The material stands on a pin holder, concealed by moss and some of the echeveria flowers, in a shallow brass dish filled with water.

Bottom, The curving branches of berberis have clusters of small sprays at intervals along their stems. They are arranged here on a pin holder in a small brown earthenware dish standing on a broad piece of wood. In all line arrangements it is essential that they are seen against a plain background.

principle applies to other flowers too, and simple though it is, it makes all the difference to the final effect.

Another reason for varying the length of stem is that a small amount of material will go farther.

Take, for instance, a bunch of cornflowers bought in a shop. Just a small bunch will go much farther and give a broader effect if the stems are cut to different lengths, quite apart from the fact that each flower benefits from being seen separately.

Varied cutting of the stems gives not only width but also depth to the group if those placed towards the centre are cut much shorter than the outside ones. If some are cut almost to the flower this should help produce the in-and-out effect which is so necessary when arranging a quantity of the same kind of flower.

This fact also applies to naturally tall flowers such as gladioli or chrysanthemums. Try cutting some of the stalks much shorter than their full length – in this way one avoids having an array of thin stems with a uniform line of rather top heavy flowers. Other flowers which seem to me to benefit from this kind of cutting are golden rod, tall campanulas, Achillea The Pearl, delphiniums and Michaelmas daisies.

The most important reason why one ought to cut the stems at different lengths is to achieve a good 'line'. (In England we have possibly been much more concerned with colour than line, although the comparatively recent interest in Japanese flower work has awakened us to the importance of this factor.)

A good line arrangement can be difficult to achieve, for it has to have a certain kind of background and position, otherwise it will be completely wasted. Basically it needs, I think, a great deal of patience and skill in selecting material. To my mind, a natural arrangement, typical of an English garden, is difficult to improve on, but it must be based on a skeleton outline that is essentially good. One could liken the necessity for a good skeleton outline to the necessity for good draughtsmanship in a painting or good structure in the erection of a new building.

Correct judgement is important when cutting the stems. If one or two cornflowers are cut too short they can easily be replenished. But if you have only five roses, or three carnations, and they cannot be replaced from the garden, or are too expensive to buy, then it is most important not to make a mistake. It is always better to cut too little rather than too much. I personally find it most helpful to hold the flower in position against the arrangement before cutting it.

Like every art, flower arrangement has certain rules, and the ones connected with line are very basic ones. Here is a short summary of them:

1 The stalks must come from a central point and not cross each other, thus giving the effect that the flowers are still growing. They must all spring from the same base, wherever it happens to be in the arrangement (i.e. if it is a central arrangement, they will spring from the centre). If, as in some long, flat dishes, there are two separate groups of flowers or branches, they must be arranged as two distinct arrangements, with the stalks emerging from a central base in each one.

2 An uneven number of flowers should be used whenever possible.

3 The stalks should be cut in different lengths.

4 The height of the arrangement should be about one and a half times the height of the container, except where a very wide base gives added balance.

5 Heavy flowers should never be used towards the edge of an arrangement. They should be used towards the centre, and not in a straight line one above another.

6 Flowers should be seen separately, except, perhaps, in an all round arrangement where this may be impossible.

7 The general effect when finished should be as natural as possible, and there should be no need to contort branches or to strive after dramatic appeal. (A stylised effect can sometimes be interesting, but very soon looks contrived and artificial.)

These are all very simple, uncomplicated rules, which will come so naturally after a time that one will not need to think about them consciously. Like most rules they can, and should, sometimes be broken – all except numbers 1 and 3. I have found myself using an even number of flowers on one occasion, which seemed to look right (but I think this very seldom happens). I have, also, seen a rather dumpy arrangement of heavy flowers look effective in a tall container. (There is the still life by Chardin where a tight bunch is arranged in a tall, thin vase and, of course, looks perfect). On the other hand, I have never seen crossed stalks look quite right, or flowers and branches cut exactly the same height.

It is important that rules are not misused, otherwise stereotyped results could well result. Rules are there for the guidance and development of personal style and taste, rather than their eradication. It is the 'line' in a group which is the sole creation of the arranger and as such should be expressive and characteristic of the individual. This can never be culled from all the flower books in the world.

Top, Here branches of Japanese quince *(chaenomeles)* are arranged against a plain background in an early Italian lead dish which gives the branches extra importance on account of its shallowness and pedestal effect. When cutting and trimming fruit branches for a line arrangement it is essential to take great care so that each detail stands out as much as possible and that they are arranged in the same positions as they have grown on the tree.

Right, Knobbly branches of witch hazel (hamamelis) with their charming yellow tufted flowers provide the outline for this January arrangement. The clear yellow holly leaves come from the lower tufted branches of a variegated holly shrub; a plain background is essential in this type of arrangement to show up the bare branches. There are five main branches as aesthetically it is best to have an odd number.

Mantelpiece arrangements

In a position of this kind where the candelabra takes up a good deal of room a tall thin arrangement is needed. The design of the container provides a link with the small jar next to it; the creamy-white background colour of the jar is a link between the white of the mantlepiece and the off-white lampshades.

Top, These three roses arranged with their buds and leaves and with clusters of elder flowers still in bud, show an example of an arrangement suitable for a narrow mantelpiece. In this case the flowers need to be kept low on account of the picture above. The group is arranged in a porcelain boat but a gravy or sauce boat would be equally suitable.

Bottom, Branches of forsythia in a tall narrow-necked glass container provide a point of emphasis at the end of a mantelpiece. The arrangement shows up well against the plain wall, and does not intrude on the painting next to it.

Many of the large, wide fireplaces of old country houses and cottages did not have a mantelpiece, they were fronted with a large supporting beam which lay flat in the brickwork. But there were some houses with beautiful Adam mantelpieces— a good, wide, well proportioned shelf with plenty of space, suitable not only for the usual candlesticks or precious ornaments but also for a vase. But it is difficult to say with any certainty that when mantelpieces were first installed, flowers were in general usage for decoration on them.

The Victorians, in contrast, went in for mantelpieces in a big way. Solidly built perhaps of dark, shining mahogany or grey and white marble, they were wide, capacious and able to accommodate all kinds of decorations, including flowers. Mr. Shirley Hibberd, in his book *Rustic Adornments for Homes of Taste* (published in 1865), illustrates what he likes to describe as a 'simple fireplace decoration'. In the middle of the mantelpiece there is a large pedestal bowl supporting a heavy leafed plant. There are four other vases all containing flowers, and below, in the fireplace itself, are three large vases, one full of foliage, one full of flowers, and one full of grasses, flowers and leaves. In a later publication entitled *British Floral Decoration* (published in 1910), there is an illustration of a heavily decorated Georgian fireplace. This has a clock in the centre with a vase on each side filled with carnations and greenery, some of these being doubled in effect due to their being reflected in the large mirror.

Now I should like to discuss mantelpieces and their decoration with reference to our own times. The mantelpiece is usually the focal point of the room, and the wall or mirror behind it will give any group arranged thereon an added importance and emphasis. This kind of arrangement depends on its surroundings and its relationships to other objects for its effectiveness. Thus the line of a mantelpiece arrangement is determined by whatever else is standing nearby and by the picture hung above it.

The surrounding ornaments, pieces of porcelain or glass, may suggest a certain colour scheme. But one must remember that if the floral arrangement is sited directly underneath a painting, it must not be allowed to overpower the painting for if harmony is to be achieved, the flowers must be subsidiary and complementary in every way. Another factor to take into consideration is the texture and colour of the mantelpiece – some may be made of wood, others of wood painted over, and others of marble.

If there are any candelabra or other methods of close lighting, it would be as well to turn them on, since colour changes in artificial light.

In winter the mantelpiece decoration depends to a large extent in the way in which a room is heated. The answer then, if there is a fire in the hearth or some other form of heating below the mantelpiece is a dried arrangement. Few fresh flowers will put up with waves of heat coming from underneath them. If the shelf is a wide one and the flowers stand well to the back there is more of a chance for them, but it is essential to choose hardy flowers. One of the winter flowering plants I remember as being most successful is spurge (*Euphorbia fulgens*) with its long sprays of bright orange flowers. Anemones are usually rather long suffering as are the spray chrysanthemums.

Summer time obviously presents no such difficulties and great use can be made of the central position of the mantelpiece. The empty grate will also make an ideal background for large containers filled with leaves, grasses etc. standing inside the fender, and if big enough will take a suitably sized vase, full of flowers coming up over the front iron bars. I have seen an electric fitment arranged so that the flowers in this position are illuminated from inside the chimney and this can be most effective.

It may be difficult to do the flowers in position and if this is the case they should be arranged elsewhere but at the same height from the ground. Otherwise they have to be altered considerably when they reach their destination.

Certain flowers and branches are more suitable than others for this type of arrangement, depending, of course, on the container you have selected. (One ought to try out the vase in position first.)

A small amount of material will show off well in a tall, narrow necked vase like a decanter or an attractively shaped bottle, and a few flowers arranged in an attractive piece of old porcelain can be placed in a prominent position.

A certain type of mantelpiece may call for a central arrangement, whilst another one may cry out for the flowers to be placed at one end. Whatever is decided it is usually better to have a simple vase of flowers than an over elaborate concoction. From this sort of position a group may easily seem top heavy or over decorative.

Top right, The lithograph by Barnett Freedman and the sculptured group of dancers in bronze dictate the colour scheme of this mantlepiece arrangement. The deep toned berberis picks up the colour of the bronze and the blue-grey carnation foliage and hydrangeas emphasise the lithograph colourings. The creamy-white of the snowberries links up with the colourings of the shell.

Right, The type of container used for a flower arrangement is of special importance for a mantelpiece arrangement. In this group a cornucopia gives the required spreading effect and fits in with the white wood of the mantelpiece and with the porcelain candlestick holder. The whole arrangement stands out clearly against the dark wallpaper.

194

Mirrors
for flower
arrangement

A round wall mirror if simple in outline
can make an attractive base for
a table arrangement. In this group
the structure of the spurge leaves is
reflected giving double interest
to the arrangement. The means of
anchorage is concealed by stones.

The use of mirrors might appear almost to be too obvious to need mentioning. But it is not as easy as it looks to make good use of them. They can, in fact, be a snare and a delusion if certain points are not considered carefully. If, for instance, the arrangement is too big and solid, with too much material in it there will be no reflection and the mirror will be very little help, then the flowers might just as well stand against a plain wall. It is only when the flowers are arranged as separately as possible, with plenty of space between each flower, that the mirror really multiplies. I once did decorations for a large room which contained two fireplaces immediately opposite to each other. Over these were two enormous mirrors. If I was successful with the flowers their reflections could be seen across the room in each of the mirrors there, then reflected each other again and again, so that one got the effect of a hall of mirrors filled with flowers. But it was very easy to muddle this effect, and it took a good deal of extra thought to make it work out as I intended. The final effect should be such that it is difficult to tell which flowers are actually in the vase and which are reflected in the mirror. When this happens a mirror is not only an added attraction to the flower but it also becomes a real economy measure.

The position of the mirror will dictate the type and shape of arrangement. For example, if the mirror is over a mantelpiece (as so often happens in Georgian fireplaces) the flowers should be selected, remembering that not only the flowers but much of the room will also be seen through the mirror. The object lesson is to be careful not to block out too much of this reflection with the arrangement. If the mirror is a small one over a wall bracket there will probably not be quite the same amount of reflection and it is only the arrangement which will be reflected. In these two cases a line arrangement is almost certainly indicated.

It is essential when arranging flowers in front of a mirror to do them in the position where they will eventually stand, since one can only tell after each flower is put into the vase how the reflection is going to show up. I imagine that it might be quite impossible to get the required effect if they had to be done elsewhere and then carried through. The same point applies even more when flowers are being arranged so that they stand on a piece of mirror for a table decoration, for one must remember the flowers which will be most reflected are those nearest to the brim of the vase or those hanging over it. The flowers at the top may not be seen in the reflection at all.

A piece of mirror used as a table decoration is invaluable, since it increases the feeling of size by the reflection it gives. Only quite a small strip down the centre of a dining table is needed and it is remarkably effective. It must be washed

and polished well, especially after the flowers have been standing on it for a day or two, as so many drop pollen etc. which shows up at once on the mirrored surface. But whatever trouble it takes to keep the mirror clean, it is worthwhile.

All containers to be used in front of mirrors need careful selection, but even more so those which stand on a piece of mirror. This must be realised, because if the dimensions of the container are not reasonably narrow, little will be seen of the flowers in reflection.

For instance, I have used with some success a white basket-work bowl for flowers. It is low and rather wide, and although I have found it most attractive for the usual flower requirements it was quite a different matter when I needed it to stand on a mirror. The width of the bowl obstructed the view of the flowers into the mirror, and almost all that was seen was the underside of the vase.

Again, if a container which is too tall is used the flowers will completely disappear from sight in the mirror reflection, and only an elongated view of the base of the container will be seen. Therefore, it is of the utmost importance to try out the vase beforehand, thus ensuring that the flowers get their share of 'double vision'.

Where a mirror is hanging on a landing or in a hall it is better not to have too tall a flower arrangement, so that the mirror can reflect the material. In the group in the photograph just the tops of the flowers are seen in reflection.

A large mirror is useful for reflecting an arrangement—
and if it is opposite another it will reflect
the arrangement even more. It is important not to stand
the flowers too near the mirror as a great deal of
the material will be lost. Reflection is the best
method of doubling the number of flowers and leaves.

Right, A mixed group of late summer flowers is arranged
in a white vase placed in front of a small gilt mirror.
The height of the group is kept low towards the centre;
the taller delphinium spikes are arranged towards the
sides so that they can be reflected
and emphasised in the mirror.

There are certain flowers which are more suitable than others for this tricky business of reflection, and the majority of these I have found from experience are the more simple uncomplicated shapes.

First of all there are the single flowers, rather than clusters, like some of the better shaped roses, lilies, ranunculus, carnations and gladioli. Although the gladioli strictly speaking does not come into the category of single flowers, the spikes are well covered with colour once most of the flowers are out and they do have a distinctive shape. This mention of shape brings to mind some of the flowering shrubs like forsythia and Chilean gum box *(Escallonia),* but these must be used with restraint so that the outline is clearly seen and the flowers are given a chance to appear at their best advantage. I remember one dramatic arrangement which was reasonably successful and

consisted of two or three bird of paradise flowers *(Strelitzia).* Perhaps this was due more to their shape than to their colour.

Another arrangement had an outline composed of large green arum leaves which were arranged with a few clivia. But the best of all I think was one which consisted of large white marguerites which seemed to take kindly to being reflected.

Where mirrors are concerned–as at any other time – interesting shapes in foliage are most helpful in getting a good outline. Iris leaves, bergenia, horse chestnut, *Magnolia grandiflora* and rhododendron (these last two must be carefully trimmed to remove overlapping leaves which would give a muddled effect) are invaluable.

The guiding principle, when arranging flowers in front of mirrors, should be to use much less material than would ordinarily seem to be necessary.

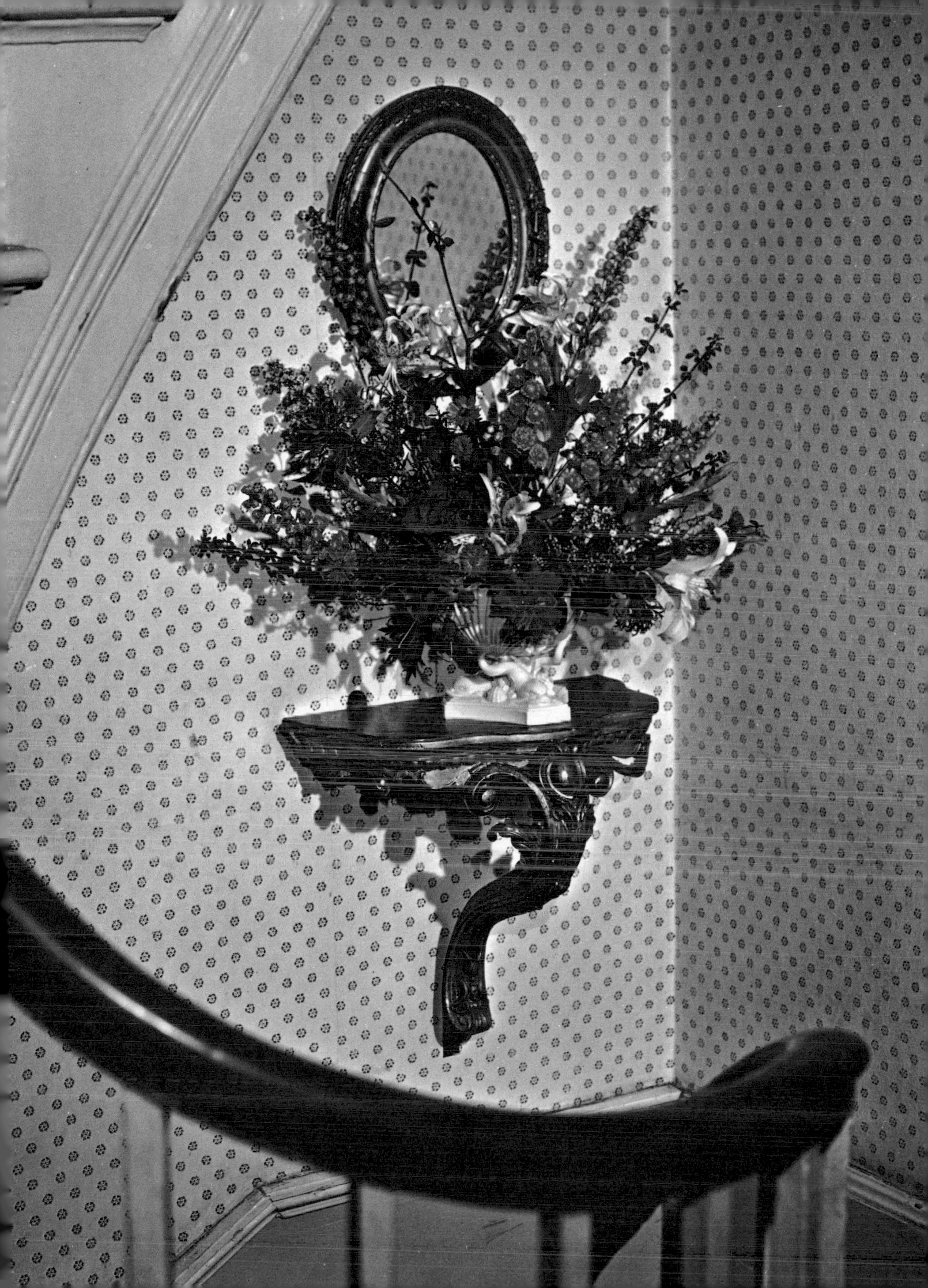

Top, The bright clear orange of marigolds is sometimes a rather harsh colour on its own; in this arrangement it is softened by using the yellow type of marigolds as well.

Left, One of the most attractive marigolds (tagetes) is the French marigold with its orange, red and brown colouring. It can produce a startling splash of colour even in a small arrangement. In this group the leaves and buds are just as important as the flowers as they provide a contrast of shape and colour.

Far right, In this group the tawny orange Henrii lily is arranged with its own glossy dark green foliage. This arrangement stands well on its own, but is also suitable for use with certain shades of blue.

Orange arrangements

Orange flowers are often difficult to deal with in furnishings or interior decorating schemes because they present problems of colour, shade and tone. Marigolds and nasturtiums are obvious examples and although these are excellent flowers in their own way, they are sometimes unsympathetic in colour when asked to co-operate with softer tones, especially when used in quantity. But a few marigolds combined with either pale yellow daisies from the border, the creamy white of meadow-sweet from a country hedgerow, a few pale lemon zinnias or creamy white sweet peas, will become so much softer in tone while still retaining the brightness of their original colour.

There are other flowers which come to mind that are orange – a deep burnt colour or yellow streaked with orange, which are magnificent when arranged alone or can act as a good contrast with other colours, especially with certain shades of blue.

Herb lilies *(Alstroemeria)* are one of the prettiest orange hued flowers, as indeed are montbretias. Herb lilies are now grown in a great variety of colours. The older *Alstroemeria aurantiaca* is the original flower grown in many gardens and considered almost as a weed because of its spreading habit of growth. This is a true orange, although looking closely into each individual flower many other tones of yellow, brown and a tawny gold will be seen.

Montbretias are charming in shape and usually a good deep red orange in colour. They last well (as the lower flowers die they may be taken off the stem and the smaller buds will eventually come out) and the iris shaped leaves are a good contrast with the lightness of the flowers.

There are some bright orange roses and of these Talisman is perhaps one of the best and certainly the one most often available at the florist. Not in itself orange, though giving this effect from a distance is Masquerade (in fact, the Baby Masquerade – a small edition – is pink). Grandmère Jenny is almost a peach orange and Alison Wheatcroft is nearer a deep apricot. Shot Silk is orange in bud but opens out showing almost as much yellow as Masquerade.

Perhaps lilies provide the greatest selection of

orange flowers and of these *Lilium henryi* is one of the hardiest to grow. In the wild state in its native China it reaches a height of about three feet but cultivated and growing in gardens it has been known to reach a height of eight feet with as many as seventy flowers on one stem. *Lilium henryi* is a tawny orange and flowers later than most, coming at a time when flowers for tall arrangements are not easy to find. *Lilium davidii* has recurved Turk's cap flowers in bright orange, also on a tall stem which may need some support. Enchantment is another well known lily with a colouring described as a hot nasturtium red and in a similar vein there is another called fire-flame. Among the deep orange golds, is Croesus, a good garden lily and Paprika, although a much shorter stemmed lily, has fine flowers of a burnt cinnamon colour.

Some of the Dutch honeysuckles have a tawny, orange colouring, streaked with yellow, and in fox-tail lilies *(Eremurus)* there are some good orange and apricot colourings. Snapdragons, too, have amongst their many shades a bright orange

Herb lilies *(alstroemerias)* in their original tawny orange and gold colouring arranged in a brown early glass decanter. These are valuable flowers for cutting and can be grown easily in the garden—they are even sometimes difficult to keep in check.

scarlet flower, whilst Iceland poppies produce a clear colour rather like the skin of a tangerine.

Now we come to two slightly more complicated orange flowers – complicated from the point of view of hardiness in the garden. The first of these is one of the loveliest clear, deep-orange flowers, bordering on scarlet – *Euphorbia fulgens* (one of the spurges) and the other is the clivia that comes from South Africa, with bright orange flowers. In England both these plants are only half hardy but in many other countries they may be grown out-of-doors. The clivia is one of the most long lasting plants for cutting; it sometimes has green tipped orange flowers, yellowish towards the centre. The flowers are in an umbel at the head of a long stalk rather similar to the African lily *(Agapanthus)*; and the tight buds towards the centre of the cluster will eventually come out in water.

There are also deep orange zinnias, closely resembling a marigold but with deeper tones towards the centre. Branches of the orange ball tree *(Buddleia globosa)* will also serve to introduce a note of orange into a large arrangement. At the other end of the scale, for small groups, are the charming small flowered French marigolds, *(Tagetes patula)*. They come in a clear orange yellow and make a good colour scheme with some of the light lobelias.

When considering the possibilities of orange as a contrast with blue it is important, I think, to try not to have a purple blue unless the orange colour is a true one. For instance, the original *Alstroemeria aurantiaca* is quite good with dark delphiniums or monkshood but not with the light delphiniums, they need more of a yellow orange to counteract the almost green shade in their blue. The rather purple-blue of bellflowers *(Campanula lactiflora)* will go well with the tawny orange of *L. henryi* and their respective heights would be most suitable for tall arrangements. It is a question of seeing the colours together and then deciding whether the contrast is right or not.

A touch of bright orange in a yellow group can be interesting and, the bright orange colour of nasturtiums and some dahlias can be the highlight of an autumn group consisting of dark brown, yellow, white and grey.

As with variegated foliage, remember a small amount of a clear orange goes a long way when it is introduced with other softer tones.

One of the most exciting plants for drying if used in small quantities are Chinese lanterns *(Physalis alkekengii)*. It has been grown for hundreds of years (in the great *Juliana Anicia Codex of Dioscorides* now in the Vienna Library, there is an illustration of it) and used to be sown in gardens then, much more than they are today. Perhaps this is because of the rather crude orange of the

A few Talisman roses arranged with eucalyptus sprays in a white porcelain vase decorated with an orange and gold motif; the orange motif links up with the orange of the roses.

dried bunches one sometimes sees hanging up for sale. But its true beauty comes before it loses its foliage and before all the lanterns have completely turned, that is while they are still varying in colour through mellow shades of green, pale lemon, yellow and orange. In this state the Chinese lanterns is a most decorative plant and at the time of the year when it reaches this stage of its development any of these tones are useful. When all the lanterns have turned to their eventual deep orange, and the plant is denuded of its pretty fresh green leaves, it is not nearly so attractive and the hardness of this overall colouring makes it more difficult to incorporate with other colour schemes.

Chinese lanterns, while still fresh and growing, have often proved useful to introduce a little bright orange as well as softer tones of lemon, and perhaps best of all, a pale lime green (before the younger lanterns have even begun to turn at all) into a group of autumn colourings. For dried arrangements they are invaluable. Added to a group of chocolate brown dock seedheads, globe artichokes, (which have turned so brown that they look as if composed of wood), nipplewort, teasels, etc., a few yellow and orange immortelle and the tall stems of orange Chinese lanterns will lighten up the arrangement in a most satisfactory way. I have also used them with dried blue delphiniums, alliums, reed-mace, sweetcorn seedheads, silver honesty and white pearly everlasting.

Here a group of peonies are arranged against a background of their own leaves in a porcelain basket.
Peony foliage is particularly beautiful and in the autumn takes on shades of wine, copper, deep purple and bronze.
For arrangements, it is better to cut peonies fairly short as they are rather heavy flowers.

Peonies

To make a list of favourite flowers would be difficult indeed. W.H. Davies in his poem *Flowers* expresses the dilemma more than adequately:
'What favourite flowers are mine, I cannot say –
My fancy changes with the summer's day . . . .' a few lines later he goes on to say:
'Sometimes I think the rose must have her place –
And then the lily shakes her golden dice . . . . '

Certainly, when they put in their first appearance during May I think that the peony would be near the head of my list, with roses winning by a short head. Among the peonies my first favourite would surely be the well known dark red, despite all the wonderful new introductions from China and elsewhere. As Peter Hunt says, in his book *Perennial Flowers for Small Gardens*, ' . . . there is nothing quite like the old cottage-garden peonies, the great double varieties of *P. officinalis* with their heavily fragrant flowers'.

But what about peonies for flower arrangement? Could anything be more valuable to introduce a solid touch of colour into a large group, or more charming to use alone, allowing the full beauty of the simple flower to be fully seen? Perhaps the only other flower which comes fairly close to the peony in the first of these requirements is either the rhododendron or the hydrangea, but yet neither of these have the same depth and quality of colouring. Going on to the second, I have found one peony arranged either with its own foliage or with short sprays of a suitably toned flowering shrub can be quite enough for one arrangement.

These are occasions when peonies, especially the much loved red cottage garden ones, seem top heavy on their stems. This is because the weight of the heavy flower head on the comparatively slight stem causes the flower to hang forward and give the impression of drooping. In such a case I have found it is best to cut the stem fairly short, though not too short (if too short the flower just falls forward and out of the vase altogether) and to make sure that the flower is well supported by other material in the arrangement.

One of the greatest charms of peonies, apart from lovely flowers, is their magnificent foliage. Of a most original shape, it is usually finely coloured, sometimes dark wine with a damson bloom, sometimes grey-green with mahogany coloured veins, and sometimes dark blue green veined and edged with a lighter green. In the autumn, before the leaves finally fall off, these colours become intensified.

The position of peonies in the garden is of some importance and should be studied carefully. They are excellent plants for semi shade and are usually happy if situated where the sun can get through light overhead foliage, such as that provided by cherry or almond trees. They seem to flourish on the borders of a shrubbery or even in open woodland. Miss Jekyll grew them together with Lenten roses as both plants like the same kind of feeding – a rich moist soil, supplemented in the spring and autumn with a good mulching of leaf mould.

It is sometimes suggested that peonies once planted in position in a garden do not like being moved. But this is not always so if great care is taken when the plant is dug up and re-planted. A friend told me of having to move from one house to another and of her unhappiness at the thought of having to leave a favourite peony behind. (She had been brought up on the theory that they must on no account be moved.) At last, and with the greatest care, taking much of its surrounding soil, she dug up the peony. On arrival at the new garden it was immediately planted in its already prepared situation. The peony has not only survived the move but has flowered luxuriantly ever since.

The following short list gives a variety of types and colourings; most are listed in catalogues of well known nurserymen who deal in peonies:

Sarah Bernhardt – a soft apple blossom pink which looks almost as if it is tipped with silver, large frilled flowers.
Duchess de Nemours – a splendid white, sweetly scented, a very free flowering plant.
Karl Rosenfeld – a bright but deep red (one can imagine this colour being especially useful for a mixed group), crinkly petals and full, open flowers.
Reine Hortense – this is a large, compact pale pink flower flushed with a deeper pink.
Madame Calot – a soft, pale pink, shading almost to cream. A good formation in the flower.
All these peonies are hardy herbaceous plants flowering usually in late May and June. Tree peonies come out earlier in May, and are the first to flower and grow into sizeable shrubs. They like a well drained soil, dislike cow manure and in the autumn prefer matured leafmould.

Here are a few recommended for planting:
Yachiyo-Taubaki–(which in Japanese means long hedge of camellias is a very lovely bright pink with foliage of a deep bronze colouring. It is free flowering and lasts exceedingly well when cut.
Alice Harding (Kinko)–a good yellow tree peony.
Tama-Midori (known as green jade)–one of the finest of the tree peonies in what is described as a 'brilliant scarlet.' Free flowering with good foliage. Here are a few suggestions for using peonies with other flowers:
The dark red cottage-garden peonies, mixed with honesty seed pods – the pods must be at the green stage, i.e. before they dry off (they are still moist now and will need water). The red is a good foil for the deep green colouring of the honesty.

The same red peonies with dark blue delphiniums and white marguerites, for a large arrangement. For a group in varying shades of pink, a few pink peonies like Reine Hortense and Madame Calot with pink larkspur (the palest pink and the raspberry pink), pink valerian, some of the earliest of the Dr. Van Fleet roses, silver grey foliage – either garden ragwort, immortelle or Artemesia ludoviciana (lad's love or southernwood) – and pink foxgloves. In a dark green and white group comprised of white peonies, perhaps Duchess de Nemours, with white larkspur, white campanulas, peony foliage, camellia foliage, and large hosta and bergenia leaves, with masterwort (Astrantia). In a pink and white arrangement made up of (Philadelphus), a soft pink peony, perhaps Sarah Bernhardt, white campanulas, both soft pink and white larkspur, white delphiniums and a few magenta roses to add a deep touch of colour.
The double pink cottage peony, flowering in May, with pink Canterbury bells, pink tulips and early flowering pale pink false goat's beard (Astilbe) and a background of copper coloured prunus gives an arrangement in soft pinks.

Apart from the usual dark red peonies there are now many other varieties available.
Here a few of the less rare ones are arranged towards the centre of a large group of lilac
columbines and sweet rocket and provide the focal point of the whole arrangement.

Two peonies included in a mixed bunch of garden flowers.
Their size and colouring provide the most important point of interest in the whole group.

208

What have flower paintings in common with flower arrangements? In both cases it takes someone who really appreciates the use of line and colour to produce a work of art, and since no art is completely divorced from the other arts, one may help us to appreciate the other more.

Religious paintings of the thirteenth and fourteenth centuries (at this time art was often connected with the church) depicted Madonna lilies arranged either in a vase or held in the hand (if carnations were shown instead of lilies, they could well have represented a protection against disease, for the juice of the carnation was supposed to be a specific against plague.)

Sometimes a group is shown, perhaps cut from the garden with a specimen of each flower that is out at the time. In the painting by Gerard David (1460–1523), of the *Virgin and Child*, the small group consists of one dark blue iris, a spray of blue columbine, a stem of sweet rocket with two or three other small flowers difficult to identify. A charming still life by Baugin, about 1630, depicts the five senses, one of these, smell, is represented by three red carnations in a simple glass bottle. During the fifteenth and sixteenth centuries Flemish artists painted still lifes of extraordinary beauty, and these lead on to the Dutch flower paintings of the sixteenth, seventeenth, and early eighteenth centuries. There is a well known story about flowers in these times. Flowers were rare and expensive to buy, and a poor Dutch woman asked Jan Brueghel (1568-1625) to paint some flowers for her. She could afford to have them painted, owing to the low value of artists' work, but she could not afford to buy them. This story may suggest a reason for the flower paintings of the Dutch schools.

These Dutch flower paintings have obviously been constructed bit by bit as the various flowers came out into season, (this is illustrated by the more obvious instances of tulips, narcissi, apple blossom and birds' nests arranged and painted with grapes, morning glory, and ripe peaches).

One of the greatest of all still life painters, Jean-Baptiste-Simeon-Chardin, (1699-1779), showed in a painting of tuber roses and carnations quite a different approach from the Dutch school which preceded him. This is a simple painting, almost unadorned, of a small cluster of flowers in a single blue and white vase. This particular flower arrangement is a natural one, the flowers have been appreciated for themselves, observed closely and then carefully selected. "There is no seeking after purely decorative effects, no superfluous accessories round the base of the vase... It stands there simply and it is, at last, an example of a vase of flowers which we might place in our own rooms today though it was painted more than a hundred and fifty years ago." THE FLOWER-PIECE IN PAINTING, H. van Guldener.

Paintings of flower arrangements

Top left, 'Fleurs dans un vase vert painted about 1910 by Redon. It was at this time that Redon's wife inherited a beautiful country house with a large garden near Paris. 'In my new home I enjoy so much felicity that I must abstain from telling you about it: the subject is inexhaustible'. The still life of this painting is supposed to have been painted from flowers in this garden.

Left, Fantin-Latour must surely be one of the greatest flower painters of all time. This picture 'Trois roses dans un verre' was painted 1873 at the time when Monet and his friends were preparing their first impressionist exhibition in Paris.

Far left, August still life by James Fosburgh painted in 1954. James Fosburgh is also an art historian and a former lecturer at the Frick Collection in New York. He 'shows sensitivity in his work, a love of nature and endeavours to strike a balance between tradition and a new visual experience'.

The Chardin painting was an important milestone not only in itself but because it paved the way for further developments – Edouard Manet (1832-83) influenced by Chardin, loved especially the richness of red peonies as is shown by his painting in the Louvre of red and pink peonies with their pointed leaves. Fantin-Latour (1836-1904), who is perhaps best known for his paintings of roses, especially the basket of white, yellow, pale pink and deep red ones in the National Gallery, London. (Fantin-Latour roses in paintings are as characteristic as the Billingsley rose in porcelain.) Following on came the flower paintings of Renoir, Cezanne, Henri Rousseau le Douanier, Van Gogh, and Gauguin. Then moving into contemporary paintings, the work of Picasso, Matisse, Georges

A group of herbaceous flowers painted
by Henri Fantin-Latour (1836–1904).
The group includes plenty of foliage
which shows up the white of the phlox
and the other colours in the group.

A group of flowers in a painting by Bonnard (1807–1947) comprising part of a domestic scene. The flowers are of equal importance with the homely brown teapot, cups and saucers on the breakfast table.

Braque and Marc Chagall. James Fosburgh (born 1910) puts a bunch of wild flowers into an earthenware jar and stands it on the edge of a cottage type chair. It is simple, unaffected, and brings to mind the 'Fleurs dans un vase vert' by Odilon Redon (1840–1916). This represents a bunch cut from the garden of his country home near Paris. He was very happy there. 'In my new home', he wrote to friends, 'I enjoy so much felicity that I must abstain from telling you about it; the subject is inexhaustible'. The peace and happiness in that garden comes out in his flower painting.

Now the flowers are presented as an entity. They complete the picture, with very little need of supplementary decoration.

Any number of beautiful, exciting and unusual colour contrasts and harmonies are suggested by paintings. In *Fenetre Ouverte Collioure* by Matisse there are bright blues, greens, yellow and reds. This painting opens up channels of ideas for contrasting or combining these colours – ideas which one might otherwise not have discovered. One's mind immediately produces a picture of blue love-in-a-mist, the Himalayan poppy, and delphiniums, with bright red geraniums and clear yellow daisies, and leaves of different greens, perhaps hosta, fennel, hydrangea, and hollyhock foliage.

Van Gogh's *Ripe Sunflowers*, whilst at first sight seems to be purely in blues, and yellows, is found on close inspection to have deep van Dyck brown shadows enriched by streaks of dark red and purple in the background.

The first impression of the well known Cezanne *Tulips and Apples* is red and green with small touches of yellow and white; it is only at close quarters that one can see the deep mauve and pink shadows on the white petals of the narcissus flowers and rich aubergine in the green tulip leaves.

In this arrangement of carnations, stocks,
lilies-of-the-valley and short sprays of broom
the candles give the group a party air.
The material and candles are fixed firmly into wire netting.

Right, Long branches cut from a climbing rose are ideal
for inclusion in a party flower arrangement.
The branches in this group were cut from a Chaplin's Pink.

Party flowers

'Special occasions' occur in everyone's life sooner
or later. It may be a celebration for two people,
an engagement, a wedding anniversary or a gather-
ing such as a party or a wedding reception at home.

Some of them may be accompanied by specially
composed music, many of them may depend on
ceremonial dress and procedure, but almost all of
them demand decorations with flowers. Flowers
can adapt themselves to any mood and any occasion. They can express the spontaneity of light
hearted celebration just as well as the dignity of
solemn ritual. This has been demonstrated by
the use of wreaths and garlands from the time of
the Ancient Greeks, long before flowers came to
be arranged in vases.

However, different approaches are necessary
when arranging flowers to be seen by a number of
people rather than a few, and when decorating a
large room rather than a small one. The finished
product always looks quite simple and it is only
when doing the actual work that one comes across
the difficulties. These may not be involved but
rather unexpected. The first point to consider
is the position of the flowers. You are probably
used to having a vase in a certain place in the room
or hall, but that particular place may not be suitable
now. What might show up well with just your
family about will not be seen at all amongst a lot
of people. For example a group in a fireplace
(which can look most attractive in the summer

212

Top, A typical collection
of roses from a garden
including Paul's Scarlet,
Ophelia, Albertine and
Zéphirine Drouhin.
For a group for a buffet table
it is helpful to arrange
the flowers with sprays
of their foliage, in
a pedestal dish so that they
can be seen above the food.

Left, An ideal party flower
for the house is the rose;
in the arrangement
in the photograph
Queen Elizabeth roses
are used which are in flower
from the middle of June
until early November;
they grow to a good height
and their dark green foliage
provides a good background.

Right, Tulips may be
included in an early summer
arrangement for a party.
In this group
pale pink, soft petal pink
and deeper rose pink tulips
tone in with viburnum
sprays, pale pink astilbes
and sprays of
Japanese quince (*chaenomeles*)
with its off white and
deep pink buds and flowers.
Curving branches of
Spiraea arguta are
included to counteract
the heaviness of
the other material.

This silver rose bowl on its black pedestal is an excellent container for party flowers, as it shows the flowers off so that they stand out well. The arrangement consists of larkspur, in various shades of pink, palest pink border carnations and deep rose hydrangeas.

Right, This is an arrangement of flowers chosen by Anna Neagle to celebrate her wedding anniversary. The white gardenias and violets are fixed in moss and wire netting in the bowl of the dish. The lilies-of-the-valley are at their full height to give a contrast and to show off the pale green of their leaves.

Far Right, A collection of wild flowers including hedge parsley, privet, grasses, jack-by-the-hedge and wild elder is given a party look by the addition of a few roses. The rose in the centre of the group is the shell rose 'Madam Pierre Oger', a pale cream pink flower flushed with a deeper pink.

months) may be less effective in a small room with many people, although if it were to be in the same room but without the people this would not be the case. In effect the maximum impact one needs to have is such an arrangement in a large room with plenty of space.

Obviously the best position for flowers is on a piece of furniture or a mantelpiece, or on a wall bracket. This will ensure not only the minimum risk of their being knocked over, but also the maximum opportunity of their being seen. Pedestals are useful, but they must be sturdy and secure and most definitely out of the way. Perhaps a good plan is to go round the house with a note book and pencil, imagining the rooms you are going to use filled with standing people (the occasions when there is a chance to sit down are unfortunately rare) and to notice where an arrangement of flowers would look most effective. After you have made your list, then work out how many containers you will need and of what size and shape.

Even though one may use one or two big arrangements, remember that something small in the right position can be equally effective. Large quantities of material are not a necessity as in some cases just a few flowers of the right colour are better than a large mixed group as long as the vase is in a key position.

The second point is that before beginning a large arrangement which is to stand against a flat background, the vase must always be weighted down in some way. The method does not matter very much, as long as it is successful and does not

show. (The smaller weights from the scales are quite good.) If large mesh wire netting is used it should be held firmly in position, either anchored down by string, tied round the sides of the container, (which can be cut away afterwards), or by wire, especially if the container has a rim or convenient handles through which it can be knotted and twisted round. To provide extra security sand can be poured into the bottom of the vase, or a small bottle of lead shot can be hooked inside on to the wire netting. Any small bottle will do, as long as it has a top. Ultimately the best means of weighing down a large container is the water inside.

The third point is the relationship between arrangements and their surroundings. Fitting in with the furnishings is vitally important. This applies particularly if the 'occasion' is to be held in a house belonging to a friend or relative.

At one reception where I worked it was almost impossible to arrange the flowers. The walls were covered from floor to ceiling with prints of all shapes and sizes and the furniture, (where one could have reasonably hoped for a clear surface), was also covered by porcelain and books. Unfortunately, the house was being lent, so it was impossible to take down some of the prints or remove any of the porcelain. Oh for a piece of blank wall!

Perhaps the celebration may take place in a very different background. Perhaps your home is a modern flat with contemporary furnishings, plenty of space and no cluttering up. You may use a small arrangement composed of very little material, well lit, and this you feel fits in perfectly.

My fourth point is the choice of flowers. If you want to be exotic without too much expense, have a collection of garden flowers and add two or three lilies and soft toned carnations, or have a collection of wild flowers and add two or three garden roses: Ophelia is a beauty and blends in well with the simplicity and soft colourings of grasses and hedgerow flowers.

Branches of laburnum, arranged in a tall narrow necked decanter to lend support to the stems, give a wonderful touch of yellow (a particularly clear yellow which is almost unobtainable in any other flower). One is often told that laburnum does not last, and so is not worth bothering about, but my own experience has been to the contrary, I have found it quite reliable if it is cut when still in bud and at a cool time of the day. Of course the woody stems should then be smashed and given a good drink.

Marguerites are a well known standby. Their lasting powers are astonishing: they seem almost to go on for ever. But what a beautiful flower this is, and how we do take it for granted! Its yellow centres surrounded by the pure white petals seen against a dark green background of foliage, provide a worthwhile lesson in contrast. Being sturdy flowers marguerites can stand up to draught and are suitable for arrangements in the hall or on a landing.

Country flowers can be most attractive. Everyone who knows the West Country has seen masses of pink, red and white valerian growing out of stone walls or cascading down grassy banks. One of the colours is bound to fit in, so use it with your colour scheme. Valerian is slightly deceptive, in that it takes quite a lot of it to fill a vase of any size. But since it usually grows in profusion, this is not a difficulty. I have already extolled the virtues of Queen Anne's lace and here would like to suggest that it be arranged with the flower of the white dead nettle. This flower is so modestly hidden beneath the rather heavy leaves that until some of these are cut off it is really not visible. Both the nettles and the hedge parsley drink quantities of water, so you should watch the water carefully and make sure it is kept well topped up.

Foxgloves and ferns have such dignity and such beautiful flowing lines that they almost arrange themselves. If the pinky-mauve foxgloves are not suitable for your colour scheme, try the white. Sometimes, later on in the summer, one finds a tall foxglove with four or five smaller flowers much lower down the stem. If these are cut off and used separately they will tuck in nicely towards the centre of the group. And don't forget to use the leaves.

Branches of pink and white Chilean gum box (*Escallonia*) give a good effect, curving naturally in an arrangement as they do on the shrub. (*E. exoniensis* is a good example.) All of the escallonias have charming small flowers and they are ideal for a pedestal vase.

These are only a few ideas for using simple flowers which can be obtained easily. One additional suggestion which I should like to make is for the use of pinks. Their scent is so reminiscent of an English summer garden, and they come in an extensive variety of colours suitable for any colour scheme.

Equipment needed for an 'occasion' is very much the same as you would normally use, though perhaps a few extra buckets would not be amiss. This way all your material can have a good drink beforehand. One or two more dust sheets are a good idea.

Having dealt with the more practical aspects of this section, I should now like to give certain bits of information which have interested me and which I hope you will find equally interesting.

Certain flowers have a special significance for certain occasions, and many of these associations are based on customs and legends, some of them hundreds of years old.

The lily is perhaps the flower that comes to mind first in this context of grand occasions; this may be because of its early connections with the Church and its appearance in many of the paintings of the Angel of the Annunciation. The lily pictured is often identical with the Madonna lily of our cottage gardens.

Mock orange (*Philadelphus*) and myrtle are flowers connected with weddings. The custom of wearing orange blossom is thought to have originated in the east with the Saracens, and since the Crusades, European brides have worn wreaths of orange blossom. Certainly, in this century, the sight and scent of *P. coronarius* immediately suggests a wedding. It is still considered lucky to have a sprig of myrtle in the bride's bouquet and this may have been derived from Jewish brides who wore myrtle wreaths during the days of the Babylonian captivity. In most Mediterranean countries myrtle is worn at a wedding and it has always been associated by legend with the Goddess of Love.

Roses, carnations, and orchids are flowers also associated with 'grand occasions'. Roses of any colour seem to give a feeling of celebration and often of sentiment, and carnations and orchids, perhaps because of their long lasting qualities as well as their charm, are especially useful for decorations which may have to be prepared ahead of time and at the critical moment still look fresh and beautiful.

The Victorians and Edwardians certainly used orchids and carnations to a vast extent in bouquets. A large bouquet made for Queen Alexandra was composed entirely of orchids in tones of lilac

Sometimes the container can give an indication of a party almost as much as the flowers. In this group,
the basket designed to hold a bottle of wine, immediately suggests a festive occasion.
A few sprays of white snowberry and button chrysanthemums with two or three carnations
and a stem of scarlet nerine lily are arranged with branches of rosemary.

and pink with sprays of maidenhair fern tied with lilac satin ribbon. There is a record of this as well as of another one made of red and white Marmion carnations tied with white ribbon for the Empress of Russia.

Roses on their own were used for decoration in 1906 at the Great International Horse Show at Olympia. The Royal Box was decorated with trellis work featuring intertwined pink and red roses. Nearer our time, the bridesmaids at the wedding of the Duke and Duchess of Gloucester carried bouquets of the 'palest of flesh-pink/creamy roses'.

At the turn of the century the foliage used for 'grand occasions' was limited, compared with what one sees today. It was then the hey-day of the potted palm tree for platforms and churches, and large quantities of maidenhair and asparagus ferns for bouquets.

Hardly an occasion went by without its attendant palms and bamboos (these were said to give height, and what is described as 'backbone' to the floral decorations.) In *British Floral Decoration* by Mr.

R.F. Felton, published in 1910, there is a photograph of the church decorations for a wedding at St. Margaret's, Westminster. The flowers are arranged to look as though they were growing out of palm and bamboo groves and interspersed with fronds of fern. One can well imagine the overall effect must have been in great contrast to a more present day arrangement which Mrs. Constance Spry executed in the same church many years later, then the whole decoration was composed of Queen Anne's lace. Today lilies, carnations and roses often form the central point of a group composed of country flowers or even vegetable seedheads. Queen Anne's pace is mixed with arum lilies, to give a lighter touch, and leek flower heads used to make a stately foil for fox-tail lilies *(Eremurus)*; roses, even simple climbers like Chaplins Pink climber rise beautifully to 'grand occasions'.

At last our appreciation of more humble flowers is showing itself, and we are learning to make the most of such material together with an equal regard for various kinds of foliage.

Red arrangements

In this group bright scarlet gladioli are cut short, removed from the main stem and arranged in a white dish.
The clear colouring of the gladioli is emphasised by the addition of a few silver-grey sprays of *Senecio cineraria*.
This type of arrangement would be suitable for a table arrangement, particularly at Christmas time.

Red in itself is a difficult colour to define. There are, after all, so many different shades of red–crimson, scarlet, rose, pink, etc. Miss Jekyll describes red and pink in this way: 'It is very easy to say pink, but pink covers a wide range, from warm ash colour to pale salmon red, and from the tint of a new born mushroom to that of an ancient brick. One might prepare a range of at least thirty tints, and this number could easily be multiplied, all of which might be called pink; with regard to some room, or object, or flower of any one kind of red, only a few of these will be in friendly accordance, a good number will be in deadly discord, and the remainder more or less out of relation'.

Some people say with certainty that they require a flower decoration in 'pillar-box red'. This remark is not as simple as it sounds, for no two people see colour alike. To some 'pillar-box red' may be a red brown and to others a cerise red. Therefore when one is asked to do an arrangement in 'pink' flowers it is only too easy to feel a certain sense of confusion as to exactly which 'pink' is wanted.

On the other hand, colours need not always be in the same range, one can have a great deal of 'clashing' colours on purpose. Introducing, for instance, Frensham roses into a group of salmon-orange begonias, pink-red geraniums, (Pelargonium), crimson gerberas and a Zéphirine Drouhin rose–that would almost take one's breath away. Occasionally, and for a short period of time only, such effects can be startling and dramatic.

If one is thinking in terms of red, pink or crimson flowers, roses and carnations seem to be the obvious choice. There are so many of them from which to make a selection–try turning over the pages of a rose book or carnation catalogue. I am now going to mention a few specific roses: Anne Poulsen, a good clear red; Garnet, a deep, dark red, very long lasting; Carol, the same small type in a soft pink, also long lasting; Kathleen Ferrier, a bright cerise pink; Betty Uprichard, salmon pink; Queen Elizabeth, excellent for cutting, with strong, long stems and deep pink buds which open into paler pink flowers; Ophelia, one of the loveliest pale pink roses of all, with long stems for cutting; Frensham, a dark red; Dusky Maiden, dark wine red; Moulin Rouge, a flat red; Super Star, has a quality of dazzling brightness, rather garish; Magenta, a soft pink mauve, with full flowers and good foliage; Josephine Bruce, a frequently planted dark velvet red; Rosemary Rose, flat, full flowers, bright rose pink with deeper colouring towards the centre; Zéphirine Drouhin, bright cerise pink, wonderful colouring, reliable, long flowering period.

Apart from roses and carnations there are many other pink, red or crimson flowers–*Anemone*

fulgens, which is early flowering and comes in a good, clear bright colour. Gerberas excel in many shades of red, pink, salmon and rose. Geraniums, also, provide an infinite variety of colour in these shades. Some of the bergamots come in a soft pink as well as the old-fashioned ruby red so often seen in cottage-gardens. Camellias, rhododendrons and azaleas are all available in these colours, which range from deep wine through many shades of delightful rose and pink to, in the case of the azaleas, a soft, almost salmon pink.

Clematis are inclined to come in a mauve pink, one of the best known and most frequently grown is Comtesse de Bouchard, flowering from late June until either the end of October or the beginning of November. Barbara Dibley is a charming violet pink with deep carmine bars across the petals and Ville de Lyon – a carmine red with petals shading to deep crimson, and finally bright red. Ernest Markham, better known as 'the best of the red clematis', flowers from August to October.

Here dark red fuchsias are arranged in a white vase. The vase together with the clear background makes the red of the flowers seem even brighter.

Red ranunculus are arranged here with a few pale green
hellebore flowers on a green Wedgwood plate.
The red ranunculus is particularly good
for a Christmas group and could be arranged
with mistletoe or sprigs of holly.

None of these clematis are 'red' in the sense of the
'pillar-box red', but they do have pink, mauve
pink, a wine rose, or deep pink in their colouring.
(A few stems of clematis on a flat dish make, what
seems to me to be a perfect arrangement for a
dining table.)

Dahlias, geums, zinnias and snapdragons also
come in various shades of red and pink. The
zinnias in particular defy description, for their
colours are at once subtle, exotic and brilliant.

Another reliable red flower is the fair maids
of France *(Ranunculus aconitifolius)*. Its red
colour varies very little, and this makes it especially
useful at Christmas. Beard tongues *(Pariste-
mon)* also come in a good, deep red, and because
of their shape and colouring make a valuable
contrast with pale blue delphiniums. Both tulips
and poppies come in a great variety of reds and
pinks. Other valuable and charming additions,
though not 'reds', are the pink and white flowers of

Chilean gum box *(Escallonia)* and Japanese quince.

Tobacco plants *(Nicotinia)* and pansies come
in a definite wine red; then there are the pink
mauve border carnations and pinks. Herb lilies
provide many soft touches for they come in shades
of pink, mauve pink, cherry, dark rose and salmon
pink as well as the better known orange and deep
yellow. Then the startling, dramatic, clear red
of the red-hot pokers, and the sealing wax red of
certain stately gladioli. (Chrysanthemums produce soft tones of pale pink and an almost Chinese
pink, as well as mauve pinks and deep wine red,
coral and crimson.)

Two more shrubs with prolific pink flowers are
flowering currant (which can look most attractive
arranged in a blue and white jug) and hydrangeas
in various shades of pink, from a pale ballet pink
to a deep rose-pink. Phlox and fox-tail lilies also
come in shades of pink, the phlox in a deep raspberry red and the fox-tail lilies in a soft flesh pink.
Canterbury bells are charming in a clear pale pink
and heuchera provides a more coral colour. The
delicate pink and white flowers of London pride
are most attractive for small arrangements, and
the spreading but also delicate flowers of Bouncing
Bet *(Saponaria)* equally effective and useful.

I have left one of the best of all red or pink flowers
until the last – it is the peony. Apart from the
well known deep red, grown for many years in
older gardens, there are now available many rare
and exciting peonies, especially among the tree
variety. One of the most delicate is Sarah Bernhardt, a clear pink; Karl Rosenfeld, a good wine
red colour; and an especially charming rose pink
with quantities of yellow stamens is Gleam of
Light.

To complete this section on red arrangements,
one may mention that red is known as a cheerful
colour, ('Have something bright to cheer you' a
friend will say in a moment of disaster, and one
may well buy a red handbag, an umbrella, or even
go into the garden and cut some bright crimson
nerines or some Paul's Scarlet roses), and also
a warm colour and I feel that certain shades of
red can introduce a feeling of warmth to a north
facing room or to furnishings in a cool, soft colouring. But it is important to remember that a small
touch of red colouring goes a long way.

These bright red gladioli illustrate the colour in which this flower was probably first introduced. The grasses are soft in colour and form and help to reduce the stiffness of the gladioli.

Rock
plants

Top, This small group from the rock garden
includes sprays of *Convolvulus cneorum,* blue-green
clusters of rue, the feathery silver-white curry plant,
blue-grey branches of *Helichrysum splendidum,*
purple spikes of the dwarf *Lavandula stoechas*
and the green flowers of the tobacco plant.

Centre, Short sprays cut from the *Helleborus foetidus*
with its dark finger like leaves and from the grey foliaged
garden ragwort *(Senecio leucostachys)*
provide a background for the smaller flowers
in this compact basket arrangement. (These two plants
help to give the extra dimension to a rock garden.)

Here is a small collection of leaves and flowers
from a rock garden; the blue-grey rue foliage predominates
the group and forms a setting, with the silver-grey artemesia,
for the bright yellow achillea flower.
Sedum, artemesia and achillea are all deciduous,
but the rue will go on throughout the winter
and provide attractive cover for bare stems.
The plants are fixed on a pin holder
placed at one end of a baking dish which holds the water.

If one has only the smallest garden, or even no garden at all, it is often possible to grow what are commonly called rock plants either in a small raised bed or an old converted sink trough constructed between two rows of bricks.

Most rock plants speak for themselves–the very name indicates that here is a plant which likes conditions similar to those it would find if growing amongst rock, though this does not necessarily mean enormous boulders or mountainous crags. The ideal situation naturally would occur in areas of the English Lake District, where such gardens are often made out of a sloping hillside with protruding bits of grey rock emerging through the green grass. Here there can be little difficulty in growing rock plants. Suitable conditions do occur in other parts of England as well as in many other countries, especially Italy and the Dordogne region in the South of France.

Excellent examples of fabricated rock gardens (in neither instance were the natural constituents of a rock garden originally there) can be seen at Wisley and at Edinburgh in the Royal Botanic Gardens. They are two of the finest rock gardens in England. These are, of course, extreme cases, but the same principle can be applied on a much smaller scale by those with just an ordinary small garden, or as I have already mentioned, those with no garden at all.

The first condition that rock plants demand is good drainage. Many of them also like a sunny position, though this is not quite so essential. Good drainage can be obtained in small gardens where there may be no natural slope to utilise for this purpose, by raising an area of soil above the ordinary level. The soil, if it is raised up in this way, will probably need some support, and it can be provided by two or three layers of bricks built to surround the area. Large pieces of logs will also be adequate and look attractive, but they will have to be of some size to hold back the weight of soil. A certain number of stones or pieces of rock-like substance can, of course, be also included, but they are not really necessary – this particular side of rock gardening is often taken more seriously than something which I should say is far more important, namely, the quality and type of soil used.

Let us suppose that there is no garden at all, but that there is some space where an old sink could stand, lifted off the ground perhaps on four short pillars made from bricks. First of all one must ensure that the water can drain away. For this reason the plug hole must be cleared and a few bits of old flower-pots broken up and spread over it so that the water will get through to the soil and then down through its outlet. One of the most effective ways of making sure that this drainage system will keep flowing freely is to cover the broken flower-pot pieces with turf laid with the grass downwards. This will then remain an efficient drain for some years to come.

The soil should be replaced once all this part of the operation is done, with a quantity of what might be described as 'lightening' material, that is substances which will help the drainage as well as give goodness to the plants. A universal mixture would be difficult to define, for all rock plants do not have the same requirements. This is not surprising if one remembers the different conditions, climates, etc. from which they come and in which they grow naturally. What is possible with a rock garden is to provide small areas described as 'pockets' and these can have different aspects and indeed, in special cases, different soils.

Without thinking too much in terms of rare alpines there are quantities of small flowers suitable for planting which are invaluable for cutting, especially when a table arrangement is required. Some suggestions follow for this type of planting:
Achillea Moonshine – there are a good many smaller achilleas suitable for the rock garden, but this is an especially good one with clear yellow flowers and soft grey blue leaves. It is long lasting when cut for arrangement and will eventually dry off and can be used in a dried group.
Anemone hepatica–one of the loveliest of all spring flowers and most suitable for a small table arrangement, where they can be well seen. They look especially charming in a small plate garden standing in moss, with perhaps primroses and windflowers.
Campanula alba – the spires of some of the campanulas make an interesting contrast in shape amongst shorter stemmed flowers. I like to have the white campanula planted near to the achillea or next to a clump of Jerusalem sage *(Phlomis)* or a deep blue iris. The same applies when I use them for cut flower arrangements. *Campanula alba* is also attractive on its own with a few chalk buds of garden ragwort.
Dianthus – these come in a great variety and are most suitable for rock gardens. It is best to see them growing in a nursery garden and to make a selection there. The foliage is most valuable.
Summer starwort *(Erigeron alpinus)* – introduces a note of lilac mauve, which I have found useful for a small mixed group of late summer flowers.
Gentiana acaulis–gentians are invaluable for cutting and like dianthus it is advisable to study a catalogue or to see them growing before making your selection.
St. John's wort–grows into a sizeable shrub with masses of golden yellow flowers. Useful for cutting as a flower. In the autumn the leaves become bright crimson or dark mahogany.
Iris–it would be impossible to give a list of names of iris for a rock garden. Again it is advisable to see them growing or to study a catalogue, before making a choice. Iris are invaluable for cutting,

A collection of rock plants including rock spiraea
with its dark green feathery leaves, pink-mauve thyme,
yellow curry plant, white pinks and border carnations,
sedum and cotton lavender (santolina).
These plants are charming arranged on
their own or with other flowers; they will last well,
sometimes for as long as a fortnight.

Right, Gentians are one of the most delightful of
rock plants, lighting up the garden with their radiant blue,
either in spring or late September.
Here they are arranged with a few sprays
of bright pink pelargonium which are
very little trouble to grow once they are established.

they give that essential shape and height amongst cushion type flowers.

Catmint *(Nepeta)* – a soft blue-grey, coming in long, curving spikes which look enchanting when arranged with white pinks.

Phlox–the rock phlox give bright touches of colour and go on flowering over a long period of time.

Pulmonaria–known also as 'soldiers and sailors', these are amongst the prettiest of early spring flowers, coming in mixed colours of pink and blue. The leaves, rather furry and well-marked, are useful for arrangements during the summer months.

Primula–are most suitable for a rock garden and come in so many colours and types.

Saxifraga (London pride) – there are so many

different types of this enormous family, but London pride is one of the oldest and best loved. Its small pink-and-white clusters of flowers on the thin red stems add a charming light touch to arrangements and later on, when fully developed, will grow into longer stems.

Maidenhair plant *(Thalictrum adiantifolium)* a small edition of the larger border plant with very delicate foliage.

Thymus citriodorus argenteus–almost any of the thyme family are charming as rock plants and useful for cutting.

The periwinkles are incredibly useful, especially the variegated ones, for their curving stems which they produce throughout the year.

Roses

The Rose has been one of the best loved of all flowers for many hundreds of years. Pliny, in his *Natural History* published in A.D. 77, writes of its medicinal properties: '. . . the rose is astringent and the petals, flowers and heads are used in medicine', and another note by the translators of Pliny describes its further uses: 'One ancient author states that even in the middle of winter the more luxurious Romans were not satisfied without roses swimming in the Falernian wine; — and we find Horace repeatedly alluding to the chaplets of roses worn by the guests at banquets'.

In England some of the first references to roses are found in Chaucer and two hundred years

Top, When roses are bought in bud from a florist
to arrange in a particular colour scheme
it is important to make sure of their colour
when fully open as with certain roses this varies.
An example of this is the Talisman rose
shown in the photograph. In bud the outside of the petals
is almost yellow but when fully out the rose
gives an impression of scarlet.

A formal arrangement of five roses with stems
at different lengths, against a background
of ceanothus branches and bergenia leaves.
The roses are yellow in colour and the container
has a yellow and green border
which carries on the colour of the flowers and leaves.

228

later in Shakespeare. In the seventeenth century Andrew Marvell writing in *A Garden* said:

'... shall we never more
That sweet militia restore,
When gardens only had their towers,
And all the garrisons were flowers;
When roses only arms might bear,
And men did rosy garlands wear?'

For many years the gardens of Ely Place and the Inns of Court (Lincoln's Inn Fields) had been renowned for their roses, especially for the *Rosa gallica* and the *Rosa alba*. But it was not until the early nineteenth century that rose growing became a national art and was established once and for all as an institution by the holding of the first National Rose Show in July, 1858, inaugurated by Dean Hole.

There is now a Rose Society and at any Rose Show in any part of the country one can see besides the well known favourites, the new roses which are being currently introduced. There is always a great deal to learn, either about modern roses, which increase in variety year by year, or the old roses which have already been written about, grown and loved. Certain roses seem to grow and thrive almost anywhere under a variety of conditions. They will flourish against a north wall, in a London basement garden, in an exposed situation open to the east winds in the fields of Kent or on the northern slopes of the Pennines.

Some roses though need extra care and sheltered positions, and one of these is the Banksian rose. There are the roses which flower profusely for a short period whilst others go on steadily throughout the summer months. Particularly relevant to flower arrangement, are the roses that are suitable for cutting, those which are long lasting and those with exceptional foliage. These two points make the selection less formidable.

Perhaps before embarking on a selection it would be as well now to consider a few general items which may be helpful when arranging the roses later on.

Firstly, there is the well known and common-sense point of cutting them when they are not yet fully out, at a cool time of day, and after that giving them a deep drink of water before arranging. Rose stems are usually woody compared to the soft and pliable stalks of many flowers, and so they must be split, crushed or peeled to ensure a greater intake of water.

There seem to be various schools of thought on this matter of splitting, crushing or peeling the stems. Certainly with some of the smaller roses such as Carol and Garnet I have found the peeling method to be most effective, but with the stouter stemmed roses such as Ophelia, Albertine, Madame Butterfly, Chaplin's Pink and Paul's Lemon Pillar crushing or splitting the ends

Top, This group shows the rose Alberic Barbier arranged with its foliage in a basket. The deep cream buds are enchanting and open out into paler flowers. This rose will grow cheerfully in almost any situation and does especially well in a town garden.

A collection of garden roses in a porcelain basket; they are arranged with a few buds and leaves and cut short so that it is possible to see over the flowers. This type of group would be suitable as a table arrangement.

229

A collection of garden roses including the yellow Mermaid, deep red Frensham, small yellow and pink roses known as Baby Masquerade, deep pink Rosemary Rose and Ophelia, Iceberg and Penelope buds.

The virtues of a climbing rose for cutting for flower arrangement cannot be overestimated. The group in the photograph shows Chaplin's Pink climber, arranged with their dark glossy leaves in a 19th century pewter urn, which holds plenty of water.

of the stem appears to be sufficient.

It is important, too, to cut off the thorns and any surplus foliage, though I want to make a strong plea for the use of the leaves in rose arrangements. Cutting off the thorns makes them much easier to arrange, as anyone who has ever tried to remove a rose from a group or to arrange it differently knows only too well. Removing some of the foliage if there is an over abundance may prolong the life of the flower, as in the case of Zéphirine Drouhin.

When arranging roses I find crumpled wire netting easier to use than anything else, although there are occasions when pin holders are suitable and roses will survive on them (certain flowers will not). But it seems to me that, on the whole, roses prefer to have as much of their stems as possible in the water and last better this way.

Like other flowers, roses will not last long if they have to stand in a draught or to suffer extremes of temperature and, as usual, the water in the vase should be filled up every day and faded flowers trimmed off to allow the buds to come out.

Roses seem to me to fall into two categories. One is the climbing rose and some of the bush roses. The other, the type of rose which looks best arranged in very small quantities.

Climbing roses can provide valuable material for large arrangements if they have been given the chance of spreading in the garden. It is then possible to cut long, curving branches which are suitable for pedestal groups to be used for a party, church decoration or a large conference meeting in a big hall. Contrary to the usual belief, these branches can last well, but they must be cut when the flowers are still in bud, and treated as I have suggested in an earlier paragraph. (I have known a large arrangement of Chaplin's Pink climber last about a week without any difficulty.)

Among the roses which look their best when cut quite short, so that one can see right into the flower and enjoy the charm of its scent and colouring is the Fantin-Latour rose, palest pink with a flushed centre and crinkled petals. Louise Odier with deep rose flowers on rather slender stems is another one, (unfortunately the stems seldom seem to stand erect, and it is only when the rather drooping flower head is cut short and supported that this rose can be seen to advantage.) The deeper pink of the buds is especially attractive when arranged in contrast with the lighter rose of the full blown flower.

Left, A trug basket of polyantha and shrub roses
from the garden. It is important when arranging a group
of roses together to remove all the thorns
and crush or split up the stems
to allow a greater intake of water.
With smaller roses such as the dark red Garnet
and the pale pink Carol the stems can be peeled right up
the stalk and they will last for two or three weeks.

A bunch of various coloured and sized roses arranged
well down in the vase to form a posy.
A small group of this kind, especially if arranged
in a glass container, gains more importance
if it is placed in the immediate light of a table lamp.

My own preference is for the old roses. I find
it hard to believe that there can be anything more
beautiful than the shell like charm of Madame
Pierre Oger or the softly flushed cream pink of
Blairii No. 2.

Despite this, I believe that the more commonly
grown roses do have their place and ought to be
more appreciated. Some gardeners and flower
arrangers look horrified at the mention of an
American Pillar or a Paul's Scarlet, but both
these roses can be of immense value when certain
colours are needed. So often it is not the fault
of the rose that it looks vulgar or too profuse, it
is the way in which the rose has been grown, (I
have seen a Chaplin's Pink climber looking radiant
against a dark evergreen, and the creamy white of
Alberic Barbier, lightening up a dark London
garden). Before one condemns a rose on any
count consider all its assets carefully, for many of

these mentioned are strong growers and last well
when cut for the house. They provide an abundance of bloom and, in the case of the last two,
also an abundance of valuable, glossy foliage.

To illustrate how tastes in roses change let me
quote Miss Ellen Willmott in her *Genus Rosa*
(one of the great rose books of the world) who
praised the charming Dorothy Perkins, whose
beautiful, pure pink flowers resemble a clustered
Rose de Meaux (this was twenty years after its
introduction to this country in 1890). Today it
is unpopular amongst many rose lovers.

Miss Rosemary James writing in the *Gardeners
Chronicle* on 'The Rose as a Cut Flower' specially
mentions Peace, a rose unsurpassed for large
flower arrangements, having good lasting qualities'. Virgo she regards as a producer of 'the
most perfect blooms among the hybrid teas', but,
she goes on, White Christmas is almost as good,

and certainly better as a garden plant, for it flowers more freely and is stronger in growth'. Miss James then recommends that these two roses 'should be arranged sparingly in simple containers of plain white, or sparkling crystal, for the perfection of form to be appreciated'.

Other recommended roses are Lilac Charm, a beautiful lilac floribunda; Lavender Princess, with soft pinkish shadings; Magenta, a warm rosy tinted lilac, which pales to delicate shades of grey mauve and Sterling Silver, still one of the best 'blue' roses.

This is obviously only a small selection of the new roses, many of which can be seen at the Royal Horticultural Society Shows, at local fruit and flower shows or growing in some of the National Trust Gardens open to the public. One of the most famous rose gardens convenient for Londoners is the Queen Mary's Rose Garden in Regent's Park. Here, there are beds and beds of modern roses in all shades and varieties. One of the finest is devoted to the beautiful white rose Iceberg.

Having already mentioned that I am strongly in favour of using foliage in arrangements, I should like to emphasise the beauty of the leaves of certain roses. The glistening green of Alberic Barbier; the large, elegant foliage of Ophelia and Penelope; the red tinged leaves of Albertine; the soft grey green of the Wolley Dod's Rose; the charm of the delicate, feathery foliage of *Rosa hugonis*, interlaced with its clear yellow flowers. One can almost find as much variety in the leaves of individual roses, as in the flowers themselves, and roses do so often show to greater advantage when arranged with their leaves. On occasions it is useful to have rose foliage included with flowers other than roses.

In each of the colour photographs illustrating this section you may notice a quantity of foliage with the flowers. This is how I have found roses look their best.

Containers for roses can be made of glass or porcelain, copper or brass, silver or basket ware. They may be coloured or plain, white or black, opaque or transparent. It is difficult to find a vase which does not suit roses, but since there are different types of roses with quite different characteristics, some containers are more suitable than others. For example, some roses are robust and can stand up to a heavy solid type of vase, whilst others are delicate and look best either in plain glass or fine porcelain. A wine glass can be just right for one or two old roses cut short, or a Worcester plate for a flat, dining table arrangement of two or three Fantin-Latour roses. Again, a bunch of Queen Elizabeth, strong and sturdy, look attractive in a large, white Staffordshire teapot, and a bunch of mixed roses from the garden can look well in a trug basket.

In conclusion I can only say 'study the rose, its style, habit, character, and appreciate it'. Perhaps the most important thing about roses whether arranging or growing them, is to feel affection for them. As Dean Hole writes in *A Book About Roses:* 'He who would have beautiful roses in his garden . . . must love them well and always'.

Top right, This cornucopia holds a small bunch of special garden roses, known as 'old' roses and includes the striped Rosamundi and the shell rose Madame Pierre Oger. To answer the criticism that old roses do not last well when cut it is worth taking the trouble to cut off the dead roses so that the buds can come out.

Right, Paul's Lemon Pillar are arranged here with foliage, buds and a few contrasting roses to give depth of colour, in a Leeds pedestal dish; this rose is prolific in growth, generous in its flowering and its soft lemon colour is almost unique. The soft yellow colouring of the dish tones particularly well with the roses.

Shells for flower arrangement

Shells, I think, without question, are some of the most delightful flower containers. They are charming to look at, interesting to arrange flowers in, since they offer so many possibilities of shape and colour, and economical, as they hold only a small amount of material.

First, let us consider their shape and range of colour. Between shells there are obvious differences in shape and texture, some are wrinkled round the edge, others are waved round the edge, others are semi-circular, oval, upright, others again are smooth edged, rough edged, covered in bumps, striped, smooth, glossy, rough etc. But colour is another matter. 'Shell pink' in most people's minds is quite a definite colour, but what is 'shell-pink'? This might refer to the insides of some shells, which seem to change into different shades of pink as one looks deeper down into them, though not all shells have this particular colouring. When the shell is pale pink or creamy-white it is a suitable container for off-white or pink flowers, such as pinks or roses, especially Carol and the small frilled Grootendorst, and when slightly apricot in colour, they encourage the use of blue-grey foliage, for example rue or lavender, with perhaps two or three small buds of an apricot rose such as the floribundas Alison Wheatcroft or Circus.

Then there are yellow shells with an orange tint. A small cluster of yellow, apricot, off white flowers with just a touch of orange make an excellent toning of colour scheme. Cream roses such as Message (white faintly shaded to cream) with two or three yellow carnations, and their grey-

Right, The soft colouring of this shell tones in well with the mixed colours of the flowers.
The group consists of snapdragons, in various shades, fuchsias and border carnations.
A relatively small amount of material is required to give a bright effect.

Left, A shell can be suitable for both small and upright arrangements. Here is a bunch of mignonette, one of the sweetest of all garden flowers, with two or three yellow roses.

blue foliage, a few yellow and orange ranunculus, or, instead of the roses, creamy yellow polyanthas with some of the deep copper coloured ones to give depth, and a few stems of garden ragwort *(Senecio laxifolius)* are also an attractive decoration.

In a large shell which held a good many stems, an arrangement with curving branches of copper berberis looked attractive, with blue hydrangeas cut short towards the centre and a few cream coloured carnations. The long open shape of this particular shell was suitable for the finished spreading outline and the deep curves on its lip were admirably placed from which to arrange them. The flowers seemed to fall quite naturally into place.

This brings one to the matter of 'fixing' the flowers in position so that they remain firmly where they have been put when a real shell is used. To ensure that the water does not spill over the edge or seep through the porous surface, it is generally wise to pack the shell with either 'Flora-pak' or 'Oasis', (which should be kept well damped) in order to avoid any leaking. If either of these materials are used it also obviates the possibility of water pouring out over the sides of the curved lips, which can mean not only a serious loss of water to the flowers but also havoc to any polished surface on which the shell may stand. Another good method of fixing the flowers in the shell is to pack it with either sand or moss, which, of course, must also be kept moist. It is also possible to use a pin holder and/or wire netting, if the shell is large enough and steady enough. (If the shell is an imitation one, made of porcelain, this problem does not apply.)

Shells, especially small ones, make most attractive arrangements for a dining table and can be used to extend an original decoration or to form the whole of a new group, and this can be done by using matching shells, one large one, or four small ones— one at each corner of the central group. If these smaller shells are filled with the same kind of flowers that have been used in the large group, they all link up and form one extended arrangement. In the case of flat round shells, a candle can be placed on the centre of one of these and a holder for flowers may be fixed over the candle, resting on the base of the shell. Flowers can then be arranged on this, spreading out over the flat shell itself, with the candle rising up in the middle. Two, three or four of these, lit up for a dining table, can make a most attractive arrangement.

Small shells can be an integral part of an arrangement, but, like driftwood, etc. should be used with discretion. They must not only be perfect and sparkling but also a suitable shape and in proportion to the main group. It is worthwhile whenever one is anywhere near the sea to look about and make a collection of shells which are not only interesting to look at and a delightful reminder of days spent on the seashore, but which will also produce, when required, something suitable for almost any type of arrangement. One will probably find that certain kinds of shells can only be found on the shores of certain coves. In much the same way different kinds of stones with a particular marking often predominate in just one section of the shore. Stones may not legitimately come under the heading of shells but they do sometimes serve the same purpose as that of additions to a flower arrangement. White ones are especially useful and I have found that in the case of a favourite colour scheme of dark brown and white—perhaps white foxgloves or white tobacco plant against either copper beech or the deep purple-brown prunus arranged on a dark brown dish—a white stone will pick up the white in the group and will show up well in the dish, especially if there is water in it. (The stems might be arranged in a small container on a dish, if it is completely flat, but it is well known that stones look quite different when they are wet and just a small amount of water which even a flat dish will hold may just make that difference.)

The use of shells and stones as additions to an arrangement is not a new idea and takes one back to the days of the Dutch flower paintings when they were often depicted along with caterpillars, cherries, butterflies, and lizards. In one panel painting by Balthasar Van der Ast, there is only a rose, a stem of lily-of-the-valley, two crocus and a few carnations, but there are quantities of stones and shells. When shells or stones are suitable for arrangements, then it is quite in order to use them. But if they are not suitable, then it is a mistake, and only one's own taste and judgement can make this decision.

Right, The soft cream and pale yellow colourings in this arrangement tone in with the grey foliage and off-white porcelain shell with its grey base of imitation waves. With this porcelain shell there is no chance of the water leaking, which can happen with naturally porous shells.

Top right, A porcelain shell makes an attractive receptacle for a few flowers; in this case it makes the most of a few carnations cut short with a small bunch of ranunculus, carnation foliage and buds and sprays of the grey-leaved *Senecio leucostachys.* This is a long lasting group and so it is important that the water level is kept up.

239

Small arrangements

So much pleasure can be captured in small flower arrangements, which do not require a lot of flowers nor cost a lot of money.

Spring is the time for small arrangements of violets, anemones, and snowdrops, or for foliage and branches. As a small arrangement, hellebores, – the beautiful greenish white Christmas and Lenten roses – are both charming and effective. They last well, and one needs to have only a few of them in a flat dish. Sometimes the purplish tinge on the outside of the petals goes well with the pale pink and purple anemones, particularly as the shape of the flowers is so similar (both are typical members of the same family); anemones or violets in a wine glass on a small table, Christmas roses or freesias in a small jug or vase – all of these small arrangements take on a new significance on a winter evening, if they stand in the light of a reading lamp.

Three carnations with a background of evergreen foliage can be arranged in a tall, narrow necked, early scent bottle. Mixed geraniums in a small glass dish are cheerful and welcoming but quite different in character from mignonette and soft tea roses, or the sturdy brightness of nasturtiums, or a rainbow bouquet of flowers from the rock garden in a curved porcelain trough.

Other ideas for using simple material in small arrangements are:

A mixed group of early summer flowers, sweet rocket, mock orange (*Philadelphus*), elder flower, columbine, lungwort foliage and various grasses; this little collection of rather soft and very simple flowers conveys a feeling of summer days as effectively as would more sophisticated material.

White viburnum flowers cut short with wedding grass in a simple wicker basket painted dark green; green and white makes a fresh colour scheme, and the graceful, spear like shape of the wedding grass combined with its colouring, makes it a most useful addition to a flower arrangement.

A few roses in a porcelain basket; if some of the

Left, Here a bunch of violets is arranged in a small ornament; this small arrangement will last for seven to ten days if the stems are trimmed off occasionally and the flowers given a drink upside down in a bowl of water.

This small Victorian piece of porcelain is ideal for a small arrangement. The group consists of gentians, ivy leaves and a few white cyclamen.

rose foliage can be spared from the bush, there is nothing better for showing off an almost fully blown rose. To be more effective some of the flowers should be cut much shorter than others and placed well down towards the centre, to show their full face.

A single rose with its own foliage, either in a tall, plain champagne glass or an old scent bottle; a tall branch of a climbing rose can be arranged in a dark green well-shaped wine bottle (especially attractive if a yellow rose such as Emily Gray or Gloire de Dijon is used).

Queen Anne's lace could be cut short with geums and lamb's ears *(Stachys lanata)* arranged in a low bread basket.

Peonies, two or three, or only one with either their own most attractive leaves or two or three sprays of mock orange *(Philadelphus)* in flower, Chilean gum box *(Escallonia)* or Japanese quince (depending on the colour of the peonies).

Foliage of iris and sprays of masterwort *(Astran-*

tia) cut quite short, with their own leaves; the masterwort contrasts well with the iris spears.

Columbines with Queen Anne's lace, cut short, in a porcelain sauce or gravy boat (preferably with yellow columbines).

Clematis, two or three flowers with their curving stems and tendrils, arranged either on a flat dish for a table decoration, or in a decanter to show off the stems and leaves.

Geranium or pelargonium – green leaves banded with white (perhaps Dolly Varden), just a few short sprays arranged with white pinks cut short in a piece of white porcelain–perhaps a figurine or a white basket.

Ox-eye daisies in a small wicker basket, with Queen Anne's lace cut short and a few buttercups.

Mignonette arranged with the dark silver grey foliage of *Convolvulus cneorum* and some of the lighter grey of immortelle and love-in-a-mist, all cut quite short and arranged rather in posy style in a small jug or tumbler.

This arrangement shows off a few flowers to their best advantage. The ranunculus and sprays of rosemary are cut quite short giving a greater effect of colour.

A Victorian 'hand' vase is an ornament in itself and will therefore only need a few flowers.
In this group freesias are arranged with a few cyclamen leaves.
The water level must be watched very carefully in this type of vase.

Something as small and delicate as Heart's-ease needs a plain background of soft colours to pick up the shades of the flowers. The stems are cut long and stand in a small dish of water on a lilac coloured plate.
The group is arranged as far as possible, so that the centre of each separate flower can be seen.

Spring flowers

The joy and delight always to be found in flowers seems to be sharpened, accentuated, and brought more vividly to life at this time of the year. Spring brings feelings of freshness, hope and renewal, and the flowers which grow and blossom in the spring seem to be particularly sweet and precious.

So many spring flowers have a woodland home, the earlier flowers, snowdrops, primroses, and violets, are associated in the mind with a mossy bank on the edge of a hazel copse, or growing in drifts at the foot of trees. Arrangements at this time of the year are particularly suited for inclusions of wood and moss.

So much attractive material too is available at this time (many shrubs and young trees at their best) that it is difficult to know what to select.

In the first three months of the year there are snowdrops and winter aconites; some of the Christmas and Lenten roses with their dramatic foliage; small sprays of witch hazel *(Hamamelis mollis)*, *Daphne odora* or *Rhododendron praecox*; twigs of pussy willow; hepaticas (quite enchanting with their clear colouring); violets (either two or three single ones or a bunch arranged with their own leaves); the soft pink bergenia (known previously as *Megasea cordifolia*) the light blue purple sweet scented flowers of *Iris stylosa*. *Viburnum tinus* and *Jasminum nudiflorum* are both in bloom throughout most of the winter in milder districts, and they last on well into the spring.

There will be many others to choose from in the shops – anemones and ranunculus being two

This woodland setting of bark, a stone, moss and a piece of wood is used to give flowers which grow in copses or under trees a natural background. The lilies-of-the-valley are placed in a narrow necked glass container holding the water.
This type of background is equally suitable for primroses, snowdrops, winter aconites, grape hyacinths or cowslips.

of the most suitable. Ranunculus can sometimes be found in a soft coral pink, which is especially attractive, although the clear red is a good, cheerful colour. I do not find it easy to get the full effect from these flowers without some patience. They are difficult to arrange naturally, although they look so straight-forward. The bareness of their stems can be part of their attraction, but they often need something with them to give a softer line. Ranunculus are usually tied and sold in bunches of only a few flowers and they seldom seem to have any greenery with them. I find the rich green of violet leaves a good background for the soft pink of the flowers.

Eucalyptus gunnii which has tufted salmon-pink flowers and lanceolate leaves make, together with a cluster of purple sprouting broccoli, a favourite colour scheme. Later on as the broccoli grows up it reveals the palest of fresh green shoots, this completely alters the character of the arrangement, which is, none the less, interesting. If purple and pink stocks are added to the broccoli, they again give quite a different aspect to a group.

A similar colour scheme could be effected in blues and purples by using blue iris, blue and purple anemones and violets, all together. Iris leaves, particularly useful for their shape and rather unusual blue-green colour, can be cut either in different lengths, kept to their full length or cut much shorter. Violet leaves are beautiful both in shape and colour, and the flowers float quite happily in shallow water.

The most important thing to remember when arranging flowers in the early weeks of spring is that the small amount of material must be conserved. In the south west of England and parts of Scotland this may not be necessary. (In the shelter of a walled garden in Broadford Bay, Skye, I have seen a good many spring flowers coming on in January. But in most English gardens there will not be many plants or bulbs in flower until well on into March.)

One useful method of making the most of a few flowers is a miniature indoor garden composed of material, that has either been bought or cut from one's own garden.

A small garden may be made in a shallow cake tin, a square strawberry punnet, or an average sized plate or dish. For a larger one, meat dishes

Top, An arrangement in a tall hyacinth bulb vase of sprays of eucalyptus and daffodils. This is a long lasting group.

A few sprays of flowering branches are seen to their best advantage when arranged in a narrow necked glass decanter, which helps to keep the branches in position. In this group there is a cluster of *Pieris floribunda* (a hardy evergreen flowering shrub with racemes of creamy-white flowers), a branch of guelder rose and viburnum coming into leaf.

245

A large group of late spring flowers including
eucalyptus foliage, branches of guelder rose,
pale pink flowering almond, pussy willow,
purple and yellow iris, double and single tulips, daffodils,
hyacinths and echeveria. An arrangement of this kind
must have a container which holds plenty of water.

Right, A pink and white spring arrangement
in a shallow porcelain fruit dish.
The mainstay of this group is provided
by the gleaming branches of camellia foliage
and the unusual green-white colouring of the guelder rose;
touches of pink are provided by
almond blossom and a few lilies.

might be useful, a tray for serving coffee or a shallow copper cooking dish. If a flat baking tin is used it should have holes pierced in the bottom and be kept on a plate or dish in case dampness comes through on to the surface it is resting on. This treatment applies equally to a strawberry punnet or any other porous container.

The flowers can be fixed sometimes on a pin holder, either in moss or damp sand, or arranged in small clumps in two or three separate glass jars. I think the latter method allows the flowers a greater supply of water and obviates the need for moss or sand.

Grape hyacinths, crocus, snowdrops, the first early wild daffodils, dwarf hyacinths, scillas, winter aconites will provide freshness and colour at very little expense. I prefer not to inflict the stiffness of a pin holder on any of these tender stemmed flowers, and infinitely prefer to have them in small glass jars.

Most evergreen foliage seems to be content with a smaller supply of water, and the moss or sand need only be damp, not saturated.

Two or three branches of an evergreen--budding flowering currant or whitebeam--will give height, and if arranged in damp moss, the appearance of growing naturally. The shape and colour of evergreen foliage, a clump of velvet moss or some stones or shells, may be very helpful by way of producing a solid or definite shape as a background for rather spindly material. Without one or all

three of these the general effect might be rather indefinite and lacking in strength.

A group of this kind is especially suitable for a hall or landing, since it stands up surprisingly well to the varying temperatures caused by draught or central heating. The branches may last for a matter of weeks, and only the smaller flowers need then be replaced.

It is essential to ensure that the outline of such a group can be clearly seen. This does not necessarily mean a light or completely plain background, but it is helpful to have good lighting from a window or lamp. *Viburnum tinus,* camellia and laurel from the garden, or hazel catkins and pussy willow from the hedgerows, are all useful. Grevillea is available in the shops, also eucalyptus and pittosporum both of which can be easily grown in milder parts of England (in warmer climates they grow all the year round). The sturdy eucalyptus stems are most suitable for arrangement on a pin holder.

Aconites gleam like sunlight usually long before March but they last surprisingly well when brought indoors, especially if one takes the trouble to cut them low down their long white stems. I think they last almost better in water than when they are left growing naturally.

Viburnum fragrans is a joy, sometimes flowering improbably in October and November, and often right through into March. This shrub is indeed welcome both in the garden for its appearance and in the house because of its sweet perfume.

This may be a good moment to say something about the whole viburnum family. We all know one of its familiar members, the guelder rose or snowball bush, a garden form of *Viburnum opulus*.

It seems to me to be an invaluable shrub to have in the garden for flower arrangement. It grows contentedly on a north wall and provides clusters of almost bright green flowers, which later turn through various shades of pale green and off-white into white snowballs.

Viburnum opulus flowers at about the same time as *Viburnum burkwoodii* which enjoys a damp, shaded position (I know one which has grown into a large bush overhanging a pond) and produces masses of flowers usually at the beginning of May.

Another member of the family is the popular

V. tinus which I have already mentioned. It is useful not only for its clear green foliage but also for the very charming pink and white flower clusters which last, in some districts, throughout the winter months.

I have heard some people complain that hazel catkins are inclined to drop quickly and that the pollen has to be continually swept up. Having had some in my own home for over two weeks I think I can answer this criticism (they only began to drop towards the end of the fortnight.) Hazel catkins should be cut in good time, before they reach the open stage, in this way they last well, although a little extra dusting may be involved. The shapes of the branches, the pendulous hanging of the flowers and lightness of the colour seem to be reward enough for any slight trouble.

Spring is the time of year when bare branches, particularly of fruit trees, can be most useful. If they are plunged into hot water, kept in a warm atmosphere, and the container filled with warm water, some of the buds will obligingly break into leaf. In any case, if they are placed against a bare wall, the branches themselves will bring into the house the illusion of the beautiful outlines of trees in a winter landscape. Pussy willow, usually available in the shops, makes a good contrast with branches of laurel, magnolia, camellia, grevillea, or eucalyptus. Branches of witch hazel (*Hamamelis mollis*) are a delight with their yellow flowers.

The leaves of the whitebeam are always beautiful, but even more so when they are just coming out. Turned away from the front of the arrangement

and showing the grey underleaf, they look very effective with anything white. (The stems should be slit or crushed with a hammer.)

Although primroses have the reputation of fading quickly I have never found this to be so. They must be fresh, and one should always remember that if one or two of the flowers have died an arrangement will at once look faded. This often seems to happen with a bunch of primroses, picked all at the same time, a few odd ones go off more quickly – but taken out the bowl will look fresh again.

At this time daffodils, primroses, tulips, freesias, and even lilies-of-the-valley all make their appearance now on the market fairly inexpensively.

Bluebells have wonderful staying power. The white and the blue both look cool and delicate, especially with double white jonquils in a blue and white bowl. The jonquils do not last as well as the bluebells, but they could be replaced by anemones. This would alter the colour scheme and would certainly give the appearance of a new arrangement. The bluebell stems would, of course, have to be cut shorter to match the length of the anemones and also to freshen them up.

Three arrangements using anemones with other flowers are suggested: blue and purple anemones with yellow tulips; red anemones mixed with a bunch of yellow daisies; pink anemones in a pink and white scheme composed of white bluebells and pink tulips with a streak of white in them.

Later on Queen Anne's lace (white hedge-parsley) first appears in the hedgerows, and goes

Far left, A few sprays of ivy can provide a charming
background for certain flowers.
Here they form the background for a few daffodils.
The group is arranged in a glass jar with a narrow neck
which helps to keep the material firmly in position.

Left, A bright touch of colour is introduced in contrast
to the soft, fluffy, grey pussy willow branches
by a few sprays of orange-gold clivia.
The shape of the branches against a plain background
emphasises the tall narrow container
which is particularly suitable for a small amount of material.
This arrangement lasted for at least a fortnight.

An arrangement of hazel catkins and laurustinus.
The laurustinus is placed towards the centre
of the group to give depth to the arrangement.
The material is arranged on a pin holder,
concealed by moss, in a shallow dish of water.

on – or rather, various members of the hedge-parsley *(Umbelliferae)* family go on – throughout the summer months. (A friend often brings me some from the country, and this seems to be a good opportunity to suggest that any chance of getting wild flowers should be taken. Most people get into the country now and again, but too many of them come back empty handed.) Hedge-parsley is one of the easiest flowers to find and most useful and accommodating for arrangements. It combines well with most garden flowers, is light and delicate, and lasts quite well. In my own experience it has formed a worthy basis for a wedding decoration in the more exotic company of lilies, carnations, and roses. With white broom and white bluebells, hedge-parsley would make an almost bridal arrangement.

Forget-me-nots with the double white narcissus Cheerfulness are cool looking and give the impression of a porcelain pattern. They also make an excellent contrast with yellow daisies or purple anemones.

Columbines (in a sauce boat) and hare's tail grasses mix well with the smaller heads of giant cow-parsnip. Solomon's seal, that delicious white pendulous flower edged with green, looks well alone or with a cluster of guelder rose, some of which should still be green.

I think that one should not conclude this section about spring flowers and foliage without mentioning the euphorbias, or spurges. This is a family of plants so large and often so different from each other that between them they cover some of the most diverse types of plants as well as some of the most unusual.

One which gives great delight from early spring right through the year and only begins to look rather tousled and delapidated during the coldest weather, is *Euphorbia wulfenii.* This grows to a height of about five feet and into a sizeable clump. Its foliage is interesting, consisting of rather long strap-like blue green leaves coming off from the stout stem all the way up and stopping just below the flowerhead. The flowers and bracts are in clusters, giving an effect of green and yellow, and when they first start to come out the new leaves nearest to them provide a good contrast by appearing in a dark wine colour.

E. wulfenii being large in itself and lasting well is useful for large decorations. But it is important to mention that its stems ooze a milky sap (as most of the euphorbias do) when it is cut and so one should wear gloves or take care not to get it on one's hands, in case of trouble. As it goes through the various stages of bud, flower and fading flower, it varies in appearance, but each is always interesting, unusual and attractive in colouring. In the garden *E. wulfenii* likes a sunny position, shaded from sharp winds. If it is expected to stand up to severe frosts it should have some protection from bracken or other suitable material.

Another charming spurge, but much smaller, is the green and gold, bright flowered *Euphorbia pilosa.* This is one of the best plants for the front of a border and is usually one of the first to flower. Its flowers are especially suitable for small arrange-

Top, A compact late spring arrangement in tones of yellow, white and orange. The daffodils and some of the freesias provide creamy-white which is emphasised by the variegated hosta leaves; two atoms of orange clivia, towards the centre of the group give a depth of colouring and the touches of yellow in their stamens and flower centres provide a link with the daffodils. This link is repeated in the iris. The dark green wild arum foliage contrasts with the narrow iris leaves.

In early spring it is sometimes necessary to collect small bunches of whatever is available in the garden. In this group a few branches of hazel catkins and pussy willow are arranged on a pin holder in a jar of water to form a background for other early flowering material.
The snowdrops are arranged in another jar of water, concealed by moss, as though they were growing; the winter aconites are arranged in damp moss towards the front of the dish with,
behind them two or three sprays of laurustinus and to the right, the charming pale pink flower of an early viburnum. This group stands in a pewter dish and if the jars are kept topped up and the moss damp the arrangement will provide a long lasting 'spring garden'.

ments, and its cheerful colouring is a good sight in the spring.

Euphorbia griffithii which doubles itself up in quantity in almost no time at all, is one of the most dramatic of this exciting family of plants. Its colouring is even more vivid and exotic than the two just described, and for cutting it is fascinating.

Euphorbia fulgens is half hardy but is often seen in the shops during spring. This is a lovely curving spray of bright orange, with small dark green leaves to set it off to perfection. It may seem expensive, but two or three sprays will be sufficient arranged in a tall jug or decanter, for a table or mantelpiece group and will last well.

Each spring without fail I always try to sow in my garden love-in-a-mist *(Nigella)* and the old-fashioned sweet-scented mignonette. Everyone naturally has his own special favourite and these two are mine. I shall always hope to find a place for them in my garden.

Summer flowers

A basket of summer flowers with a background of bergenia leaves which show up the variety of colours in the flowers.
A few carnations are arranged with different coloured stocks and sprays of white heather.
The basket is lined with a shallow cake tin to hold the water and flowers are kept in position by wire netting.

White Shasta daisies are effective, long-lasting, and adaptable. They mix well with other flowers, looking particularly charming with forget-me-nots, or can be used on their own quite happily. Blue cornflowers look pretty mixed with white daisies, or two or three red roses, or a spray of scarlet geranium. Just a small bunch will go a long way and give a broader effect if the stems are cut to different lengths. The pink and white ones do not always seem to last quite so well but they do help to make up subtle colour schemes if mixed with other flowers, especially sweet peas.

This is the time for elder flowers, which can look very delicate when still in bud and arranged with sweet rocket, mock orange (*Philadelphus*), columbines and peonies.

A few short flowers of white astilbe cut from the garden with some wedding grass will make an arrangement by themselves, as will branches of honesty seedpods (still a clear green) with bright tulips.

Early summer is also the time for mock orange. It doesn't have the reputation for lasting well, but the delightful sight and smell of its flowers make it worth trying. Mock orange will last better if it is cut when still in bud. Chilean gum box (*Escallonia*) is rather a prickly shrub to arrange, but it, too, is well worth the trouble.

More than anything this is the time for roses, (I have discussed these at some length in the Rose section). One of the smallest members of the *Compositae* family, known as feverfew (not the yellow leaved variety sometimes called Golden Feather) is exceedingly pretty, of simple shape, and lasts well. It looks effective broken down into small sprays either on its own or mixed together with other flowers – like white phlox, and white Shasta daisies.

For a mixed arrangement of garden and wild flowers, summer jasmine with everlasting peas and wild parsley is most successful.

Pink larkspur mixes well with pink cornflowers, and poppy heads rescued from the wheelbarrow on their way to the compost heap contrast well with soft purple-grey allium heads, a bunch of carnation foliage, and two New Zealand flax (*Phormium*) leaves. Golden rod and gladioli go together well but both are equally good on their own. Golden rod need not always be used to the full length of its stem. It looks more delicate cut quite short, with the longer sprays of flower stripped from the main stem and arranged individually. In this way it can be combined with even shorter flowers, white antirrhinums and white larkspur being especially good (it looks prettier with white than almost any other colour).

There should be no difficulty if you decide on gladioli. Nowadays there is hardly a week throughout the calendar when it is not possible to buy or have growing one of the many different kinds of gladiolus. But this has not always been the case. During the seventeenth century only three common kinds and two rare ones were mentioned.

Alice Coats in *Flowers and their Histories* quotes Sir Thomas Hanmer on one of these: 'The Aethopian . . . which was brought from the Cape of Good Hope in Africa . . . It hath light red toward scarlet flowers . .' later on she tells of the history of the plant. *G. primulinus* was found by Sir F. Fox, engineer of the bridge across the Zambesi at the Victoria Falls. The plant was growing close to the spray from the tumbling water of the Falls.

Only fairly recently have the possibilities of the gladiolus been appreciated in flower arrangement. Tall sprays of white gladioli are extremely useful for large wedding groups, and coloured gladioli are often indispensable for interior decoration at parties, dances, receptions, and so on when height is an essential factor. But should a low arrangement be required it can be cut shorter and be just as effective. One cannot say too much in favour of its lasting qualities, for gladioli is reliable under conditions where many other flowers would droop.

One American writer, Matilda Rogers in her book *'Flower Arrangements'*, chooses gladioli for her first lesson for beginners. She writes: 'If you want to impress your family and friends with your first arrangement, start with six gladioli and a few sprigs of lemon leaves. They are available at florist shops most of the year, are inexpensive, last fairly long and are easy to manage effectively'.

The name 'gladiolus' derived from the Latin word for sword, was earned by the stiffness and shape of the foliage. This, in itself, is an indication of a certain formal line and feeling to be expected from a gladiolus arrangement.

Who has not seen gladioli planted in gardens in regimented stiff straight lines? Often they are propped against the wind by equally straight bamboo sticks. A better arrangement would be gladioli planted among lupins, to have their stiffness broken by the softer lupin foliage.

Obviously something similar can be done when arranging gladioli by introducing other material of more spreading and delicate habit. Grasses help to reduce this rather stiff effect, I think.

When large and heavy spikes are used for the outline or background of a group it is specially important to arrange other material close up to them. Gladioli are rather large flowered for an outline, (as the whole spike unfolds, its separate flowers soon look heavy), unless the group is built up well from the centre out towards them. Sometimes gladioli come with curving stems, this is a gift if they happen to curve in the right direction. I have found that it helps to hold the stem in one's hand to make sure which way the natural curve goes and then to put it in the vase at the same angle.

If using gladioli for a smaller group, cut their stems in graduated lengths and arrange them on a pin holder with the shortest and fullest flowers towards the centre, and the taller, thinner spikes forming the top and edges of the group. Each stem must be fixed firmly in position before the next is added. The pin holder itself standing in a shallow dish, must be a large and weighty one, kept in position with Plasticine. In this case the spiky gladioli foliage is most useful, although one may still need a few larger, round or oval-shaped leaves (geranium, bergenia, camellia, ivy, laurel or magnolia) towards the centre to conceal the pin holder.

Gladioli flowers can be used individually. It is quite possible, given one full flowering spike of gladiolus, to make a complete arrangement by using the separate flowers as though they came from individual stems.

An original idea using the gladioli foliage is one from America: 'The leaves were separated from the stems to make the flowers last longer and to create green areas of interest', says Patricia E. Roberts in *Flower Arrangements Through the Year*.

As with most other flowers, the container plays an important part in the arrangement of the gladioli. Gladioli in a tall pedestal group:
Here the flower spikes will be of the large and heavy variety at the end of long stems and will need a container which will give enough water and enough support to stop them becoming top heavy.

Gladioli used individually makes an attractive group for a dining table, if a flat plate or a shallow dish is used as a container.

I have also seen individual flowers used to decorate candles which were standing in small containers holding water. The flowers were so arranged that the candles seemed to come from the centre of two or three of them.

Yarrow (*Achillea*) is one of the most economical flowers one could wish for. It goes on and on throughout the summer months, until it finally dries in the autumn, after which it can be used for winter decoration. Some have very long stems and big heads and others are quite short with smaller flowers. A touch of their very deep chrome yellow goes well with purple asters and

A pale pink and mauve summer arrangement in a mauve and white dish consisting of funkia flowers, masterwort and old-fashioned roses. These three materials are completely in contrast with each other— their only link is the softness in their colouring.

with certain shades of antirrhinums. It also goes well with most delphinium blues.

An attractive arrangement can be made of sea holly *(Eryngium)* with godetia. The soft blue grey of the sea holly is a good foil for the rather deep salmon pink of the godetia cut very short so that the full beauty of the flower centres may be seen. Both these plants last well, the sea holly for weeks and the godetia for a long time if the dead flowers are removed at once to allow

the buds to come out. Godetia can also come in many shades of pink, deep red, and purple.

Clematis is useful for small arrangements, which can be gathered from a garden. They come in different tones of blue, purple and pink, and the flowers almost arrange themselves, and last well. Love-in-a-mist *(Nigella)* with blue flowers looks charming with the clear yellow double African marigold cut short. White love-in-a-mist arranged with white larkspur, and two clove carnations added

A delicate arrangement in a shallow yellow dish of yellow-green lady's mantle flowers and deep purple prunus. Both the lady's mantle and prunus are available from the beginning of May until the end of October and are invaluable for cutting.

towards the centre make a good arrangement, the clove colour contrasts sharply with the rather greeny white of the love-in-a-mist flowers.

Japanese anemones come on at about the same time as gladioli. With their tall, straight stems and soft pink or clear white flowers, all emerging from a mass of dark, spreading green leaves they make wonderful clumps either in the border, by a wall or at the edge of a bank of shrubs. These flowers are sometimes regarded as being unsuitable for arrangements because of their habit of drooping their heads when cut and put into water. This is contrary to my own experience, as only occasionally have I found them to be slightly unreliable, and this is usually when they were older flowers and ready to fall anyway. In fact, I have often used them in church decorations and been grateful for their colouring (either white or pink, whichever was needed) for their height and for their dignified and beautifully-shaped foliage.

The tobacco plant (Nicotiana) is another lovely summer flowering plant, but this time, an annual. It comes in deep rose or starch white or lime-green, all of them sweet smelling, with fine, fresh green foliage. For cutting they are most admirable, lasting well and going on into the autumn months with still a hint of summer about them.

Lilies are among the best of all summer flowers and I have dealt with these in a separate chapter. Agapanthus is not a true lily, but is often known as the African lily, and is a splendid flower for cutting. It comes either in white or in a rather deep purple-toned blue, with lily like foliage to set it off. The African lily is one of the most long lasting of all plants suitable for tall flower groups. It looks especially attractive when contrasted with deep cerise coloured gladioli and blue globe thistles.

Delphiniums, yet another summer flower, have been discussed in a separate chapter too. The yellow meadow rue (Thalictrum) is a good contrast with delphiniums.

Dahlias and zinnias are both summer flowers and both have been dealt with in separate sections. Sweet peas are among the sweetest smelling of all summer flowers, the best for cutting and one of the most exciting and exotic where colour is concerned. Arranged with some of their tendrils and buds they give a charming feeling of lightness to a group of flowers. White sweet peas are especially charming with Iceberg roses and white snapdragons.

Coneflowers (Rudbeckia), chamomile (Anthemis), nasturtiums, phlox are all valuable flowers in their different ways, depending on the colour needed or the type of arrangement one has in mind.

Table arrangements

It seems to me to be a great pity that flowers for a dining table should only be attempted when entertaining. I personally always like to see flowers on a table where one is having meals, whether it be the kitchen table or a polished Regency table in a large dining room.

The tradition of elaborate table decorations has been handed down to us from the days of the epergne, (this may well be the reason why people sometimes feel they have not got the time or money for flower arrangements for the table on an everyday basis.) Decorations then often included fanciful ornaments filled with exotic flowers placed at intervals on damask cloths. Elegant colour schemes were worked out in coloured glass, heavily crocheted lace, candles and napkins, and these were picked up by the flowers. A glance into an early edition of Mrs. Beeton's cook book will show what I mean.

Nowadays this kind of domestic splendour would be impossible to keep up, our mode of living dictates a very simple form of decoration. Almost more than anywhere else in the house, it seems to me to be vital to arrange flowers for the dining table in position. How can you tell what two little silver egg cups full of snowdrops are going to look like with silver candlesticks beside them unless they are where you are finally going to need them. They will look quite different on the kitchen table or the pantry draining board. And so polish your table top as much as you like, and then do the flowers in their positions, laying a small dust sheet on the table beside them to ensure that no spot of water, leaf or petal will fall upon your polished surface. Let us now concentrate on ideas which can be carried out simply, quickly, and economically.

There are a few general rules for table decora-

tions, whether for a dinner party or for breakfast:-

1 The flowers and leaves must be in *perfect* condition.

2 The means of anchorage must be disguised.

3 A decoration should not be big enough to necessitate peering round or over the flowers in order to engage in conversation.

4 The colour schemes of the flowers, candles, containers, and table napkins must be considered, but it is possible to introduce some variety by the use of silver or plain glass, porcelain or coloured glass, as the occasion demands and as one's possessions will allow.

5 The need to use long lasting flowers does not arise for a dinner party, and water lilies, for example, come into their own here. Phlox, cut right up to the flower head, can be charming, and poppies, though they may drop the next day, can provide just that touch of colour which fits into the scheme.

The smaller the quantity of material used the more essential it is that it should be in perfect condition. If, for example, there is a bunch of yellow chrysanthemums in a glass container and a leaf is crushed or one of the flowers is beginning very slightly to droop, their slight defects might not be noticed. But where there are only two iris, a few anemones, or a spray of clematis any defect, however small, would be very noticeable.

The means of anchorage *must* be well concealed. This is an obvious fact, but it is not always easy to carry out. It is simple enough to hide a pin holder when it is only seen from one angle or at a distance. But on a dining table it must stand up to close observation from all directions. There are various means of subterfuge. Sometimes moss or stalwart leaves are used, or the flowers themselves are cut short towards the centre.

Leaves are easy to find during the summer months. At other times geranium and bergenia are both available (this is one of the uses of keeping a geranium through the winter and not throwing it out after taking cuttings) or else one or two flat

A bunch of anemones can provide an economical table decoration, if the flowers are cut short so that the full beauty of their centres is seen. They also look attractive for a table arrangement, floating in a flat dish.

Left, In this table decoration small bunches of violets are arranged in individual containers.
The soft woodland scent of violets seems to be more noticeable when they are arranged in bunches and a greater emphasis of colour is provided.
Primroses, snowdrops, grape hyacinths etc. could be used in place of violets.

Right, A candlestick holder can be an attractive container for a table arrangement. A few Paper Whites are arranged here with sprays of dark green ceanothus and are reflected in the silver base of the holder.

257

globular eucalyptus leaves cut from the lower stems, if you already have some in the house. From the garden a short spray of camellia or rosemary or garden ragwort might provide the cover needed. When selecting leaves for this purpose it is important to think of them not only for the purpose you have in mind but also in relation to the flowers. Otherwise they will look just what they are, a camouflage, and not an integral part of the arrangement. Still another method of deception is the use where suitable of a small piece of bark.

On one occasion when only a single spray of spurge *(Euphorbia fulgens)* was used on a yellow plate, a silver thimble was kept in position with yellow Plasticine, and held enough water for the evening.

If wire netting is used in a table decoration it can be helpful to paint it either white or green, according to the colour of the container and the flowers. I have found white most useful on many occasions, but if a lot of foliage is used green would be less obvious a colour. Small containers, like silver egg cups, do not require anchorage of any kind and this saves a great deal of trouble.

The size of the decoration in relation to the size of the table is also a main consideration. A small table dictates a small arrangement, but with a bigger table there is more scope for variety. It is not always necessary to have one central decoration, and some hostesses have found that two or three small matching groups arranged at intervals, either down the centre or towards the corners of the table, make an interesting change. Small porcelain troughs are excellent for this purpose. They do not take up much room or use many flowers and much interest can be achieved by the way in which they are grouped on the table.

One way of making a small decoration larger is by the use of a strip or circle of mirror. The amount of reflection obtained is not great, but it is enough to give an extra emphasis to the flowers.

If length is required, as on a long, fairly narrow refectory type of table, it is wise to remember the importance of cutting stems into different lengths, using short flowers towards the centre.

Colour schemes of flowers, candles, containers, etc., are so personal that I hesitate to make suggestions. They are fun to think out oneself and satisfying when complete.

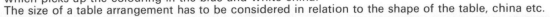

A suitable arrangement, in size and colour, consisting of mock orange blossom which picks up the colouring in the blue and white china.
The size of a table arrangement has to be considered in relation to the shape of the table, china etc.

As we have already said, flowers used for a dining table need not be long lasting, neither do they need to come in any specific size, shape or colour. But there is one restriction, they should not have a strong perfume. The smell of the food should not have to compete with the perfume of heavily scented flowers. Furthermore, a scent which appeals to one person may not do so for another, and the warm atmosphere of a dinner party will bring out the scent even more.

Small flowers are, of course, especially suited to small arrangements, though one or two single large blooms, cut *almost* up to the flower so that one can see right into them, also make excellent decorations. One of the most successful of these I have found was a head of giant cow parsley, cut right under the umbel. This was arranged on a flat plate that had been painted black, and showed up the white clusters of the smaller umbels like so many stars.

Violets are invaluable for many reasons. They have a faint, sweet, rather woody smell, which is not likely to offend anyone. They are cheap, and obtainable at almost any time of the year and if they are given a good drink through their heads before arranging (they like being submerged upside down) they will retain a sparkling look throughout the evening, as though they have been sprinkled with dew.

I should now like to discuss briefly larger groups for a buffet or side table or for a dinner party of some size.

One of the best containers for flowers on such an occasion is a dish from an early dessert service with a pedestal, or a glass tazza. The former may have some depth to it and be capable of taking water, if this is the case a great deal of trouble is removed. Otherwise, as in the case of the flat topped tazza, something to hold the water has to be included. A shallow sandwich cake tin is quite suitable for this purpose and may be held firmly in position by covering it with wire netting. This type of pedestal container means that the flowers are seen well above the dishes of food, etc. and by having one or two such arrangements quite a lengthy floral decoration can be achieved.

To sum up, although dining table decorations need not cost a lot of money, or use a lot of flowers, or take up a great deal of time, they require some thought to be successful.

Here a few bright red carnations are arranged with camellia foliage in a white porcelain vase. The colour of the carnations is picked up by the curtains and emphasised by the white of the vase.

Top, A tall glass bottle is used here to give extra height to carnations and a few branches.
A group of this kind should have a plain background so that the outline can be seen clearly.

Left, In this tall group the graceful curving stems of fuchsia are arranged in a glass decanter. Shrubs of fuchsia should be allowed to grow freely and untrimmed if the branches are to be used for tall arrangements.

Right, It is not always necessary to have a tall container to produce a tall arrangement. In this group foxgloves are used and if the lower flowers
are cut off as they begin to fall, the tight buds will come out giving longer life to the group.

Tall arrangements

Tall arrangements need not necessarily be edifices of great height and vast proportions. On the occasions when a vertical effect is required in a room, height can be achieved by merely using a tall, thin container. This is the usual method employed and some flowers lend themselves especially well to this sort of arrangement. In this category one could probably include without exception all lilies (they grow so straight and tall in their natural habitat). Iris is another upright plant, as are delphiniums, gladioli and foxgloves.

Another way to achieve a tall effect is by using a perfectly flat dish or plate, which does not in itself give any height. The floral arrangement in this case might only need the addition of two or three spear like leaves or flowers to give an appearance of height to a rather squat, squarish group. This is a more difficult type of arrangement to arrange, I think, but it can be effective in its way if done well, and it also allows the material to be spread out at the base in a manner which would be impossible in a tall, thin vase. The question of balance is a difficult one but one well worth studying, for width at times seems to be an essential counterpart to height. If a flat container is used, the width of the dish helps to give balance and the large leaves at the base will also add weight when dealing with tall arrangements.

Returning to the previous point of tall containers, when using a tall container a great deal must depend on the amount of material to be arranged. For only a few stems there is nothing better, to

salmon and pinky-yellow. It flourishes, once established, to such a degree that it has to be trimmed occasionally to keep it within bounds.

The alstroemeria, known as the Peruvian lily, is a native of South America. In England it flowers in the open from late June onwards.

The flowers of the Lenten roses, *Helleborus orientalis*, and their hybrids are delightful for decoration, although sometimes inclined to droop their heads, but their foliage is always rewarding.

Dramatic foliage in a tall group may be provided by the iris, gladioli, hosta, and hellebore plants. The contrast here is one rather more of shape than colour.

In *Flowers in House and Garden* Mrs. Constance Spry writes about the dark gleaming foliage of *Helleborus corsicus*. 'This is a magnificent species with its dark shining holly like leaves and clean strong stems carrying quantities of flowers'. The flowers are especially attractive, they come in clusters of a clear, pale green, always an unusual and difficult colour to find in cut flowers. Helleborus produce flowers of a shape (large and drooping, or small tight clusters) and colour (white, mauve and mauve-green, and pale lime green) rarely equalled. They are certainly plants to be cherished, as much for their decorative value in the garden as in the house.

Both iris and gladioli have rather similar spear like leaves, invaluable in an arrangement, but sometimes their wide, rather fat stems are difficult to fix in position, though once they are firmly in place they will last for a long time without showing any signs of wavering. Two other leaves which give the same kind of clear outline, but which are even more solid and definite, are those of the New Zealand flax *(Phormium tenax)* green streaked with yellow, and clivia, dark and gleaming. The gladioli flowers themselves are perhaps one of the most valuable for giving height with a spire effect and more solid colour lower down their stems.

Hostas, or funkias as they are still sometimes called, also come in a great variety. They like a cool, shaded position in the garden and are especially suitable as clumps towards the edge of a shrubbery. *Hosta fortunei* and *H. sieboldii* are among the most decorative of all. Apart from their rather lovely colouring – either pale green, dark green or green and yellow, or green and white, their shape is a good clear cut and simple.

When leaves on the older plants have grown to a good size and have a stem over one foot long, hostas are tremendously useful in large pedestal arrangements. They will last well, especially if they are given a good deep drink before they are arranged.

Branches of trees will provide the extra height needed in certain tall arrangements, and flowers

my mind, than a decanter. This is usually an attractive shape, and its narrow neck acts as an excellent holder for the flowers.

An important fact to remember is that water soon disappears down this narrow neck and that unless the stems are all safely reaching down into the bowl, the water level must always be very carefully watched.

A tall jug, a coffee pot or certain early pewter tea urns are also excellent. (The spouts of these can be removed and the hole soldered over.)

Here is a selection of tall flowers and foliage:

A few stems of the already tall Peruvian lily *Alstroemeria aurantiaca* when arranged in a decanter can be given extra height. This plant, comes in many beautiful soft shades of pink,

Right, An arrangement of carnations
and snapdragons in a pedestal vase.
The material is kept in place by large mesh wire netting —
the level of the water needs careful watching
with such a large arrangement.

A tall arrangement not only needs tall flowers but often
a stand or some type of pedestal to give it extra height.
In the photograph the flowers are arranged
in a pedestal vase which stands on
a specially constructed pedestal.
The tallest flowers in the group are fennel,
teasels and branches of viburnum; globe artichoke leaves
and branches of Persian iron wood (branches of beech
would have been equally suitable)
give width to the arrangement.

can be arranged inside a framework of such branches as beech, silver birch, prunus (copper),
Persian iron wood *(Parrotia persica)*, whitebeam
and hazel. Delphiniums will give height but not
with quite such a tapering effect as gladioli. False
goat's beard *(Astilbe)* or bush spiraeas are also
valuable and well worth growing specially for such
arrangements. (Any of the flowers or flowering
shrubs mentioned are reliable and are not in any
way difficult to anchor in position.) To me the
best flower of all for height must surely be the
Eremurus robustus.

It can grow to a height of about eight feet, and
in this case the stem is sometimes so stout and
heavy that it becomes very difficult to fix it firmly
in a group of flowers. However, the extra height
and size of *E. robustus* makes it almost indispensable for especially tall arrangements. The smaller
fox-tail lilies *(Eremurus)* are not nearly so tall or
solid of stem, and will present few problems.

Tall larkspur are often helpful in introducing
colour and giving a clear outline. Certain lilies
can also be of great value. *Lilium candidum* and
L. longiflorum are both excellent, and are often
used for wedding decorations.

Finally, there is a way of making tall arrangements even taller, but it must be done with great
care. This means using tin containers in the
shape of cornets, and painting them dark green.
These are then attached by wire on to thin sticks,
which are inserted into the flower arrangement,
with the stem of the stick going into the water
and being fixed in the wire netting underneath.
The tin cornet is now filled with water, after which
the flowers may be arranged in it, thus giving them
an extra height, approximately the length of the
stick from the base of the cornet to where it touches
the water. It is essential to put only flowers that
look as though they could possibly achieve this
height into this device otherwise the falseness of
the apparatus will be seen at a glance. For
example, most gladioli, delphiniums, larkspur,
etc. would be a safe choice, but something which is
naturally much shorter such as a stock, or snapdragon, or marigold, would look absurd. This
may seem only a small point, but it is worth
remembering since using the wrong flowers can
spoil the whole effect.

Tulips

Tulips are one of the pillars of flower decoration in the late spring. Reliable, usually stout stemmed, coming in a variety of colours, and always with good, green leaves, they will add colour and dignity to any vase of flowers.

During the seventeenth century in Holland the well known *Tulip Books* were being painted. They are, in fact, illustrated catalogues of the tulips then available for purchasing. At this time one could have not only striped tulips (the British Museum has a water colour drawing of one in dark red and white) but also ones with coloured borders and in plain colours. In a painting reproduced in Thornton's *Temple of Flora* (1799-1807) there is a group of tulips which are like Joseph's coat of many colours – a yellow tulip with dark purple lines at the edges, another striped with blue purple, and yet another in what seems to be a rose-pink with white stripes. Describing them in his text, Thornton sadly remarks on the inability of the artist to depict truly the wondrous colours of these splendid flowers: 'How much does the imitative

painting fall short in trying to represent these ravishing beauties of the vegetable world'.

Nevertheless the Dutch painters of the time did depict this beauty fairly effectively, for we feel that we know the striped tulips in the paintings of Ambrosius Bosschaert the Elder, Abraham Bosschaert and Ambrosius Bosschaert the Younger, Balthasar Van der Ast, Jan Van Huysum and Nicholas van Veerendael. In their military colourings these tulips are reminiscent of regiments of cavalry standing proudly out amongst the softer tones and shapes of the roses, bluebells, love-in-a-mist, and butterflies.

Present day tulips come in an unbelievably wide range of colours, from the primary shades of clear, bright pillar-box red, sunshine yellow, and white, to the secondary colours of orange and deep purple, to the 'mixtures' of pink, cream, rose, ruby, scarlet, crimson, etc.

There are plain tulips, tulips with pointed petals, tall tulips and short tulips, and tulips with frilled edges or striped petals. One of the most enchanting for flower decoration is, to my mind, the small pink and white striped *Tulipa clusiana*. It is charming arranged either with other late spring flowers or on its own. It grows happily in any pocket of a rock garden or in clumps at the front of a border (only if the border is well drained and in a sunny position).

Some of the early flowering tulips (those out in April as opposed to the May flowering ones) especially the cream, white and yellow ones, combine well with daffodils, and the soft yellow of primroses. The May flowering tulips are usually out about the same time as rosemary, guelder rose and some of the brooms *(Genista)*. In a pale yellow they are especially attractive with rosemary and the yellow flowered berberis, while the off-white or cream shades are enchanting with the guelder rose – especially before it is quite out and when it still has a tinge of green in the flower-head.

For bolder and brighter colour schemes clear red tulips can be arranged with equally bright and contrasting yellow forsythia, as well as the crisp blue early flowering Californian lilac *(Ceanothus)*. Shorter scarlet tulips can be combined with grape hyacinths, *Anemone fulgens* and rosy sprays of japonica. Pink tulips contrast charmingly with white lilac and tone in with the mauve or deep purple kind. They are also a good contrast in shape with the early tree-peonies (rose, pink and white or creamy-pink). Salmon-pink tulips can

Three pale yellow double tulips are arranged here on a pin holder in a shallow dish of water. The stems are cut different lengths so that each flower can be clearly seen; there is special emphasis on the beauty of colour and shape of the pale green leaves.

Tulips can sometimes be difficult to arrange so that they do not seem stiff and formal.
Here the stems are cut different lengths and are arranged with their own leaves and contrasting foliage.
The soft green of the tulip leaves is emphasised by the shiny dark green elaeagnus.

echo the colour of the salmon tufted eucalyptus and, in any case, stand out against the usual blue-grey of the eucalyptus foliage. The salmon-orange variety go well with the same tones in clivias, and the bird of paradise flower *(Strelitzia)* make a splendid show with the more yellow orange tulips.

Besides these, there are so many more possible colour schemes, but of course all depend on the material available.

Below is a list of available tulips from which to make a selection for growing in the garden, and of course ultimately for cutting:

SINGLE EARLY TULIPS –
APRIL FLOWERING:
Pink Beauty, deep glowing pink with a snow white flush on the outer petals, about twelve inches in height.
Prince of Austria, bright brick-red shading to orange. Long lasting flowers, sweet scented.
Proserpine, large satin rose flowers, white based, one of the best available.
Rising Sun, large, well formed, deep yellow flowers on strong stems, is about sixteen inches

in height, good for cutting.
Princess Irene, distinctive apricot colouring, about twelve inches in height, dark green leaves.
Sunburst, bright yellow striped and feathered brilliant red pointed petals, about fourteen inches in height.

DOUBLE EARLY TULIPS –
APRIL FLOWERING:
Orange Nassau, one of the best of recent introductions. Large, warm orange scarlet flowers, twelve inches in height.
Peach Blossom, large full-double flowers, deep rose-pink, flushed white, twelve inches in height.
Schoonoord, the finest double early white. Large, full flowers, excellent for bedding and forcing, twelve inches in height.
Tea Rose, the same exquisite blending of pale yellow and soft rose as seen in many tea roses.
Aga Khan, warm deep orange; a really good colour and with quite distinct, large handsome flowers.
Duchess of Kent, a very large flower, full rich rose throughout.
John Dacosta, brilliant salmon pink, a most unusual shade.

A jug of tulips arranged with their leaves; the colour and shape of tulip leaves is most attractive as a background for the flowers, but it is important that they should be in a large container to allow them to breathe. Tulips are one of the flowers which provide more variety of colour than any other and which link up with almost any furnishing scheme.

Rheingold, large bright chrome yellow.
DOUBLE LATE TULIPS – MAY FLOWERING:
Allegro, large flowers of warm cerise red with white tipped petals.
Mount Tacoma, large white flowers on strong erect stems, closely resembling a double white Chinese peony.
Symphonia, a deep glowing maroon red.
COTTAGE GARDEN TULIPS –
MAY FLOWERING:
These are so named because their prototypes have been found mostly in old cottage gardens in Great Britain and France. Distinct in habit they come in many beautiful colours, and are excellent for borders and for growing naturally amongst grass.
Beverley, a lovely orange flame shade, late flowering.
Carrara, a cup shaped flower of great size and substance, snowy white with white anthers.
Conde Nast, light yellow flushed with rosy orange. A tall, shapely and strong grower.

Persian Beauty, outside carmine-rose edged with pale bronze, inside carmine-bronze shading to salmon towards a yellow base, anthers are a greenish yellow.

Rosy Wings, good lasting quality, with long five inch buds, a delightful shade of pink with a forget-me-not blue base. Blooms about three days earlier than the average cottage tulip but will remain in flower as long as the others.

DARWIN TULIPS – MAY FLOWERING:

Arabian Nights, a most unusual shade of chestnut red with a darker sheen, large, well formed, egg shaped flowers.

Breezand, intense geranium like with a jet black, gold edged base, a large flower on a strong straight stem.

Clara Butt, of perfect form, delicate soft rose pink with a salmon glow, centre white and blue.

Glacier, large oval pure white flowers with white base and white anthers. Very long lasting.

Nobel, deep geranium red with an attractive greenish black centre, edged with yellow.

Princess Elizabeth, a charming vivid rose pink flower, deepening with age and with a slight silvery flush at the margins, centre white.

Winston Churchill, light rose pink with a silvery flush at the margin, and long lasting.

PARROT TULIPS – MAY FLOWERING:

Fantasy, rose pink in colour with apple green featherings.

Sunshine, bright golden yellow with green flecks.

Violet Green, an artistic blend of soft lilac and lavender violet.

BIZARRE AND REMBRANDT TULIPS – MAY FLOWERING:

Clara, deep pink and scarlet with white feathering.

Insulinde, a lovely combination of yellow, bronze, and various shades of mahogany and violet.

Sometimes it is found that the longer stemmed tulips either droop or take on unexpected curves. In case this happens it is useful to take the tulips out of the vase in the evening, snip off the ends of the stems, wrap all the stems together in firm newspaper so that only the flower-head emerges. This must not be too tight, but it must also be firm enough to give the necessary support. Tie round with string or pin together and then stand upright in a bucket or tall jug filled to the brim with water and leave all night in a cool place. In the morning the stems should have become much straighter and firmer and can once more take their place in the arrangement.

Tulips are arranged here with sprays of mimosa, which provide a clear contrast in shape and tone with the tulips. The basket is lined with a cake tin to hold the water; the flowers are arranged in large mesh wire netting.

Wall arrangements

A wall bracket arrangement is one of the most attractive and safe ways of showing off flowers, for the flowers and branches are clearly defined against the solid background, and are well out of of the way of being knocked over.

There are various kinds of these, but the principle in most cases is the same – a small amount of material only is needed.

Perhaps it would be a good idea to go through the different types of wall brackets or wall vase one by one.

The console or bracket is often made of wood and painted with gilt. Although its top is flat it usually has a carved leg bracket which curves back underneath the console and against the wall. The bowl of flowers is placed on the flat top against the wall.

Sometimes a bracket such as this is fixed to a mirror, in which case the flowers will be seen partly in reflection. It is important when fixing the bracket on the wall, with a flower arrangement

in mind (after all these are often used to hold a special piece of porcelain or a bronze) to think of the height in relation to one's eye level. If it is too high on the wall the whole arrangement will have to be seen from below. This entails curving stems coming forward over the container, otherwise only the base of the vase will be noticeable. I think that it is almost better to be too near to the ground (at least one can see into the flowers from above) than too far away. An ideal position for a bracket is at the foot of a staircase. In this way whether one is coming down or going up the stairs one is always looking down into the arrangement.

The vase or container for the flowers is most important. First of all it must show the flowers to their best advantage, and, secondly, it must be in keeping with the bracket as some of it is likely to be visible. A flat cake dish with a low pedestal is one of the most successful containers that I have ever tried. It allows for some height and at the same time makes it possible for flowers to come

Nasturtiums come in an exciting range of colours, often on curving stems and are particularly suitable for a wall arrangement. Here they are arranged with their own attractive foliage and stand out well against the white wall.

A cluster of hop flowers is arranged here with pressed Spanish chestnut leaves. The hop flowers can be used when they are still green, before they have dried out completely or when they have acquired an attractive tan colouring.

forward and perhaps curve slightly over the edge of the bracket.

Next, the porcelain bracket to hang on the wall. It seems that some of the earliest arrangements were done in this type of wall bracket. The Leeds factory in 1745 designed and made ones which can now be seen in the porcelain department of the Victoria and Albert Museum in London. This type of bracket is not easy to find these days. One's best hope of coming across one lies in an antique shop or a junk stall in one of London's markets.

If you do find one guard it jealously. This bracket is especially suitable for a 'line' arrangement, and, as I have already mentioned, like most brackets this one will only need a little material. A few branches of cherry, quince or apple in the spring will go a long way towards making a decoration of some charm. In the winter a dried group is ideal, (in a bracket one need no longer be worried about the arrangement being easily knocked over,

especially as dried flowers are so light) where the soft colouring of the material is shown off so well, especially if it stands against a light background.

When fresh flowers are used, there is one big problem about a porcelain wall vase. This is the supply of water. The natural shape of such a vase is wider at the mouth, narrowing in width towards the tip, and since there must be a hole cut in the porcelain at the back of the vase to allow it to be hung up on a nail or hook, the water level cannot be above this hole. Unfortunately some manufacturers have not realised the importance of this hole, from the practical point of view, and it may easily be at least an inch from the brim of the vase. So watch the water supply very carefully indeed.

Again, when hanging a wall vase one must think of it in connection with the nearby decorations, curtains and pictures (this, I must emphasise, applies equally to any vase in any room and is not something extra to consider).

Sometimes a pottery will make twin wall vases

Here branches of mock orange are arranged
in a porcelain wall bracket. A few branches
are sufficient for this type of arrangement.
As branches like a lot of water
the level in the tapering vase needs to be watched carefully.

and these can be most attractive. I have a friend who has two small ones, which she keeps filled even during the winter months with material that she brings back from the country. I have seen these vases looking most charming with sprays of ivy and branches of hazel and alder with their first catkins. Later on she arranges a few wood anemones and primroses with wild arum leaves.

An old fashioned silver tureen lid cut in half and backed with metal, then hung upside down with the handle at the base (when in use over a meat dish it would have the handle at the top) is a most capacious wall bracket and this is fixed to the wall with solid screws. Although it can look delightful with a few branches it does, unlike the porcelain vase and the console, hold a large quantity of material if required. The lid itself is big enough to conceal two or three jam jars holding water, or to take one jam jar for flowers and branches and one or two pot plants which help to spin out the cut material during winter time. You can also fill this wall bracket with dried materials such as hydrangeas and teasels and only a few of these will make an arrangement of some size.

Bracket holders made in metal or wood are often to be seen nowadays. They are primarily designed to hold pot plants. The metal ones can be most decorative on the white washed (or pink washed) brick walls of a conservatory or small greenhouse. (I have also seen them filled with trailing ivy plants, used at intervals on the walls of a steep staircase going up at least three flights. The ivy was trained so that one pot connected with another, and a large bare area of rather ugly walls was completely transformed.)

Of course, these brackets can be converted so that they hold containers for water and this way they are especially useful when extra decorations are needed, like a party or wedding or at Christmas. A festive appearance can be given quickly and by the use of a relatively small amount of material. Garlands or bundles of ribbon, evergreens, smilax, ivy, etc. may be hung from one to the next. The brackets can be bought quite cheaply (there are extravagantly priced ones, beautifully made, probably by hand), since they are made in numbers by machines. The metal ones usually come in black but they can be painted white or any other colour to match the wall.

This type of bracket can also be used for church decorations at a harvest festival—if the stone pillar will not take a nail it can be held in position with a strong wire, though if used on a wooden pulpit or choir stall a nail might perhaps be possible.

A few carnations are arranged with branches of holly and evergreens in a raffia wall bracket.
The shape of the container is similar to that of a cornucopia;
it is important that this group should have a plain background.

A dried arrangement in a wall bracket can be an investment for the winter months; the flowers are not likely to be knocked or broken in this position and not so much material is needed as for an all-round arrangement.
The white background is good for the soft colours and ensures that they are seen to their best advantage.

Wedding flowers

When arranging the church flowers for a wedding the first step is to pay a visit to the church by yourself. Take a notebook and pencil and sit down in a row about half way down the aisle. You may know the church well, or think you do, but you must now look at it from a new point of view.

Colour plays a very large part in wedding flowers, and it is important to notice any bright stained glass windows or strip of carpet which may dominate the scene. Altar cloths and hangings often vary according to the church calendar, and the vicar or the verger should be consulted about these. The general atmosphere of the church should be taken into consideration. Some churches are light and airy and are lit from the sky by a clerestory or from the sides by large plain windows uncluttered by glass. Others are built of heavy stone, with only small stained glass windows. A lofty building with big windows through which the sun comes streaming in, will require different treatment from a dark church with solid architecture producing deep shadows. All these factors must enter into one's conception of the colours to be chosen, fitting in, of course, with the selection of the bride herself.

Pedestals being of special importance would probably be the next note heading. As you sit in your place looking round the church, you can probably see everything clearly. But you must imagine the church full of people standing up. In that case, only flowers which are above the height of the average person's head have a chance of being seen, except when the congregation is seated and the marriage service is one where the greater part of the time is spent in standing, hence the pedestal arrangement. A well designed one adds dignity and shows off its flowers to great advantage. The great point about a pedestal is that it should be absolutely steady and capable of firmly supporting a heavy weight.

Sometimes one pedestal is required and sometimes two. If you decide to have a pair, there is the added difficulty of matching up two big arrangements, getting flowers of the same variety, shape and size.

If the font is particularly lovely or very near to the church entrance, the bride may like some form of decoration in it or round it. Should the font stand well back in a corner of the church it is not always necessary to fill it with flowers. I once decorated a font in this position by putting a big square glass fish tank inside and almost filling it with water. I used large mesh wire netting as

This wedding group in the Parish Church of Abinger Hammer, Surrey, England, stands on a pedestal. The colour scheme is green, white, cream and yellow and includes cream eremuri and carnations, white lilies, yellow roses, green leek heads and dark green and variegated arum foliage.

an anchorage, and arranged in it tall branches of silver birch. The effect was rather like a small bit of woodland in the corner, and as it was so far away from the centre aisle it showed up in a way I think that flowers would never have done.

A subsidiary decoration may be needed in the form of a vase on the prayer book table near the door, or one on a window ledge. People occasionally ask for garlands to go from pew to pew, but the making of garlands is really strictly for the professional and should never be attempted without expert advice. At Jewish wedding ceremonies the tabernacle is often decorated in this way, and I have known three trained flower arrangers spend a whole morning on this alone.

Containers can be discussed with the verger as you make your plans. I suppose that nothing varies more in churches than the way in which they are equipped—or not equipped—for arranging flowers. With weddings one expects to provide most of the necessary vases, etc., as requirements may vary greatly from wedding to wedding.

Remember that if you are having two big groups on pedestals, you will need two matching big containers, and these may take some finding, unless, of course, the church has them there already. If you do not know, find out where the water supply is, and arrange for permission to leave your flowers overnight in buckets of water in a cool place. (Most churches are notoriously cool, but I have heard of flowers being placed near some hot pipes when the heating happened to be turned on.)

It is most important to find out if the church is free some hours before the wedding, for sometimes there is another wedding to fit in with, and you may only have enough time to whisk away those vases and put your own into position, having had to arrange them beforehand. Or, there may be a choir practice the evening before and you may have to work while it is going on. But whatever happens, you must allow yourself plenty of time, remembering that whenever it is at all possible you ought to do the flowers the day before and then just tidy up on the day itself.

This font is near the church door
so is included in the decoration scheme for a wedding.
It is filled with branches of mock orange,
partly stripped of their leaves, and guelder rose.

Right, A wall arrangement is ideal for a wedding reception as it can be clearly seen and is in no danger of being knocked over. This group includes eremuri, lupins, mock orange, arum lilies, bergenia leaves, grasses and rosemary.

wasting time looking for them.

The lead shot and the sand are used to weight down the large vases; use one or the other or both if you like. The tin tubes are valuable for getting height, but it is sometimes difficult to use them so that they remain invisible. They are fixed into the wire when most of the flowers are already arranged, and then kept in position by binding them with string or wire to the existing support. The last two requirements on the list speak for themselves.

Some special flowers in special colours have to be ordered well ahead of time, particularly if they are out of season, but it is advisable to have delivery of them only the day before. If you are cutting flowers from the garden, do so at a cool time of the day. If you are buying them from a shop, only go somewhere that you know and where you can depend on the flowers being fresh. A good reliable florist will be your greatest friend at such a time, and it is worth paying a little more to get the very best material.

When you have all the flowers together take them to the church or have them delivered there, and then unpack them, trim the ends and smash the stems of branches or split them up (any woody stemmed flowers such as chrysanthemums and roses require this).

There are a few ways of helping flowers to last well, apart from trimming the ends of the stems and giving them a good drink. Sometimes, if the stems and heads are wrapped round in stout newspaper while they are standing in water, wobbly stems will become strong and floppy flowers will become crisp and sturdy. (This applies especially to tulips.) Mock orange *(Philadelphus)* will show better and last longer if many of its leaves are trimmed away. Stocks need tender care and must have their lower stems stripped. Fox-tail lilies *(Eremurus)* may be bought ahead of time if they are in tight bud, and kept in a shut wooden box. Queen Anne's lace, cut from the hedgerows, will behave wonderfully if given a good deep drink for some hours and allowed to stiffen its stems.

Equipment needed for doing wedding flowers is almost the same as that used for doing them in the house, only on a much larger scale.

3 large dust sheets
6 buckets
plenty of large mesh wire netting
2 pairs of secateurs or special scissors
that will cut wire and trim branches
small bottles of lead shot, or bag of sand
tin tubes for raising height of flowers
watering can with narrow spout for topping up the vases
vases and pedestals

The uses of the dust sheets are obvious. The six buckets may seem mysterious, but if the flowers are to soak the night before they need plenty of water and space. Flowers like to breathe as well as to drink and being tightly packed together will not help them at all. I have put two pairs of secateurs in because it is easy to put them down amongst leaves and then not be able to find them. Without scissors one is completely lost. They will turn up in the end, but in the meantime you are

Now begins the most exciting part.

You divide your material, fix the wire netting so that an earthquake would not move it, weight down the vase, fill it three quarters full with water, then arrange the flowers.

The arrangement itself is entirely for you to create. You will have thought out the colours and and shapes, and after that it is exactly like painting a picture.

I have always found it very helpful to go and sit in various pews in the church, and see how the arrangements look from each one.

Fill the container to the brim with water when you have finished and tidy it up the next morning, topping it up where necessary.

Perhaps a few suggestions for wedding flowers might be helpful, thinking chiefly in terms of white. Other colour schemes are perhaps not quite so specific, since they vary from one wedding to another according to personal taste and selection.

WHITE: carnations, roses, delphiniums, fox-tail lilies *(Eremurus)*, Solomon's seal, lilac, chrysanthemums, gladioli, gypsophila, azaleas, narcissi, larkspur, rhododendrons, summer flowering jasmine, phlox, iris, spiraea, valerian, tobacco plant, marguerites, magnolia, peonies, tulips, campanula, mock orange *(Philadelphus)*, guelder rose, *Clematis montana alba, flammula* and The Bride, broom, myrtle.

BLUE: African lily *(Agapanthus)* bluebells, campanulas, delphiniums, Californian lilac, *(Ceanothus)*, *Clematis* Mrs Cholmondeley, cornflowers, gentian, hydrangeas, iris, larkspur, love-in-a-mist, lupin, flax, scabious, veronica, sea holly, globe thistle.

PINK: larkspur, carnations, roses, lilies *(Rubra)*, camellia, hydrangea, dahlia, nerines, peonies, fox-tail lilies *(Eremurus)*, gladioli, phlox, valerian, Chilean gum box *(Escallonia)*, bush honeysuckle *(Weigela)*, coral bells, spiraea, snapdragon.

YELLOW: fox-tail lilies *(Eremurus)*, carnations, roses, lilies, yarrow *(Achillea)*, honeysuckle, forsythia, globe flower, *(Trollius)*, broom, chrysanthemum, tulips, daffodils, leopard's bane *(Doronicum)*, chamomile *(Anthemis)*, rhododendron, winter flowering jasmine, azalea.

275

White arrangements

White flowers are no longer thought of purely in terms of weddings or funerals, nowadays, in fact, coloured flowers are often ordered for both these occasions. But there is no doubt that a white arrangement seems to have a certain distinction of its own which in some mysterious way is denied to other colour schemes.

Apart from aesthetic reasons the usual preferences for white is this–a white arrangement goes with any colour scheme in any surroundings and with any background. This means that a certain economy can be practised at a time when flowers are scarce and expensive, for a white arrangement can be moved from room to room with confidence.

A white group almost always gives a cool effect, and white flowers mixed with fresh green foliage can be as refreshing to the eye on a hot summer's day as a cool drink is to the palate. Think of Madonna lilies, or the single white moon-daisies, of lilies-of-the-valley, or Iceberg roses – all give an impression of stillness, calm and serenity, but one must remember that they might tend to give a chilling effect on a cold day in a room without sunlight.

If white flowers are small they give a feeling of lightness and, in the case of Queen Anne's lace and the single philadelphus, have an almost fairy-like quality.

What about white flowers with green, grey or yellow foliage?

Solomon's seal (one of the most enchanting of all green plants suitable for flower arrangement) arranged with other white flowers immediately turns the colour scheme into a striking green and white one. The addition of a grey, like lamb's ears *(Stachys lanata),* garden ragwort *(Senecio laxifolius or Cineraria maritima)* is most effective and there is something appealing, I think, about white roses with immortelle, or the spiky curry plant *(Artemesia)* with white sweet peas. The foliage of *Convolvulvus cneorum* is dark grey green and goes most attractively with white bluebells or white campanulas. Finally a yellow green colour such as the tight buds of meadow sweet (before the flower begins to open) is immensely pleasing.

Numerous white flowers exist, from rare lilies and old roses to herbaceous plants and wild flowers. Here is a list of some of them, which includes now

Far left, The white of the lilies-of-the-valley in this small basket is picked up and emphasised by the variegated ivy leaves. If a special 'white' effect is required for a wedding the basket could be painted white.

Left, Short flower stems of a white viburnum are arranged here in a low basket with green and white wedding grass (also known as gardener's garters). The basket is painted green which helps to show off the white flowers.

and again a variegated leaf, but only if it is a green and white one not yellow: –

Anaphalis

Aster

Broom *(Cytisus albus)*

Californian tree poppy *(Romneya coulteri)*

Christmas rose *(Helleborus niger)*

Chrysanthemum

Clematis (e.g. *C. armandii, C. montana)*

Columbine *(Aquilegia)*

Everlasting pea *(Lathyrus latifolius)*

Fox-tail lily *(Eremurus)*

Guelder rose *(Viburnum opulus roseum)*

Gypsophila

Honeysuckle *(Lonicera)*

Horse chestnut *(Aesculus hippocastanum)*

Iris

Lilac *(Syringa)*

Lily (e.g. *L.regale, L. candidum, L. auratum)*

Magnolia

Marguerite *(Chrysanthemum frutescens)*

Mock orange *(Philadelphus)*

Myrtle *(Myrtus)*

Mullein *(Verbascum)*

Ox-eye daisy *(Chrysanthemum leucanthemum)*

Peony

Phlox

Pieris floribunda

Plantain lily *(Hosta)*

Plume poppy *(Macleaya cordata)*

Privet *(Ligustrum)*

Rhododendron

Russian vine *(Polygonum baldschuanicum)*

Snapdragon *(Antirrhinum)*

Solomon's seal *(Polygonatum)*

Star of Bethlehem *(Ornithogalum)*

Summer flowering jasmine *(Jasminum officinale)*

Tobacco plant *(Nicotiana)*

Whitebeam *(Sorbus aria)*

There was a time, known as the 'white period' when white flowers on their own, or with only a few leaves, were the fashion. Cecil Beaton describes this in his book *The Glass of Fashion:*

Here Japanese anemones are arranged on a pin holder in shallow off-white Staffordshire dish (the pin holder is in a glass bowl of water and is concealed by leaves). Japanese anemones have pure white flowers with circles of gold stamens, the small buds are dove-grey and the shape of the green leaves is particularly attractive.

'Those who had white rooms considered white flowers a desideratum. The craze for pristine whiteness became so exaggerated that even the green leaves had to be peeled off the branches of white lilacs and peonies. This stripping process, though a lengthy one, produced its surprising metamorphoses, and a bunch of syringa denuded of its leaves became something finely carved out of Japanese ivory'.

Another fashion of a more recent date and of rather a different kind, has been the vogue for the white vase. Whether this does, in fact, derive from the 'white period' already mentioned is difficult to decide, but it is true that the vogue for white was not, at that time of the early twenties, confined to flowers.

Even before these years, Mrs. Earle, author of *Pot-Pourri from a Surrey Garden* advocated the use of white paint in houses for bookcases, panelling and woodwork. This must have been something of a revolution at the time, as a great niece of hers remembers the interest she aroused and how unusual it was. Much later Mrs. Constance Spry recommended giving the walls of a sitting room, coats and coats of whitewash to make a good background for flower arrangements. She first noticed this idea carried out in Tunisia and 'saw afresh the beauty of flowers set against whitewashed walls.... it certainly gives full and true value to every flower and leaf set against it'. *(Flowers in House and Garden)*.

In exactly the same way a white container makes an effective background for most flowers and it is also a way of introducing white into an arrangement. There is an extra emphasis if white flowers are arranged in a white container. A very special and subtle effect is obtained.

Although white flowers are no longer connected *only* with weddings, they are, nevertheless, of great value on these occasions. The bride is often dressed in white and likes to carry white flowers, and some of the decorations will probably be carried out partly in white, although their chief colouring may be that of the bridesmaid's dresses.

The beauty of these flowers is equalled by their delicious scent; the small, delicate bells of the lilies-of-the-valley show up well against the bell-like flowers of the freesias in the arrangement. The dark evergreen leaves help to show up the paler green of the lily-of-the-valley leaves and to hide the bare stems of the freesias.

Wild flowers

For a long lasting arrangement there is
nothing to equal the wild ox-eye daisies or
field marguerites. These daisies lasted for
nearly a fortnight although the hedge parsley
had to be replaced after a week.

The general objection to using wild flowers for
indoor decoration is that they do not last. This
is something I have seldom found to be correct.
Of course there are some wild flowers which die
quickly, but this fact applies equally to some
garden flowers. Many wild flowers last surprisingly well when they are treated with the same
respect and care which is usually reserved for
specially cultivated blooms. They can hardly be
expected, any more than florist's flowers, to stand
up to the journey home unless they are well wrapped
or have their stems in water. Clutched in a hot
hand, exposed for some length of time to the
sunshine and, almost as bad, to draughts (of all the
discomforts that wild flowers have to suffer draught
is the most dangerous), and kept out of water for
some hours, it is hardly surprising if they droop
at the end of it.

They have been known to survive (in excellent
condition) first a local bus journey and then three
hours in a train, when wrapped in a compact
parcel of newspaper, (if they are wrapped in strong
newspaper, and covered completely so that no
outside air gets into the parcel, they will repay any
trouble taken over the packing), or settled in a
tall enamel jug with their stems in the water.

Here are a few which have proved their staying
power: the little white flowered jack-by-the-hedge,
with its curved stem, pale green pods and heart-
shaped leaves.

Bluebells and primroses which should be carried
home wrapped in a cool dock leaf or some damp
moss, and given a long deep drink as soon as
possible on arrival.

Spurge, one of the most decorative plants,
which goes on for weeks, to add to a green group.

Cowslips, buttercups (if picked in bud and the
older flowers cut off, as they die.)

Grasses make a delicate arrangement;
they should stand against
a plain background
so that the lightness
and design of the various
grasses can be seen against it.

White valerian, often seen
flourishing in walls and along grassy
banks is particularly useful for
flower arrangement. If cut when
still in bud it will last well.

Garlic, sheep's bit scabious, all these, together with some of the hedge-parsley family (particularly angelica), white campion, ox-eye daisy, clover, meadowsweet, and foxgloves. Another flower and a most graceful plant, coming this time from the hedgerows is wild clematis. (Instead of dying in the usual way by becoming limp or dropping its flowers, it actually dries while still in water, and the small bunches of flowers become soft, grey, fluffy clusters, looking almost more attractive than before.)

I once had a bowl of ox-eye daisies, Queen Anne's lace, and spur valerian which lasted perfectly for eight days. After that time the valerian and the Queen Anne's lace began to fall, but the daisies lasted for a further five days. A week is usually considered a good record for most cut flowers and these little field daisies, which often last beautifully for as long as a fortnight, ought to have

a special mention.

There does seem to be one difficulty which sometimes arises when arranging wild flowers. By their nature they are usually more delicate and very often smaller than most plants, which means that they may not produce such a definite effect or such a firm outline. It is important then to arrange them against a plain background and to be sure that they are not overpowered by too many ornaments or Victorian paraphernalia. Of course, there are some wild flowers and leaves which can compete perfectly well, but on the whole wild flowers show off best in simple surroundings.

There is a charming and interesting appeal for the use of wild flowers in a Cassell's *Household Guide* of about 1860, which shows a refreshing approach to the whole subject: 'It is to be regretted that a more general use is not made of our lovely field flowers for purposes of table decoration.

Foxgloves and hedge parsley are two of the most familiar sights growing in many hedgerows
and are both invaluable for flower arrangement. The tall spires of foxgloves are useful in large arrangements
and the lightness of hedge parsley contributes a delicacy to the group, often unobtainable in any other material.

Of all wild flowers the honeysuckle is perhaps the one with the sweetest smell and the one which goes on flowering for the longest. Even without many flowers the leaves and curving stems have a special charm; if cut when in fairly tight bud the flowers will come out in water and last for some time.

Even the most skilful and professed bouquet makers know of no substitute for the 'totter', or quaker grass, and ...the ragged robin, scarlet poppy, wild clematis, butterfly orchis, honeysuckle, lady's mantle, bluebells, wild anemones, and the ever welcome daisy...abound wherever there are green fields and hedgerows'. It goes on to suggest that 'a handful culled at random in an evening's walk' should be kept from day to day 'to gladden the eyes of those whom daily toil debars from outdoor pleasures'.

Finally there is the fun of collecting wild flowers and seedheads for a dried arrangement for the winter. I have covered this in its own section.

Growing in the hedgerows, amongst many other treasures, are foxglove seedheads, knapweed, and meadowsweet. The foxglove stems are useful and decorative, but, for some reason, often rather difficult to find; the growth of knapweed (this ordinary weed is condemned for 'blunting the mower's scythe') is its chief attraction.

Let us turn now to the subject of branches and leaves suitable for decoration, especially in the spring. Willow, alder and hazel are three of the most valuable trees for cutting in the first months of the year, when their catkins adorn the hedgerows and bring indoors the expectation and cheerfulness of the season. Although they are sometimes accused of dropping their pollen badly, I think that they are worth the trouble of a little extra dusting and I have noticed that if they are cut as soon as they show signs of coming out, this practice will not happen.

The fresh green of wild arum leaves is a welcome addition to a small arrangement of flowers, especially coming early on as they do before many other plants are even showing. Foxglove and primrose leaves also provide some of the first patches of green and they are closely followed by bursting buds of beech, silver birch and hazel.

Winter arrangements

Flowers available during winter months vary according to the climate and the country where one lives. The problem is which flowers will survive the heating, whether it be a wood fire with flames leaping up from cheery logs into the wide recesses of an early cottage chimney, coal burning in a neat modern grate, oil stove heating, or the less dramatic but possibly more effective means of central heating.

It seems to me that the two most obvious solutions are:
The use of foliage and/or chrysanthemums, and dried flower arrangements (the drying process has been dealt with in their own section). Now I shall suggest ideas for typical winter arrangements, using evergreens, a few flowers, early branches of fruit trees, berries, pressed or preserved leaves and a few house plants which can also be useful for cutting.

The most important thing is to have as large a selection of the above mentioned material as possible in your garden. It is often just a question of making the most use of a small space. Periwinkle with its shining dark or variegated leaves, will grow on most shaded banks, and the dramatic Christmas and Lenten roses will produce their magnificent foliage almost all year round, demanding only a cool place for their roots and not too much sun on the bed. Then there is variegated holly—with a dark leaf like laurel or camellia—a wonderful contrast. Golden privet is another possibility for most of the year and Portugal laurel always has branches of beautifully pointed dark leaves.

Rosemary and garden ragwort go bravely into the frosty weather, as do *Garrya elliptica* with its grey green catkins, and *Pieris japonica* whose leaves grow in fan like clusters with racemes of white flowers. These will add interest and give variety of shapes and colours. Also very useful are bergenia and bay which take up very little room.

In the shops one can buy eucalyptus, and silk-bark oak *(Grevillea)*, branches of pussy willow, bunches of pittosporum, laurel, yew and box. The two most important things to remember about this particular material are that the tips of the branches must be split open or smashed to allow a greater intake of water, and the water supply must be kept up well.

Right, This winter arrangement of sprays of shining camellia foliage and branches of variegated privet is long lasting and needs little attention, apart from topping up with water, once it has been arranged. This type of arrangement is best seen against a plain background.

Dried flowers come in many different shades and the material in this group ranges in colouring from the dark brown of the flat achillea seedheads, and the burnt tones of the iris seed pods to the light tan of the hop flowers. The group is arranged in a white cornucopia and will last throughout the winter months.

Sprays of winter jasmine are arranged here with variegated periwinkle in a Staffordshire jug. The periwinkle helps to pick up the soft yellow of the flowers and the lightness of the group is accentuated by the cream and gold colouring on the jug.

285

The contrast of one kind of foliage against another, either in colour, texture, or shape, can give interesting outline material. Arrange, for example, two or three short sprays of dark camellia foliage with branches of golden privet, or some long thin branches of broom with either three or four fat leaves of bergenia towards the centre of a group or with clusters of hydrangea foliage. Garden ragwort rather solid and velvety, and rosemary, grey green with an etched outline, show up well against copper beech, (if the copper beech leaves have not fallen) or the brown of beech leaves which have been preserved in equal parts of glycerine and water.

It is possible to collect as many as fifteen different types of dried material during one summer from quite a small garden. (The only exceptions are the great reed which comes from dykes – it grows abundantly in any flat area, especially in Cambridgeshire and Romney Marsh and East Anglia – eucalyptus and the yellow cud-weed *(Gnaphalium)*. Cud-weed is usually grown in France and imported. Sometimes it is bleached and sometimes it is dyed but yellow is the natural colour.)

One finds that there are some misconceptions about dried flowers as a whole. First of all, it is said they are only suitable for certain positions in the house and for a definite period of time in the year i.e. winter. Secondly, that they are not as suitable for table decorations as for a large group, and that certainly one should not have too many of these arrangements about at once.

In defence of dried flowers I should like to say that they are excellent in November and towards Christmas time and that they come in most attractive and interesting soft shades. But I would suggest that they should never be arranged in groups of over a dozen of one kind (the variety of seedheads and flowers is part of their charm). Ferns and bracken are especially suitable for wall brackets on account of their beautiful outlines and almost paper like flatness, here they can be seen to their best advantage. However, I have seen them used most successfully in a large vase as a background to hydrangeas of various colours. Sprays of crimson and wine Virginian creeper may add interest and colour to a dried group.

Dried flowers will also decorate a large corner or fill up a gap in a hall or on a landing at a time of year when fresh material would be either expensive or almost impossible to procure. They do not flinch under the sometimes stuffy conditions of central heating, and they can be easily packed away, to be brought out the next year looking as fresh as ever. (Anything which has crumpled can be replaced by a newly dried spray, perhaps of delphinium or larkspur, which will at once give a new look to the whole group.)

Then there is the material which has been dried

An early winter group may be composed of many different kinds of material from the garden. This arrangement includes some branches of late summer jasmine, copper coloured *Rosa hugonis*, the mottled grey and green leaves of lungwort, scarlet oak and forsythia (the scarlet oak could be preserved by pressing or by steeping in equal quantities of glycerine and water). Branches of camellia, rosemary, buddleia, pressed bracken and the dramatic dark winter foliage of *Fatsia japonica* could also be used.

Right, Chrysanthemums are a standby throughout the winter months and here they are arranged with dark green rosemary and branches of variegated privet. Privet introduces a cheerful note of colour during winter and also provides material at other times of the year.

off by allowing it to drink up quantities of water and glycerine. This may include branches of bronzed beech, leaves of Persian iron wood *(Parrotia persica)* in a rich chocolate brown, and bear's breeches *(Acanthus)* flowers, hydrangeas, wild rose foliage, eucalyptus (which may go a deep wine colour) and sweet chestnut. Poppy heads may also be dried off in this way as an alternative to the usual drying in a warm room or cupboard, with varying results, some of them interesting.

In conclusion, I feel that with a little forethought during the summer and autumn, and with the help of one or two valuable evergreens, it is possible to produce at least one large decorative arrangement at little cost to last through the winter.

A few stems of clear yellow calceolarias are arranged here on a pin holder is a shallow dish of water.
These flowers are better when not seen in too great a quantity and bring a feeling of sunlight into a furnishing scheme.

The rather burnt yellow achillea heads are arranged here with branches of *Lonicera nitida* which help to soften the achillea. If left on the plant until November the achillea will dry to a nut brown colour.

Yellow arrangements

There is nothing quite like a group of yellow flowers to give the illusion of sunlight in a room. For, in the minds of most people, yellow is the colour of spring and spring is the time when one hopes for some hours of sunshine after winter gloom and greyness. Winter aconites, daffodils, primroses, laburnum, cowslips, buttercups, mimosa, forsythia – are all the first flowers of spring and all are yellow.

What a difference in shades there can be in this one colour. From the glistening yellow of a buttercup, looking as though it has been varnished in its brightness, to the paler, more gentle, yellow of primroses growing in a cluster on a mossy bank.

Yellow is nearly always a safe choice when taking or sending flowers as a present. Some people do not like to be given white flowers, ('too funereal' I have heard them remark). Blue is not a good colour in artificial light, neither is purple, and red can be difficult with furnishings.

Apart from the spring ones already mentioned,

there are many other yellow flowers, some in the herbaceous variety are blanket flowers (*Gaillardia*) tickseed (*Coreopsis*), golden rod and yarrow (*Achillea*). Then there is a good lemon coloured snapdragon (this looks most attractive when planted with white) and, of course, those most magnificent lilies, Limelight, Destiny, and Charity. Roses include Paul's Lemon Pillar (rather pale but very fine blooms), *Rosa hugonis* (charming small single flowers interspersed with feathery foliage), Nevada (pale when it is fully out and a soft charming colour), Lydia, Spek's Yellow, Mc-Gredy's Yellow, Goldilocks, Highlight, Allgold. (These last six roses are all well known and frequently grown. Amongst climbing roses a good yellow is Emily Gray and, even more famous, Mermaid, although this is perhaps not one of the most lasting of blooms when cut.)

Strangely enough, most of the grey foliaged plants have yellow flowers and some of these are most suitable and attractive for arrangement. (garden ragwort is perhaps one of the best.) But on the whole, it is best for the plants if the flowers are removed, though it is permissible to keep a few for cutting.

There are some good yellow foliage plants which, if not completely yellow, are at least variegated. These include golden privet, variegated periwinkle, holly and silver berry *(Elaeagnus)*.

Some wallflowers, tulips and primulas come in a good yellow, as do pansies and lupins. The same is true of certain flowering shrubs like broom, berberis, honeysuckle and azalea. Fennel, from the herb garden, has a most charming clear yellow flower, which lasts exceptionally well, and in the same colour range is the stately eremurus. Equally pleasing are columbines, iris, monkey musk, globe flower and evening primrose (although this last flower is not a lasting one in spite of the fact that as each flower fades a bud will come out).

Winter jasmine, with its showers of pure gold cascading down from a fence or the side of a wall, cheers many a cloudy wintry day – witch hazel *(Hamamelis)* will do the same. Its small starlike flowers on bare branches are delicate and enchanting. If a few branches can be spared for cutting they will make perfect material for a 'line' arrangement. (If brought in before the flowers are fully out, it is fascinating to watch this process indoors.)

Chrysanthemums, reliable and long-lasting, come in all shades of yellow. One of the most charming colours is the pale lemon yellow of the spray chrysanthemum, which usually has a fresh green foliage. The colour of this foliage sets off the flowers to their best advantage and contrives almost to produce a springlike effect in the late autumn.

I must not omit from this list a well known flower which is sometimes regarded by arrangers with distaste because of its habit of developing curving stems. This is the leopard's bane *(Doronicum)*. Its daisy like flowers are a clear golden yellow and are especially attractive when cut quite short and arranged with white flowers such as white bluebells, white broom, or Queen Anne's lace. If fixed right down into the bowl amongst the white flowers the general impression will be of white studded with gold and this arrangement will show off the leopard's bane since the beauty of their faces is often lost owing to the curving stems. They last well and are available at a time when other herbaceous plants are only just beginning to show some growth much less produce flowers.

Another positive point in favour of yellow flowers is their usefulness in bringing harmony to an arrangement in a mixed bowl. Sometimes a splash of colour is required in an arrangement and flowers which in nature would clash have to be arranged together. How does one solve this problem? Miss Sackville-West writing on the planting of herb lilies *(Alstroemeria)* in her book *In your Garden* said 'Keep the orange away from the coral for they do not mix well together, and whoever it was who said Nature made no mistakes in colour harmony was either colour blind or a sentimentalist'. My solution to the problem is a yellow flower, for the most strident oranges, reds, purples and crimsons.

Yet another good example are decorations using orange marigolds or nasturtiums. Arranged alone or with bright reds and scarlets, these flowers

Carnations can provide a useful note of colour throughout the year. These three flowers arranged on a yellow dish with blue-grey eucalyptus foliage and with the addition of the shells with yellow and white markings give an emphasis of yellow in various tones.

Right, Various flowers at different times of the year can introduce the colour of sunlight into a furnishing scheme. Spray chrysanthemums often come in this particular shade of yellow and immediately, even in winter give a feeling of lightness and sunshine.

can have a hard appearance because of the rather flat quality of the orange colour. But immediately a paler lemon yellow is introduced the hardness of the orange seems to melt away.

I should like to suggest a few arrangements for yellow flowers:

Yellow broom with yellow tulips and white lilac.
Honeysuckle with summer jasmine and yellow roses (Emily Gray).
Yellow columbines with masterwort and sprays of *Rosa hugonis* or Nevada rose.
Tall stems of fennel, the white tobacco plant *(Nicotiana)* and pale yellow snapdragons.
Yellow and white snapdragons in a bowl.
Forsythia, cut short, with early bluebells and two or three out of door blue hyacinths.
White foxgloves with yellow iris and buttercups.
Small sprays of the slipper flower *(Calceolaria)* with white pinks.
Nasturtiums, all colours with their leaves.
Yellow tulips with blue forget-me-nots.
Yarrow *(Achillea)* arranged with St. John's Wort and blue delphiniums.

291

A few zinnias in colours ranging from pale yellow
to orange and deep bronze are arranged
in a basket with sprays of traveller's joy.

Left, Three zinnias are arranged here
against sprays of honesty in its autumn colouring
of dark grey, chocolate brown and burnt sienna.
The zinnias are in shades of yellow and orange
which lightens up the darker colouring of the honesty.
If the outer coverings of the honesty are split away
the silvery capsules will be revealed.

Right, Zinnias can be most effective
when arranged on their own. They last well,
but if the stems of the heavier flowers begin to droop,
they can be cut quite short and the flowers will thrive.

Zinnias

To decide that zinnias will have a section to themselves may well be looked upon with disapproval
by those who do not care for them, and who regard
all zinnias as rigid and difficult to arrange. I
wonder if I can convert these 'dislikers of zinnias'
by reminding them not only of the wonderful
array of 'jewel' colourings in which these flowers
come (their quality of brightness in a mixed arrangement is without any touch of vulgarity or crude-
ness), but also of their lasting qualities for cutting.

In a small area of garden a few zinnias can produce such a collection of colours as can only be
seen amongst semi-precious stones in a jeweller's
window.

And so, for the enthusiast of the one flower
type of arrangement, there can be little to compete
with zinnias. Apart from their colours zinnias
have their uses for arrangements in many other
ways. The criticism that they look rigid and
almost military in their stiffness can be met by
arranging them with other, more graceful, flowers,
and by cutting their stems at uneven lengths so
that some are quite short, which are then placed

The various colours of zinnias are introduced in this group of early autumn flowers.
The rather tight pyramid-style of the arrangement gives an effect of being studded with bright shapes in purple, scarlet, orange, white and yellow.

The glowing colours of zinnias reminiscent of precious stones can be seen to better advantage when arranged alone or with a background of soft toned flowers such as mignonette.

towards the centre of a group. In this way, too, the full beauty of the petals can be appreciated, spreading out from the dark purple centres in dramatic colours.

The zinnia, a native of America and Mexico, was only introduced into European countries at the end of the eighteenth century. The vivid brightness and depth of some of the flowers can be easily visualised as coming from a country like Mexico, with its hot sun and brilliant skies. It is this clear, Mexican colouring which is so outstanding in the late summer in European gardens.

For early autumn flower groups either the red, yellow, orange and burnt copper colours are valuable, mixed with nasturtiums, nemesias, montbretia, marigolds, etc., or perhaps the more subtle lilac-pink, deep raspberry and garnet colourings with Michaelmas daisies in the same tones, together with dark purple pansies, clematis (Comtesse de Bouchard), and spikes of lavender.

Zinnias are usually reliable and long lasting for cutting. Miss Sackville-West remarks: 'As cut flowers they are invaluable: they never flop, and they last, I was going to say, for weeks'. It should be admitted, I think, that there are occasionally some stems which bend and then the whole flower head droops owing to its weight. If this happens it is advisable to cut the stem much shorter, even if it means cutting to within a few inches of the flower itself—in this way there is more stability and firmness, and the life of the flower will be prolonged and – an added point – it will possibly be easier to see into the flower when it is cut short.

If the flowers are bought, and the stems seem floppy, or, alternatively, if they are cut from a garden and have been out of water for some length of time, it may be helpful to give them the same treatment as that suggested for tulips. Snip off the bottom of the stem of each flower and then stand the bunch in a bucket or tall jug, filled with water to the brim. Wrap stiff newspaper around the flower heads and whatever amount of stem is emerging from the bucket, and tie in position. Leave all night in a cool place. In the morning it is likely that the stems will have stiffened up and give no more cause for anxiety.

Zinnias, because they are so colourful, most attractive with soft-coloured material such as the seedheads of sweetcorn, green poppyheads, green and purple teasels, or the fresh green of hop flowers. In an arrangement with hops, I have seen zinnias, with their stems cut at uneven lengths, giving the impression of studding the group with precious gems.)

Index

BIBLIOGRAPHY

Alicia Amherst	*A History of Gardening in England*
Mary Averill	*Japanese Flower Arrangement*
Julia S. Berral	*A History of Flower Arrangement (London, Thames and Hudson)*
Wilfred Blunt	*The Art of Botanical Illustration*
Sir Josiah Conder	*The Flowers of Japan and the Art of Floral Arrangement*
J. S. Dakers	*Greenhouse Plants in Colour, with colour illustrations by Cynthia Newsome-Taylor (W.H. & L. Collingridge Ltd., 1962)*
Xenia Field	*House Plants*
Margery Fish	*A Flower for Every Day (Studio Vista)*
J. Fisk	*Success with Clematis*
Miles Hadfield	*One Man's Garden (Phoenix House, 1966)*
Michael Haworth-Booth	*The Hydrangeas (Constable)*
A. G. L. Hellyer	*Flowers in Colour, with over 300 colour illustrations by Cynthia Newsome-Taylor (W.H. & L. Collingridge Ltd., 1955)*
	Garden Plants in Colour, with nearly 300 colour illustrations by Cynthia Newsome-Taylor (W.H. & L. Collingridge Ltd., 1958)
	Shrubs in Colour, with 269 colour illustrations by Cynthia Newsome-Taylor (W.H. & L. Collingridge Ltd., 1965)
Shirley Hibberd	*Rustic Adornments for Homes of Taste (Thames & Hudson)*
Juson Hill	*The Contemplative Gardener*
Peter Hunt	*Perennial Flowers for Small Gardens*
	100 Best Flowering Shrubs, with 100 line drawings by Cynthia Newsome-Taylor (Eyre & Spottiswoode Ltd., 1963)
	100 Best Herbaceous Plants, with 100 line drawings by Cynthia Newsome-Taylor (Eyre & Spottiswoode Ltd.)
Gertrude Jekyll	*Flower Decoration for the Home*
	Colour Schemes for the Garden
	Wood and Garden
	Home and Garden
Margaret E. Jones	*House Plants (Penguin Handbooks)*
Christopher Lloyd	*Clematis (Country Life)*
W. Keble Martin	*The Concise British Flora in Colour (Ebury Press)*
George Moore (Trans.)	*Heloise and Abelard*
Thomas Rochford and Richard Gorer	*The Rochford Book of Flowering Pot Plants, illustrated by Cynthia Newsome-Taylor (Faber & Faber)*
Lanning Roper	*Hardy Herbaceous Plants (Penguin Handbooks)*
	Sunday Times Gardening Book (Nelson)
V. Sackville-West	*In My Garden*
	In My Garden Again
	More for Your Garden (Michael Joseph, 1955)
	Even More for Your Garden (Michael Joseph, 1955)
George Sitwell	*The Making of Gardens*
Constance Spry	*Flowers in House and Garden*
Graham Stuart Thomas	*Climbing Roses Old and New (Phoenix House)*
Fred Whitsey	*Sunday Telegraph Gardening Book (Collins)*

A Guide to Church Flowers, compiled by The National Association of Flower Arrangement Societies of Great Britain

Acknowledgements

My thanks are due first to Mr. John Miller of the Country Life Studio and Michael Holford for their skill and care in taking their photographs, and to Mrs. O. H. M. Sturges who, for some of the arrangements, has supplemented my own supply of containers by lending me ones from her Biddenden antique shop.

I am grateful to the following who have often generously supplied flowers and foliage from their gardens:– Mrs. Harold Blaker, Mrs. Campbell Dixon, Mr. and Mrs. Harold Raymond, Lt. Col. and Mrs. E. E. N. Sandeman, Dr. and Mrs. G. Seligman, Mr. and Mrs. L. Whitfeld, and Major-Gen. and Mrs. C. G. Woolner, and to Mrs. David Hawkins for help with the typescript and to Miss Maureen Doherty of the Hamlyn Publishing Group Limited for her kind co-operation.

To my son Adam, for his willing help in many ways, I am especially grateful.

Betty Massingham

PHOTOGRAPHIC ACKNOWLEDGEMENTS

Bernard Alfieri
Australian Consolidated Press
Barnaby's Picture Library
Reginald Eyre
Farmer and Stockbreeder
Flowers and Plants Council
Michael Holford
George Newnes
Odhams Press
Picturepoint
Radio Times Hulton Picture Library
Royal National Rose Society (pp.14 and 15, arrangements by Mrs. C. M. Bowen and Mrs. K. Wells)
Ray Ryan, Cape Town
Brian Seed, © Illustrated London News
H. Smith
Zentrale Farbbild Agentur

The painting by Henri Fantin-Latour entitled '*A Bunch of Flowers*' is reproduced by Courtesy of the Ashmolean Museum, Oxford. The following two paintings are from the Collection of Mr. and Mrs. John Hay Whitney: Henri Fantin-Latour, '*Three Roses in a Glass Vase*'; Odilon Redon, '*Flowers in a Green Vase*', 1910.

The illustrations on pp.170-171 are from '*The Flowers of Japan and the Art of Floral Arrangement*' by Sir Josiah Conder. Other Japanese flower arrangements in black and white are by Stella Coe. Endpapers from a design by Wall Paper Manufacturers Ltd.